WAR CRIMES

ALSO BY BUZZ PATTERSON

Reckless Disregard:
How Liberal Democrats Undercut Our Military,
Endanger Our Soldiers, and Jeopardize Our Security

Dereliction of Duty:
The Eyewitness Account of How Bill Clinton
Compromised America's National Security

WAR
CRIMES

THE LEFT'S CAMPAIGN TO
DESTROY THE MILITARY AND
LOSE THE WAR ON TERROR

Lt. Col. ROBERT "BUZZ" PATTERSON
(U.S. Air Force, Ret.)

THREE RIVERS PRESS
NEW YORK

Published in the United States by Three Rivers Press,
an imprint of the Crown Publishing Group, a division of
Random House, Inc., New York.
www.crownpublishing.com

Three Rivers Press and the Tugboat design are registered
trademarks of Random House, Inc.

Originally published in hardover in the United States by
Crown Forum, an imprint of the Crown Publishing Group,
a division of Random House, Inc., New York, in 2007.

Library of Congress Cataloging-in-Publication Data

Patterson, Robert, 1955–
War crimes : the left's campaign to destroy the military and
lose the War on Terror / Robert Patterson.—1st ed.
p. cm.
Includes bibliographical references and index.
1. Democratic Party (U.S.)   2. Liberalism—United States.   3. War
on Terrorism, 2001–   4. Iraq War, 2003–   5. National security—
United States.   6. United States—Military policy.   I. Title.

JK2316.P27 2007
973.931—dc22   2007006758

ISBN 978-0-307-33827-3

Printed in the United States of America

Design by Joseph Rutt

10 9 8 7 6 5 4 3 2 1

First Paperback Edition

For those who have answered the nation's call, then and now.
For those who have fallen and for those who are fighting.
For my father, who taught me that leadership is not management.
For Nichole, Kylie, Tanner, and Chase, who love me.
And, for Paul Smith, Jason Dunham, and Rafael Peralta,
may you rest in God's peace.

CONTENTS

CONTENTS

A nation can survive its fools, and even the ambitious. But it cannot survive treason from within. An enemy at the gates is less formidable, for he is known and carries his banner openly. But the traitor moves amongst those within the gate freely, his sly whispers rustling through all the alleys, heard in the very halls of government itself. For the traitor appears not a traitor; he speaks in accents familiar to his victims, and he wears their face and their arguments, he appeals to the baseness that lies deep in the hearts of all men. He rots the soul of a nation, he works secretly and unknown in the night to undermine the pillars of the city, he infects the body politic so that it can no longer resist. A murderer is less to fear. The traitor is the plague.

—Marcus Tullius Cicero,
in a speech to the Roman
Senate, 42 B.C.

ONE

THE UNHOLY ALLIANCE

Whereof what's past is prologue, what to come
In yours and my discharge.

—William Shakespeare,
The Tempest

On January 30, 2005, the face of the Middle East changed for-ever. In the cradle of civilization, whose people had never known self-determination, 8.4 million Iraqis braved attacks by Is-lamofascist terrorists and chose freedom. Sixty percent of eligible Iraqi voters turned out that day, closely approximating participa-tion in the American presidential election three months earlier (where obstacles were significantly more pedestrian). Only through the noble efforts of the U.S. military, not American politicians, did such a moment occur.

U.S. Air Force Major Eric Egland was an eyewitness to this birth of independence. A member of the elite U.S. Improvised Ex-plosive Device (IED) Task Force, Egland and his team of soldiers patrolled the many voting sites around Baghdad in anticipation of the first-ever democratic elections in Iraq. At 8 A.M., just as the voting began, Egland's group heard an explosion in the area of a polling site they'd visited the night before. A suicide bomber had detonated himself, killing two others in the process.

Egland's unit responded expecting to find that the terrorists had achieved their desired result: potential voters dispersed and retreating to the safety of their homes. As they arrived at the scene, though, the soldiers witnessed the true nature of freedom and democracy.

The lines of Iraqis waiting to cast their first meaningful votes were not at all diminished by the terror; serpentine queues stretched around the block far beyond the soldiers' field of vision. "The Iraqis were resolute in their will to vote," Egland recalled when I interviewed him in Iraq a few months later. "And we watched them file past the remains [of the terrorist] toward the polling booths, some even taking time to loudly curse and spit on the murderer." The significance of the moment was not lost on Egland, who was serving his country thousands of miles removed from his newlywed and his family. "I will put my faith in a people who, when attacked by a suicide bomber, not only do not run away but gather and stand to face the danger in order to have a say in their future," he concluded.[1]

U.S. Army Sergeant Joe Skelly of the 411th Civil Affairs Battalion, from Danbury, Connecticut, patrolled the city of Baquba, Iraq, that day. Sergeant Skelly is the American fighting man personified—the citizen soldier that Thomas Jefferson envisioned. He was a professor of history at New York's College of Mount Saint Vincent, and joined the military after the attacks of 9/11 when he realized his country was at war.

In Baquba, terrorists launched mortars and rocket-propelled grenades (RPGs) in an attempt to shatter the will of the Iraqi and American people. Skelly noticed, though, that the Iraqi security forces guarding the election sites had assumed a new posture;

they were more engaged, confident, and alert. They had "owner-ship," he realized. They knew "what's at stake."

"In a neighborhood called Al-Huwaydir, near the Diyala River," Skelly told me, "I saw an elderly Iraqi dressed in his finest suit of clothes proudly walking past us to vote. He was strutting, his head held high, he was so proud, he was going to vote. His quiet dignity was moving. That's what it's all about. I knew at that moment that's why I was there."[2]

Fearing democracy and freedom in Iraq, Islamic terrorists from Afghanistan, Pakistan, Saudi Arabia, Syria, and Iran targeted the Iraqis' courage and commitment with the maximum strength they could muster . . . and the Iraqis gave them the finger.

Flashing purple fingers to the world, Iraq's people joyfully announced their entry into the world of freedom and human dig-nity—concepts they could hardly have grasped in previous gener-ations. With fallen despot Saddam Hussein incarcerated and awaiting trial, the nation of Iraq rose to celebrate the end of thirty-five years of ruthless oppression.

In the summer of 2005, I visited Iraq to see the truth for my-self and to talk with American soldiers, whose stories had not been told in the mainstream media. What I was hearing daily from friends and peers engaged in the fight was not what I was seeing or hearing in Big Media or Congress. I had served as an Air Force officer and pilot for twenty years and been involved in com-bat operations in Grenada, Somalia, Bosnia, and the Persian Gulf. When I got on the ground, I was overwhelmed with the extremely positive nature of our soldiers' morale and professionalism. I was equally struck by the emotional commitment of the Iraqi people.

One member of our traveling team, American filmmaker Brad Maaske, was embedded on patrol with the Iraqi Army in a very dangerous former Baathist area of Baghdad's "Red Zone" when he was approached by a young Iraqi father holding his infant daughter.

"Please bless her," the Iraqi asked in broken English.

"I don't know what you mean," Maaske said.

"Please bless her," the man repeated and reached for the American's hands. Placing them on the baby's forehead, the father continued, "Please bless her with the freedoms that you have . . . the freedoms of America." Maaske suspected that he'd walked into an ambush. We had discussed the inherent danger of exactly this sort of scenario on our way to Iraq. Overcome with emotion, though, Maaske knelt over, kissed the child, and blessed her. Her father was beaming. Maaske was too.

On October 15, 2005, the Iraqi people took another dramatic step forward and again thumbed their noses at al Qaeda, as this time 78 percent of the voting-age population walked to the country's 6,000 polling stations. Where al Qaeda's soulless butchers had launched 147 attacks to disrupt the January 2005 elections, on this day they were capable of only 14.

Only two months later, in December, 11 million Iraqis elected the most representative Arab government in the Middle East.

This was remarkable progress in a nation that had never experienced democracy and had spent nearly a quarter century under the brutal tyranny of Saddam Hussein.

But to the American Left, none of this mattered, just as the wondrous democratic elections in Afghanistan the previous year had done nothing to inspire it. The Left's leaders expressed no appreciation for, or pride in, their nation's noble and historic efforts in bringing law and elections to a land devoid of civil rights. Once again, they offered only acrimony and defeatism.

On the very day that Saddam was being arraigned in Baghdad, Democratic National Committee chairman Howard Dean wildly asserted, "The idea that we're going to win the war in Iraq is an idea which is just plain wrong."[3]

West Virginia Democratic senator Jay Rockefeller claimed that America and the world would be safer if Saddam Hussein was still in power.[4]

Democratic senator John Kerry, who had come close to becoming America's commander in chief, slurred our soldiers in an interview with CBS's *Face the Nation*. "There is no reason," Kerry said, "young American soldiers need to be going into the homes of Iraqis in the dead of night, terrorizing kids and children, you know, women."[5]

Democratic congressman John Murtha, a former Marine, took the opportunity to call for a pullout of troops from Iraq. "We can't win this militarily," he said, adding, "The Army is broken, worn-out, and living hand to mouth."[6] Proving there are no depths to which this lawmaker won't stoop when undermining his nation, he then accused U.S. Marines of "killing innocent civilians in cold blood" before an investigation into the incident at Haditha, Iraq, had been completed.[7] This was an irresponsible and incendiary claim that outraged soldiers from all services who were proudly and voluntarily defending their nation.

Former president Bill Clinton joined in the pile-on. Speaking just miles from the war zone, in Dubai, Clinton told students that the Iraq War "was a big mistake." The former president, standing on foreign soil, continued to criticize the commander in chief's decisions by saying, "The American government made several errors, one of which is how easy it would be to get rid of Saddam and how hard it would be to unite the country."[8]

Such comments swelled the chorus of defeatism that had been heard since the early days of the war. It didn't matter that the United States went into Iraq with overwhelming congressional authorization, with the support of 70 percent of the American public, and with the consent of the United Nations (which had failed to enforce seventeen separate resolutions against Saddam's Iraq). The Left quickly reframed America's justification for combat to meet *their* reality, launching a ceaseless campaign of vindictive anti-American, antimilitary rhetoric.

Even when the gruesomely decapitated bodies of Americans were shown on international television swinging from a bridge in

Fallujah, the Left could muster no outrage toward the enemy. The incredibly influential leftist blogger Markos Moulitsas Zúniga of Daily Kos wrote of the American civilian contractors, "I feel nothing over the death of merceneries [*sic*]. They aren't in Iraq because of orders, or because they are there trying to help the people make Iraq a better place. They are there to wage war for profit. Screw them."[9]

After U.S. Army soldiers Kristian Menchaca and Thomas Tucker were abducted, tortured, and mutilated, their eyes gouged out by terrorists and their bodies so desecrated that DNA testing was necessary to prove their identification, the Left again found themselves incapable of choosing good versus evil. Instead of condemning the horrific crimes of America's enemy, Senator Dick Durbin, who had earlier charged American soldiers with the crimes similar to those committed by Nazis in death camps and Soviets in their gulags, blamed his own government. "Unfortunately, this is a grim reminder of the price we're paying for a failed policy in Iraq," he said.[10]

The story was much the same when, in late December 2006, Saddam was executed for his crimes against humanity. The *New York Times* editorial page did not celebrate the fact that justice had been done, and that the Iraqi people, under their new democratic government, had given the tyrant a fair trial (something he had never afforded his people). The *Times* instead condemned the "rush" to hang Saddam. The paper then seized the opportunity to trash the American war effort, adding, "After nearly four years of war and thousands of American and Iraqi deaths, it is ever harder to be sure whether anything fundamental has changed for the better in Iraq."[11]

Oh really? The millions of Iraqis who braved suicide bombers in order to exercise their newly delivered right to vote might disagree.

How could so many on the left ignore America's extraordinary achievements in the War on Terror? How could they twist every victory into a defeat for the United States?

These are questions that millions of Americans have wrestled with, and that ultimately drove me to write this book.

In my years serving as military aide to President Bill Clinton, when I carried the "nuclear football" and thus had to shadow the president at all hours, I gained an intimate understanding of how he and other Democratic leaders regarded the armed forces. Not only didn't the Left understand military culture, they regarded it with utter disdain.

Still, that alone did not explain the Left's subversive behavior in the War on Terror. It was only on my return from Iraq that I had something of an epiphany.

Sitting in the Baghdad airport waiting for a massive sandstorm to pass, I engaged in a conversation with another American who sat nearby, waiting for the same flight. It turned out she was an official for the United Nations. Quickly our discussion moved to the horrific bombing of the day before: an indescribably evil terrorist had crashed his explosive-laden car into a crowd of Iraqi children who were receiving candy from a U.S. soldier, killing twenty-seven.

"Why do the soldiers do that?" the woman asked me in her Madonna-like faux–British accent. "They must know that sort of thing only attracts the terrorists. I wish they wouldn't do that to those children."

I was stunned. She was blaming the U.S. soldier for the deaths of the children! Al Qaeda's car-bombing thugs had dictated the time and the place for their murders, and their evil scheme had claimed the lives of innocent Iraqi children and a caring American soldier. But this American official did not direct her anger at the terrorists. Instead she indicted the U.S. soldier who was compassionately passing out candy to poor Iraqi kids.

It was then that I realized why America's liberals could fail to process, or even acknowledge, the remarkable achievements in the Middle East, including the liberation of millions of oppressed people: They are so blinded by their pathological hatred for their own nation that defeatism is their only recourse. They cannot credit the

United States and its armed forces with success because, to them, America and especially the U.S. military are the real enemy.

After 9/11, the question that dominated the national discourse was: Why do they hate us? That question referred, of course, to the radical Islamic world, but as has become clear in the succeeding years, it could apply just as easily to the American Left.

In this time of national crisis, the Left has formed what my friend and colleague David Horowitz, a former left-wing activist, calls an "Unholy Alliance" with our Islamofascist enemies.[12] America, unfortunately, has overlooked this internal threat, when in fact it represents the greatest obstacle to our success in the War on Terror. This conflict is, as we knew it would be from the beginning, a long and arduous struggle, but seeing it through to victory is our only option if we want to preserve the freedoms the Islamofascists so detest.

Yet every day that passes, the Left saps more of our nation's will to fight.

This is no accident. The Left's campaign against America's War on Terror is a well-coordinated, well-financed operation that involves individuals and institutions from all parts of our society. Leading Democratic politicians, major media outlets, academia, popular culture, and a host of deep-pocketed radical organizations combine to form a Fifth Column that undermines our military's heroic efforts in this global campaign.

The frightening reality is that the United States will not win the war against radical Islam unless and until we defeat the enemy within.

IN BED WITH THE ENEMY

Throughout the Cold War, leftist Communist sympathizers and fellow America-haters across politics, academia, media, and the popular culture united in their opposition to the United States.

They sided with the Communist states of the Soviet Union, China, Cuba, North Korea, and Nicaragua, not to mention tin-pot dictators in Uganda, Libya, and Iraq.

The leadership and vision of President Ronald Reagan shattered their dreams by causing the collapse of the Soviet Union and the rest of the Communist bloc.

Still, the Left continues to see their country through the "hammer and sickle" lens. They see America as racist, sexist, repressively capitalistic, imperialist, and "too Christian".

With the horrific events of 9/11, the Left had an opportunity to change course. It was simple: they could reembrace the progressive patriotism of Franklin Delano Roosevelt, Harry Truman, and John F. Kennedy, or they could continue to oppose the U.S. military and disregard freedom, capitalism, and democracy.

Predictably and sadly, they chose the latter. The "D" in Democrat more than ever represents "defeatism" and "disdain"—defeat for America and disdain for its uniformed forces. The list of offenders is long but includes Nancy Pelosi, John Murtha, Harry Reid, Hillary Clinton, Ted Kennedy, and John Kerry, to name a few.

Liberals believe that an antiwar movement will bring them political capital, as it did during Vietnam. By inflating Vietnam into the symbol of American imperialism, leftists achieved their real goals—power in Washington, D.C. (where they could cripple the war machine) and control of the nation's universities and editorial offices.

The costs of their shameless agenda were horrifying. Not only were 58,000 Americans killed in Vietnam, but after the Left's ceaseless protests finally convinced America's leaders to pull out of a war they were winning militarily, some 2.5 million Vietnamese and Cambodians were murdered under Communist regimes.

It did not have to be that way. North Vietnamese General Staff officer Colonel Bui Tin later credited the American antiwar movement with the Communist victory over U.S. forces. "Through dissent and protest," Tin said, the United States "lost the ability to mobilize a will to win."[13] North Vietnamese General Vo Nguyen Giap agreed. "We were not strong enough to drive out a half-million American troops, but that wasn't our aim," he said. "Our intention was to break the will of the American government to continue the war."[14]

That is exactly what happened. And now our Islamofascist enemies want history to repeat itself. In a July 2005 letter to al Qaeda's then-leader in Iraq, Abu Musab al-Zarqawi, bin Laden's second in command, Ayman al-Zawahiri, remarked, "The aftermath of the collapse of American power in Vietnam—and how they ran and left their agents—is noteworthy." Thus Zawahiri reminded his top terrorist in Iraq that "more than half of this battle is taking place in the battlefield of the media." And that "we are in a media battle in a race for the heart and minds of our Umma [Muslim population]."[15]

Having lost one war for America already, the Left—led by many who came of age during Vietnam—is once again shamelessly exploiting for political gain an armed conflict and the deaths of brave American soldiers.

Leftists announced their willingness to unite with the jihadists early on. Propagandist filmmaker Michael Moore declared, "The Iraqis who have risen up against the occupation are not 'insurgents' or 'terrorists' or 'the enemy.' They are the REVOLUTION, the Minutemen, and their numbers will grow—and they will win. Get it, Mr. Bush?"[16]

On October 29, 2004, a week before the U.S. presidential election, Osama bin Laden released a videotape in which he regurgitated claims from Michael Moore's "documentary" *Fahrenheit 9/11*. "Bush is . . . engaged in distortion and deception," declared bin Laden. America was guilty of "the greatest mass slaughter of children mankind has ever known" by dropping millions of pounds of bombs on Iraqi children. The 9/11 attacks, bin Laden claimed, came as "a reply" to this oppression. The 2000 presidential election was illegitimate because of "election fraud" in Florida, he contended. When America's citizens needed him most, the president gave the terrorists "three times the period required to" destroy the World Trade Center by "occupying himself by talking to the little girl about the goat"—this a reference to Bush's reading a story to a classroom full of children, something that Moore played up in his film. And, finally, bin Laden charged that the United States was fighting in the Middle East "to pilfer Iraq's oil."[17] All these arguments were central to Moore's film.

Likewise, in May 2006 Iranian president and nuclear madman Mahmoud Ahmadinejad penned a rambling screed to President Bush in which he claimed that Bush lied about the reasons for invading Iraq and that 9/11 was a U.S. governmental conspiracy, suggested that the Holocaust never occurred, complained about the lack of legal representation for the prisoners held at Guantánamo Bay, and expressed his concern for U.S. soldiers who, he contended, returned home depressed and suicidal.[18]

It's one thing for radical anti-Americans like Moore to side with the enemy, but how disgusting is it when the U.S. Congress does? Once the Democrats seized control of the House and Senate in November 2006 they immediately went to work establishing their antimilitary agenda. Led by leftists Nancy Pelosi and her political ally John Murtha, the Democrats initiated their strategy for the "slow bleed"—the gradual withdrawal of support for our troops. Democrats defended their pursuit of a "non-binding resolution" as a signal of their opposition to the administration's policy in Iraq—one that they had overwhelmingly voted for. Unfortunately, their very public positions did indeed send a signal—to al Qaeda, that they could win if they just held on to their terrorist intentions, and to our troops, that they had in fact lost.

The Dems sent an even clearer signal in the spring of 2007,

when Pelosi and Senate Majority Leader Harry Reid pressured their party to attach specific timelines for troop withdrawal to an emergency appropriations bill—one designed to equip our troops with the funding that is vital to the war effort! The bills were, plain and simple, votes for American defeat in Iraq. And Democratic leaders were so eager to send this signal to our enemies that to get the necessary votes they larded the emergency funding bill with billions of dollars of unnecessary nonmilitary expenditures on everything from spinach to shrimp to sugar beets. By passing the bills with withdrawal timetables in place, the House and the Senate for the first time in our nation's history attempted to subsume the power of an elected commander in chief.

Speaker Pelosi went further beyond the pale when she anointed herself America's foreign policy expert and visited Syria in April 2007. Against the wishes of the White House and the duly elected commander in chief, Pelosi donned a *hijab* and paid an official visit to the same Syrian government that is a known sponsor of terrorism and, more precisely, has funneled terrorists and weapons into Iraq that have killed American soldiers.

While her attempt at usurping the constitutional responsibilities of the commander in chief didn't play well with American troops in Iraq, Pelosi did engender the support of America's enemies. Khaled Al-Batch, a spokesman for the terror organization Islamic Jihad, praised the Speaker's visit. "If the Democrats want to make negotiations with Syria, Hamas, and Hezbollah, this means the Democratic Party understands well what happens in this area and I think Pelosi will succeed. . . . I hope she wins the next elections." Jihad Jaara, a senior member of the Al Aqsa Martyrs Brigade terror cell, said, "She is a very brave woman. . . . All the American people must make peace with Syria and Iran and with Hamas. Why not?"[19] Islamic Jihad and the Al Aqsa Martyrs Brigade have been responsible for every suicide bombing in Israel over the past two years.

For those of us who have served in uniform, the Democrat-controlled congressional agenda marks the most subversive effort to undermine our military and our allies since the Democrats completely cut off funding of the South Vietnamese army in 1974. That decision led to the slaughter of millions. So, too, might this one.

THE FIFTH COLUMN

The American Left has crossed a line into disloyalty and betrayal, as their subversive actions embolden our enemy, weaken the resolve of the American people, degrade U.S. warfighting capability, and damage the morale of our men and women in uniform. This subversion occurs all across the Fifth Column.

We see it in our universities, whose faculties are dominated by radicals who arose during the Vietnam era. Thus we encounter hostile anti-American professors like Columbia University's Nicholas De Genova, who at an antiwar "teach-in" preached that "U.S. patriotism is inseparable from imperial warfare and white supremacy" and that "the only true heroes are those who find ways that help defeat the U.S. military."[20] We also meet academics like Ward Churchill, who said while a professor at the University of Colorado that he wanted the "U.S. off the planet" and suggested that "it may be that more 9/11s are necessary." Lamenting that the terrorism of 9/11 had proved "insufficient to accomplish its purpose" of eviscerating the United States, Churchill wrote, "What the hell? It was worth a try."[21] This is only the beginning of the anti-American propaganda in our schools, as this book will reveal.

We also see the subversion in Big Media, now an instrumental tool for both anti-American leftists and Islamofascists alike—whether it be obsessing over President George Bush's aircraft carrier landing; sensationalizing the falsehoods of Iraqi antiquity thefts; overdramatiszing photos from the Abu Ghraib prison (some real, some fake); highlighting false, politically motivated accusations of grandstanders like Richard Clarke and Joe Wilson; feeding the flames of Islamic hatred by publishing false stories of Koran flushings; or championing the subversive declarations of Senator Ted Kennedy and Congressman John Murtha. Some news executives cannot conceal their anti-Americanism and disdain for the military. Former CNN chief news executive Eason Jordan falls into this category, having accused the U.S. military of committing war atrocities by intentionally killing journalists.[22]

Democratic Party leaders are complicit as well. We have seen, for instance, a high-ranking Democratic senator comparing the U.S. military's treatment of terrorists detained at the U.S. prison in Guantánamo Bay to the atrocities committed by the regimes of Adolf Hitler, Joseph Stalin, and Pol Pot. We have also seen a Democratic congressman claim that U.S. Marines had killed "in cold blood" when they returned fire against insurgent terrorists, and that the military had covered up the matter.[23]

Inexcusably, the Democrats are attacking a policy that they in fact supported in the first place. Congress, recall, overwhelmingly voted for war in Iraq in October 2002, with the Senate authorizing the use of force in Iraq by a vote of 77–23 and the House approving it by a vote of 296–133. And four years earlier, under President Bill Clinton, 90 percent of the House and a unanimous Senate had approved the Iraq Liberation Act of 1998, which established that the policy of the United States called for regime change in Iraq.[24]

Another pillar of the Fifth Column is formed by Hollywood limousine liberals and champagne socialists, who always have something to say whether they're qualified to say it or not. Actor Woody Harrelson reminded us that "the war against terrorism is terrorism. The whole thing is just bullshit." Actor Charlie Sheen told a radio audience that 9/11 was a government conspiracy and the collapsing of the Twin Towers "a controlled demolition."[25]

Washed-up rock-and-roller Chrissie Hynde urged her concert crowd in San Francisco, "Have we gone to war yet? We fucking deserve to get bombed. Bring it on!" Television host Rosie O'Donnell said that President Bush "is basically a war criminal! He should be tried in the Hague!"[26]

The radical nongovernmental organizations, or NGOs, that support and finance the so-called peace movement make up the final element in the Fifth Column. All the major antiwar demonstrations, including all national protests against the post-9/11 wars in Afghanistan and Iraq, have been organized by three main groups: International ANSWER, United for Peace and Justice, and Not in Our Name. These and other groups have underwritten the campaigns of activists like self-anointed "peace mother" Cindy Sheehan, a radical who squealed, "America has been killing people on this continent since it was started," called George Bush "the world's biggest terrorist," and declared that her country "is not worth dying for."[27] These groups do much more than organize demonstrations. America-haters Medea Benjamin of Code Pink and Leslie Cagan of United for Peace and Justice personally delivered $600,000 in supplies and cash to terrorists fighting U.S. Marines in the bitter street combat of Fallujah. Left-wing congressman Henry Waxman, Democrat from California, signed a letter addressed to the U.S. ambassador in Jordan that may have helped facilitate the transaction.

This is not healthy democratic dissent. In the midst of a global war to defend national security and with American lives on the line, it's unconscionable.

WAR CRIMES

The Left has declared war on the U.S. military and the global War on Terror. For decades liberals have tried to emasculate the armed forces; now, in this global campaign against Islamofascists, their assault has become a full-fledged attack on America. While we fight evil abroad, liberals fight America at home.

It is time to indict the Left for their sabotaging of the War on Terror and their subversive actions. This indictment of the Left will be told from the perspective of the American fighting man and woman by a former Air Force officer. Through hundreds of interviews with soldiers of all ranks and services, including many conducted on the front lines in Iraq, I will expose the Left's campaign to defeat America and America's armed forces—and the scary truth: Their plan is working.

Only by exposing the Fifth Column can we hope to defeat its well-coordinated attack. Since 9/11 we have understood that Islamofascism represents the greatest threat America has ever known. But that's not quite right, it turns out. The only danger that can destroy our society must come not from abroad, but from within.

TWO

THE WAR WITHIN

Our God and soldier we alike adore
Ev'n at the brink of danger; not before:
after deliverance, both alike requited
Our God's forgotten, and our soldiers slighted.
——Francis Quarles, 1632

On July 8, 1972, piloting his F-4D Phantom in the skies over North Vietnam, Air Force Captain Steve Ritchie shot down two North Vietnamese MiG fighter aircraft—the Communists' most prized possession—in only 89 seconds of aerial combat. Two months later, he downed his fifth and final MiG, becoming the only "ace" the Air Force could claim in the entirety of the Vietnam conflict.

In another time and another war, Ritchie would have been honored as a national hero. A small-town boy and high school football star, Ritchie rose from noble roots and became one of America's most heroic fighter pilots.

But Ritchie's timing was bad. He fought in the "wrong war." As his reward for two combat tours in Southeast Asia, this brave fighter pilot received an airplane ride home and the wrath of his country. "I was spit on in San Francisco in uniform," Ritchie recalled.[1]

Fast-forward three decades.

On the Fourth of July 2004, twenty-three-year-old Army Specialist Jason Gilson, recently returned home from Iraq, the survivor of a terrorist ambush, joined his mother, siblings, and friends to march in the Independence Day parade in their hometown of Bainbridge Island, Washington. Proudly wearing his medals, Gilson carried a sign proclaiming "Veterans for Bush." It was, after all, a day for patriotism—red-white-and-blue bunting, American flags, and firecrackers—and Jason was celebrating his commander in chief.

Unfortunately for Gilson, the homecoming was humiliating. Like Steve Ritchie thirty years before him, he heard taunts and epithets from his fellow citizens—outrageous things like "Baby killer!" and "Murderer!" The parade's PA announcer picked Gilson out of the crowd of marchers and derisively asked, "And what exactly are you a veteran of?"[2]

In an earlier note from Iraq, Gilson had prophetically written, "Some of the American public have no idea how much freedom costs and who the people are that pay that awful price. I think sometimes people just see us as nameless and faceless and not really as humans. . . . A good portion of us are actually scared that when we come home, for those of us who make it back, that there will be protesters waiting for us and that is scary."[3]

The young soldier was deployed to Iraq at the direction of his president and with overwhelming consensus in Congress. He survived an enemy ambush nine thousand miles away only to come home to America . . . and be ambushed again. While the enemy had wounded his muscle and flesh, citizens from his country of birth attacked his spirit.

Sadly, many other U.S. service members have felt the sting of an ungrateful nation. In Steve Ritchie's day, protesters threw paper bags filled with dog feces over the fences at Travis Air Force Base in California, where gurneys held wounded soldiers; chanted, "Ho, Ho, Ho Chi Minh, Vietcong are gonna win!"; and vandalized and shut down ROTC offices on college campuses nationwide. Today, our fighting forces receive cards saying, "Dear Soldier, Have a great time in the war and have a great time dieing [*sic*] in the war,"[4] and endure relentless attacks from all elements of the left-wing Fifth Column—journalists, politicians, academics, "peace" organizations, and other activist groups.

The parallels between the experience of Vietnam veterans and that of the men and women fighting in the War on Terror are no accident. Vietnam changed the way America's wars were judged; America's Left disdained America's warriors then, and the years since have done nothing to temper their hostility.

THE HATRIOTS

Today's America-hating leftists are the foot soldiers of the counterculture revolution that came of age during the 1960s and Vietnam—the war liberals love to hate.

Perhaps my good friend David Horowitz has the clearest insight into the Left, having been the child of American Communists, a 1960s counterculture activist, and a key player in the antiwar movement before realizing its destructive pathologies and delusions. "Hatred of self, and by extension one's country, is the root of the radical cause," Horowitz has concluded. "My experience has convinced me that historical ignorance and moral blindness are endemic to the American left [and] necessary conditions of its existence. It does not value the bounty it actually has in this country."[5]

During the 1960s, shortly after the assassination of President John F. Kennedy, liberals abandoned the established successes of progressivism under FDR, Truman, and JFK for the increasingly polarized and radical politics of the New Left. When these liberals began to condemn the United States for its "imperialism," they came to revile a war they themselves had initiated. And, by association, they reviled those tasked with fighting it. Who else but dupes would fight for such an immoral country? And why would such dupes deserve glory? Todd Gitlin, along with Horowitz a member of the New Left and the antiwar effort, articulated this view when he acknowledged, "If you grew up in the 60s, the military is to some degree tainted. I won't say forever tainted. But it is tainted by its implication in the Vietnam War."[6]

The U.S. military thus became the object of the Left's hatred of America and a metaphor for all they saw as wrong. The military establishment represented ideals and policies anathema to the New Left: martial values, discipline, uniformity, physical courage, and moral strength derived from our Judeo-Christian heritage.

The New Left had grown out of the radical student movement led by Tom Hayden and his comrades in the Students for a Democratic Society (SDS), whose ideological manifesto, 1962's Port Huron Statement, codified their belief that America was responsible for global conflict and the social ills of racism, materialism, militarism, poverty, and exploitation. By 1968, Hayden and the New Left were staging riots outside the Democratic National Convention in Chicago in order to damage the candidacy of anti-Communist Hubert Humphrey. The tactic worked, and by 1972 the New Left activists had burrowed into the Democratic Party. The leftists pushed pacifist George McGovern to the Democratic presidential nomination and used antiwar fervor to elect seventy-six new Democrats to the House of Representatives and eight to the Senate. Included among the new congressmen were radicals Ron Dellums, Bella Abzug, Elizabeth Holtzman, Robert Drinan, David Bonior, Pat Schroeder, and former Black Panther Bobby Rush. Hayden himself, who had spent the previous decade preaching revolution, was elected to office in California that year.

The antiwar New Leftists had taken command, and they have

not relinquished it. They didn't seem to mind that their policies resulted in Communist takeovers and the unprecedented slaughter of 2.5 million Vietnamese and Cambodian peasants.

The Democratic Party—and the country as a whole—has been coping with the legacy of 1972 ever since. Many of today's anti–War on Terror politicians are veterans of the McGovern campaign, including Bill Clinton, Hillary Clinton, John Kerry, and Ted Kennedy. Many of the Democrats' key policy architects also come out of the anti–Vietnam War Left. Among them are Anthony Lake and Sandy Berger, both of whom served as national security adviser under President Bill Clinton, and Harold Ickes, Clinton's White House deputy chief of staff, money man, and dirty trickster. (In the 1970s Ickes worked with a young Bill Clinton to promote Operation Pursestrings, which aimed to eliminate all U.S. funding to South Vietnam following the negotiated peace settlement.) Today, both Ickes and Berger remain key advisers to Senator Hillary Clinton.

The New Left activists matured into positions of power outside of politics as well. They took to university faculties, teachers' organizations, the national press, Hollywood, religious institutions, and organized labor. They are our "enlightened elites"—college presidents, professors, newspaper editors, television anchors, columnists, politicians, playwrights, movie stars, recording artists, and leaders of organizations that all have their ideological birth in the 1960s.

Liberals won the Vietnam War because America lost. They are trying to pull off the same "victory" today in Iraq, in Afghanistan, and wherever else the United States must fight Islamofascism.

"NOT FOR OUR KIND OF PEOPLE"

The cultural gap between the Left and the military remains a chasm. What the Left really wants is no U.S. military at all, or at least not one that isn't shackled to the capricious United Nations and our increasingly incompetent European "allies." The only justified use of armed force for leftists over the past three decades has been flushing a religious cult out of its home in Waco, apprehending a young Cuban boy at gunpoint for deportation, launching feckless Clintonian-style CNN "wars" with overwhelming force and underwhelming justification in places like Haiti and Kosovo, and shooting missiles at empty tents and aspirin factories for ego-driven bumps in the public opinion polls or to divert attention from messy impeachment testimonies.

As a result, today's elites regard military culture as something alien and in need of dramatic transformation or elimination. Military scholar Mackubin Owens explains that "all too often, the American civilian elite see military culture not as something that contributes to military effectiveness, but as a problem to be eradicated in the name of multiculturalism, sexual politics and the politics of 'sexual orientation.' . . . That approach seeks destruction of the culture, not its reform."[7]

For this reason, America's elitists view military service as "something other people's children do" and the profession as unworthy. But this elitist approach is dangerous, explains classics scholar and political columnist Victor Davis Hanson: "The danger to a civilization has always been an overabundance of wealth, and how you inculcate to an affluent suburban youth principles of . . . patriotism, family values . . . civic duty. We have a large group of several million people in our media, government and universities who have the privilege and the luxury to almost make fun of, indeed, trash or criticize, the very culture that gave them so much abundance."[8]

A study conducted by Professors Peter D. Feaver from Duke University and Richard H. Kohn from the University of North Carolina found that leaders in civilian society were three to four times more likely than a military leader to say they would be "disappointed if a child of mine joined the military."[9]

Proving that he's traded his soul and abandoned his country for personal political aspirations, one-time Marine and combat veteran Congressman John Murtha told ABC News's *Nightline* flatly that he would not join the military today. When the interviewer followed up by saying, "And I think you're saying the average guy out there who's considering recruitment is justified in saying 'I don't want to serve'?" Murtha responded, "Exactly right." This from the top Democrat on the House of Representatives subcommittee overseeing defense spending.[10]

Even Republican senator John McCain, a former Navy fighter pilot and prisoner of war during Vietnam, confided, "The military is a career I would not recommend for my son at this period in time."[11]

Staff Sergeant Jason Rivera, a Marine recruiter in Pennsylvania, experienced the prejudice firsthand while visiting the home of a high school student who had expressed interest in joining the Marine Reserves. Hoping to discuss options with the student's parents, Rivera was met at the front door of the home in an upper-class neighborhood on Pittsburgh's north side by the student's mother. "I want you to know we support you," the mother told Rivera. "[But] military service isn't for our son. It isn't for our kind of people."[12] It's surprising she didn't ask him to use the water fountain labeled "for military only."

Frank Schaeffer, the bestselling author of *Keeping Faith* and *AWOL*, told of his upper-class neighbors' shock when they discovered that his son had joined the Marine Corps. "I live on the Volvo-driving, higher education–worshiping North Shore of Boston," Schaeffer explained. "I write novels for a living. I have never served in the military. It had been hard enough sending my two older children off to Georgetown and New York University. John's enlisting was unexpected, so deeply unsettling. I did not relish the prospect of answering the question, 'So where is John going to college?' from the parents who were itching to tell me all about how their son or daughter was going to Harvard. At the private high school John attended, no other students were going into the military." Schaeffer said one perplexed mother asked him, "But aren't the Marines terribly Southern?" Another parent said, "What a waste, he was such a good student." Still another, a professor at a nearby and rather famous university, spoke up at a school meeting and suggested that the school should "carefully evaluate what went wrong."[13]

These attitudes aren't confined to Schaeffer's town. A physician and mother in Los Angeles typified the antimilitary perspective when she said, "I've raised my sons to be sensitive to others, and to be critical thinkers, so I don't think they'd be well suited for the military."[14]

Harvard Business School professor Regina Herzlinger recounted attending a dinner party with fellow academics when the discussion turned to the war in Iraq. One guest, a "hippie-academic-turned-chef," as Herzlinger described him, was virulently antiwar and anti-Bush. When Herzlinger's husband remarked that their son, a Harvard graduate, had chosen to serve his country as a first lieutenant in the U.S. Infantry, the hippie, stunned, said, "I don't know anyone with a child in the military." All the other guests agreed.[15]

Consider how far our nation's cultural values have fallen. A generation ago the children of politicians, bank presidents, university professors, and oilmen commonly served in uniform. The families of Joseph Kennedy, Franklin Roosevelt, Prescott Bush, and, believe it or not, the Sulzbergers (of the *New York Times*) had sons who fought for the nation. Our American Republic was founded on the shoulders of the citizen soldier whose dedication and commitment, whether in peace or combat, has never been found wanting. Service in uniform was an obligation, a contribution to the greater good, and Americans from all educational, economic, and regional backgrounds answered the call.

Not today. During the mass mobilizations of World War II, almost 12 percent of the American population was active in the military and almost every family in the country had at least one

member serving in the armed forces. Today, active-duty and reserve military personnel make up less than one-tenth of 1 percent
of the population.[16]

In the 1990s, Bill Clinton became the first president since FDR
not to have served in uniform. In FDR's defense, though, he had
been the assistant secretary of the Navy under Woodrow Wilson
and had four sons who served as officers in World War II. Clinton
dodged the draft and wrote of "loathing the military." The last
president to have a child (in this case a son-in-law) in uniform
was Lyndon Johnson.

The participation gap is equally glaring in the houses of Congress. In 1971, the proportion of congressmen who were veterans
was 70 percent. In 2005, that figure stood at 35 percent in the Senate
and 27 percent in the House. Only slightly more than 1 percent of
the members of Congress could claim a child serving in uniform.[17]

Nowhere is the culture gap more pronounced than on the
campuses of America's universities, most notably the Ivy League
schools. Charles Moskos, a Northwestern University sociologist
who specializes in military issues, points out that in his Princeton
class of 1956, there were 450 students, out of about 750, who
served in the military.[18] By 2004, that number was down to 9 students out of about 1,100.

Throughout the 1950s, approximately one-half of the graduates of Harvard and Princeton entered the services for tours of
duty. Today, that's true of only 1 percent of their graduates.[19] At
one time, Columbia University was producing about as many
officers as the U.S. Naval Academy at Annapolis. ROTC has been
banned at Columbia since 1969.

LEFTIST MYTHS

It hasn't been enough for the leftist elites to abandon the military
themselves. Ever since Vietnam they have portrayed the armed

forces as bloodthirsty, racist, predators of the underprivileged, and worse. In doing so, the Left has created a false and debilitating characterization of the military that survives to this day.

Perhaps nobody is more responsible for the United States's losing the war in Vietnam or for creating false representations of American fighting men and women than former Navy Lieutenant John Kerry, now a U.S. senator from Massachusetts. In his infamous Winter Soldier testimony to the Senate Foreign Relations Committee in April 1971, Kerry, under oath, alleged that American servicemen in Vietnam were routinely committing war crimes "on a day-to-day basis with the full awareness of officers at all levels of command."[20] Specifically, Kerry, still a commissioned naval officer at the time, claimed that U.S. soldiers "had personally raped, cut off ears, cut off heads, taped wires from portable telephones to human genitals and turned up the power, cut off limbs, blown up bodies, randomly shot at civilians, razed villages in fashion reminiscent of Genghis Khan, shot cattle and dogs for fun, poisoned food stocks, and generally ravaged the countryside of South Vietnam."[21]

Kerry's testimony—later shown to be fraudulent and politically motivated—irresponsibly turned a nation's war effort into failure.

He also recklessly portrayed the returning American serviceman as broken, ruined, drug-addicted, and suicidal. With America watching, Kerry pontificated about how "the largest unemployment figure in the country . . . are veterans of this war, and of those veterans 33 percent of the unemployed are black. . . . I understand 57 percent of all those entering the VA hospitals talk about suicide. Some 27 percent have tried, and they try because they come back to this country and they have to face what they did in Vietnam. . . . There were 35,000 or some men, heroin addicts that were back. The problem exists for a number of reasons, not the least of which is the emptiness. It is the only way to get through it. A lot of guys,

60, 80 percent stay stoned 24 hours a day just to get through Vietnam."[22] This is a characterization that the Left, the media, academics, Hollywood, and Democratic politicians have perpetuated in the decades since.

Kerry sounded another familiar theme when he said, "We saw that many people in this country had a one-sided idea of who was kept free by our flag, as blacks provided the highest percentage of casualties."[23] The antiwar Left had spent the past several years caterwauling about the inequity of the military draft, which supposedly left only the poor, minorities, and the not-so-bright to fight the nation's battles. The draft, in fact, became the vehicle by which liberals turned public opinion against the war. Ultimately the protests led to the establishment of the all-volunteer military in 1973. (Of course, the high-minded arguments actually were in large part a smokescreen for being antidraft—the student activists simply didn't want to serve their country. While it is acknowledged by many that the draft was the major impetus behind the antiwar movement, it's noteworthy, but often overlooked, that antiwar activism on college campuses didn't explode until the Selective Service changed its rules and said students would no longer be eligible for deferments for graduate school or professional school.[24])

Historians and journalists have leveled similar accusations of class and race prejudice in the Vietnam-era military. In his bestselling book *Bloods,* journalist Wallace Terry claimed that blacks in the Vietnam War died in numbers far exceeding their representation in American society. "Black soldiers were accounting for more than 23 percent of American fatalities in Vietnam," claimed Terry's book jacket, "although blacks comprised only 10 percent of America's population."[25]

Appearing on PBS's *NewsHour* in April 2000, historian Michael Beschloss commented that Vietnam "was a war that, especially as it went on, was fought by Americans who were poor and African-American." Fellow historian Doris Kearns Goodwin agreed, saying, "I still think that one legacy that's left from [Vietnam], however, is that we let the draft go because we didn't want a selective draft, as we had in the war, because it seemed to weigh so heavily on those who were poor and working-class, and the middle-class, better-educated kids got out of it."[26]

Myra MacPherson, in her book *Long Time Passing,* put it more succinctly. "The best and the brightest" started the Vietnam War, she said, "but they did not send their sons."[27]

The poor boy fighting the rich man's war: It's a mantra liberals have applied well beyond Vietnam. Of course, we have not had a military draft since 1973, so the Left must now portray members of our all-volunteer military as *virtual* conscripts—*forced* to enlist for economic reasons (based, of course, on the prejudiced assumption that enlistees are unqualified to do anything else). When National Guardsmen and Reservists are activated or have their tours extended, they become, as John Kerry charged during the 2004 presidential campaign, victims of a "backdoor draft."[28]

Many other Democratic politicians have echoed Kerry's charges. In 2004, Democratic congressman Charles Rangel from New York claimed that "the disproportionately high representation of the poor and minorities in the enlisted ranks is well documented."[29] His fellow congressman John Conyers, Michigan Democrat, said that the nation has "an indirect draft of minorities and the poor."[30] Congressman John Murtha argued that the military is made up of "people who are volunteering because they could not find a job,"[31] while Congressman Pete Stark said that "just the poor and disadvantaged" serve our country today.[32]

Other liberals fall in line, especially in the media. Former CBS News anchor Dan Rather asked, "What drives American civilians [to join the military and] risk death in Iraq? In this economy it may be, for some, the only job they can find."[33] Andy Rooney of *60 Minutes* said, "We speak of [soldiers] as if they volunteered to risk their lives to save ours, but there isn't much voluntary about what most of them have done. A relatively small number are professional soldiers. During the last few years, when millions of jobs disappeared, many young people, desperate for some income, enlisted in the Army. . . . Most are victims, not heroes."[34] *New York Times* columnist Bob Herbert wrote, "The youngsters recruited most relentlessly are those from small towns, rural areas and impoverished urban neighborhoods. They are kids who are not well-to-do, and who don't have much of a plan for their future."[35] *Atlanta Journal-Constitution* columnist Cynthia Tucker agreed, writing, "Military recruits are pulled largely from . . . those whose prospects are less than stellar, from high school graduates who know they have little chance of affording college tuition, from young parents whose civilian jobs don't come with health insurance."[36]

Hollywood has joined the chorus as well. Actor Tim Robbins charged, "You've got middle-aged men who never served when they were young enough to serve in the armed forces now reaching their 50s and 60s and sending young men and women off to fight. And most of those [soldiers] they're sending off to fight are poor."[37]

Michael Moore peddled a similar argument in his pseudo-documentary *Fahrenheit 9/11*, which features a scene with Marine Corps recruiters hounding African-American high school students in an economically disadvantaged neighborhood. As he does throughout his propaganda hit piece, Moore cleverly but deceitfully intersperses edited clips with messages specifically designed to appeal to the Left. He narrates, "Where would [the military] find the new recruits? They would find them all across America in the places that had been destroyed by the economy. Places where one of the only jobs available was to join the Army."[38]

A couple of years later a supposedly respectable liberal "think tank" endorsed such claims. In 2005, the Center for American

Progress—which is run by former Clinton chief of staff John Podesta and bankrolled by billionaire George Soros—organized the Campus Progress National Student Conference, attended by Bill Clinton and other liberal luminaries. At the conference a booklet was distributed with the title *A Mind Is a Terrible Thing to Waste: A Guide to the Demilitarization of America's Youth and Students,* which said that "those of us who are poor and persons of color are aggressively recruited to fight and die for wars built on lies."[39]

There is only one problem with what John Kerry, Charles Rangel, John Conyers, the *New York Times,* Michael Moore, the Center for American Progress, and the rest of the bumper-sticker Left have to say: They're wrong! Their claims about the "helpless victims" of the U.S. military—whether forty years ago in Vietnam or today in the Middle East—are completely false.

THE GROUND TRUTH IN VIETNAM

Let's start with Vietnam, the source of so many antimilitary myths and feelings. The truth is that in the Vietnam War, minorities, the poor, and draftees did *not* represent a disproportionate share of the military or of those killed in action.

In their seminal book *Stolen Valor: How the Vietnam Generation Was Robbed of Its Heroes and Its History,* authors B. G. Burkett and Glenna Whitley debunk the myths about our soldiers in the Vietnam conflict.

To begin with, despite all the complaints about the Vietnam-era draft, only a little more than one-third of the 8.7 million Americans who served in uniform during the Vietnam War years entered service through the draft; the rest were volunteers.[40] At least 10 percent of all draftees volunteered to be drafted. And of those drafted, only 38 percent actually saw duty in the war.[41]

In addition, contrary to leftist assertions, the enlisted forces and draftees did not assume greater than their fair share of the sacrifice. Volunteers, in fact, represented 77 percent of those who died in the war, while they made up 62 percent of those serving in Vietnam. Officers—who were (and are) required to have a college degree and to volunteer—represented 13.5 percent of those who gave their lives in Vietnam, while representing only 12.5 percent of the total force.[42]

It is also a leftist fable that the poor and the uneducated bore an inequitable burden in Vietnam. In 1992, Professor Arnold Barnett from MIT and Captain Timothy Stanley from the U.S. Military Academy combined efforts to study the socioeconomic status of Vietnam veterans. Comparing the economic class of all those killed in Vietnam with a randomly generated group of their civilian contemporaries, Barnett and Stanley found that 30 percent of those who died had indeed come from the lowest one-third of the income range. But they also discovered that fully 26 percent of the combat deaths came from families earning in the top one-third. Servicemen from well-to-do backgrounds, they discovered, had an *elevated* risk of dying, as they were more likely to be pilots of aircraft or frontline infantry officers.[43]

Nor were Vietnam vets less educated than their "better and brighter" peers. In fact, exactly the opposite is true. Eighty percent of those who served in Vietnam had a high school education or better, compared with only 65 percent of those in the same age brackets in the civilian population.

Then there is the question of race. Despite what the Left often suggests, the burden in Vietnam did not fall unfairly on the shoulders of minority soldiers. African-Americans, who represented 10.5 percent of the overall U.S. population at the time and 13.5 percent of all draft-eligible males, accounted for just 10.6 percent of all who served in Vietnam.

Regarding those who paid the ultimate price in the war—

those killed in combat—the claims of John Kerry, Wallace Terry, Doris Kearns Goodwin, and Michael Beschloss are baseless. Young, conscripted blacks were no more likely to die in combat than members of other races. In all, 7,257 African-American servicemen paid the ultimate price fighting for their country in Southeast Asia; that's 12.5 percent of all U.S. soldiers killed in action, at a time when, again, blacks represented 13.5 percent of draft-eligible males. There were only two years when black fatalities exceeded national representation among their peer groups— 1965 and 1966, when there were large numbers of blacks in frontline combat units.[44] Upon realizing the disparity, Army and Marine Corps commanders implemented policies to reassign black servicemen in greater numbers to rear-echelon jobs. In 1969, at the height of the war, blacks accounted for 11.4 percent of the deaths, statistically in line with their representation in the military and below that of the population in general.[45]

White soldiers, meanwhile, constituted 88.4 percent of those who served in Vietnam and 86.8 percent of those killed in combat.[46]

So much for the canard that blacks were in Vietnam as slaves of a racist government sent to remote jungles eight thousand miles away to serve as cannon fodder.

The tragedy of the Left's continued playing of the race card is that it obscures the reality of African-American patriotism, valor, and willingness to fight for their country. In fact, blacks volunteered for the war at higher rates than did whites: 75 percent of blacks seeing duty in Vietnam were volunteers, not conscripted.[47] Twenty African-American servicemen were awarded the Medal of Honor for heroism in Vietnam, and one hundred received the Distinguished Service Cross.

Black Americans fought for their country because of their courage and patriotism, while rising above the racism they were forced to endure at home. That is the ground truth.

PATRICIANS AND GRUNTS

Though the record doesn't support the Left's outlandish claims about the Vietnam War, the myths persist, to the point that even respected historians blithely repeat them on national TV. It helps that the myths are politically useful: the falsehoods about Vietnam helped discredit that war. Medal of Honor winner Colonel George "Bud" Day, who was a prisoner of war during the Vietnam War, contends, "The false history of Vietnam has been used to demoralize our troops in combat, undermine the public's confidence in U.S. foreign policy and weaken our national security. . . . Radical leftists such as Jane Fonda lied about the war 35 years ago, and they're still lying about it today."[48]

Such lies still propel the Left's antimilitary crusade.

As the rhetoric of Michael Moore, Charles Rangel, Tim Robbins, and many other liberals indicates, the Left depicts soldiers the same way they did thirty years ago: poor and stupid. According to these liberals, America's military is built upon inner-city kids, dumb farm boys, high school dropouts, and kids who are dodging the law. These unsuspecting dupes are, according to the liberal caricature, brainwashed into shedding their "blood for oil." It's an incessant and insidious campaign.

Nationally syndicated talk radio host Laura Ingraham highlighted this bigoted elitism when she interviewed a representative from the antiwar organization Not in Our Name. Referring to the military, Ingraham asked the woman, who insisted on being called "Maya" only, "Are you saying they're all brainwashed and stupid?" Maya replied, "Yes. They only have two options, you can go to jail or you can go into the military. . . . This government sets it up very specifically so that targeted communities have to go into the military. I have many friends who joined the military because that was their option. They wanted to get out."[49]

Thirty-five years after slandering his Vietnam War–era

brothers-in-arms, Senator John Kerry told students at California's Pasadena City College, "You know, education, if you make the most of it, if you study hard and you do your homework, and you make an effort to be smart, uh, you, you can do well. If you don't, you get stuck in Iraq."[50] In the immediate aftermath of his reckless but telling statement, Kerry adopted an indignant stance and claimed he'd simply botched a punch line intended to be at the expense of the commander in chief, not the troops. But Kerry has built a political career on slandering America's military, beginning with his fraudulent testimony of 1971. His verbal gaffes in 2006—as when he accused the troops of terrorizing women and children in Iraq—speak volumes about the Left's mindset.

In fact, plenty of other liberal elites have unapologetically made the same argument that Kerry backpedaled from. Columbia University professor Hamid Dabashi, for example, told war protesters on campus that they were the " 'A' students, who think for themselves," as opposed to the " 'C' students with their stupid fingers on the trigger."[51]

Charles Rangel spoke for many on the Left when he told Fox News, "I want to make it abundantly clear. If there's anyone who believes that these youngsters want to fight, as the Pentagon and some generals have said, you can just forget about it. No young, bright individual wants to fight just because of a bonus and just because of educational benefits. And most all of them come from communities of very, very high unemployment. If a young fella has an option of having a decent career or joining the Army to fight in Iraq, you can bet your life that he would not be in Iraq."[52] Rangel also said, "It's just not fair that the people that we ask to fight our wars are people who join the military because of economic conditions, because they have fewer options."[53]

We don't and they aren't.

Like the myths about the Vietnam War, the Left's contemporary critiques of the armed forces are just wrong. In stark contrast to what the Left wants you to believe, today's military is a representative slice of our society. Upper- and lower-income families are represented proportionate to the population. More troubling for the myth spinners, the trend since 9/11 is that well-to-do families are sending their sons and daughters into uniform *more often* than lower-income families send theirs. For every two recruits the military signs up from the more economically depressed areas, three recruits enlist from the most affluent. They just happen not to come from the antimilitary liberal hotbeds of the Northeast or the West Coast.

The truth was revealed in several studies conducted by Tim Kane, Ph.D., of the Heritage Foundation. Kane has discovered that each year since 2000, the percentage of Americans enlisting from the poorest neighborhoods has decreased, while the percentage of those volunteering from the richest neighborhoods has increased.[54] In the most recent studies, only 14.6 percent of recruits came from the poorest areas, while 22.0 percent came from the richest.[55] As Dr. Kane also points out, the wealthiest 40 percent of America's neighborhoods are producing 45.6 percent of today's recruits.[56]

Moreover, Kane's studies give the lie to the claims that military recruits come from the dregs of America's schools and choose the armed forces as a last resort. In reality, today's soldiers are *more educated* than their peers in the civilian population. Virtually all enlistees—98 percent—have a high school diploma or better, whereas only 75 percent of the general population can make that claim.[57] New soldiers have, on average, 12.1 years of education, which would include some college experience. Nearly two-thirds of today's recruits are drawn from the top half of America in math and verbal aptitude.[58] Thirty-eight percent of all officers, and more than half of all Air Force officers, have advanced degrees.[59]

As for the claim that minorities are unfairly represented in the

military, the reality is that they are largely represented proportionate to their population. Overall, whites represent 67 percent
of the nation's active-duty military, compared with their 71 percent of the overall military-age population; blacks constitute 17
percent of the military and 13 percent of the population, a math-
ematically fair representation. Latinos are actually *underrepresented,* accounting for 9 percent of the armed forces and 11
percent of the population.[60]

While black Americans are slightly overrepresented in the enlisted forces, the percentage of black officers directly mirrors the
proportion of blacks in the overall population. Significantly, black
enlistees have a greater propensity to reenlist and spend a career
in uniform, as a military career offers equality and opportunity
for advancement that they might not find as easily in the civilian
world. Latinos, meanwhile, are not as underrepresented as they
used to be but still make up only 10 percent of the enlisted force
(as compared with 16 percent of the civilian population) and 4
percent of commissioned officers (as opposed to 5 percent of
comparably aged citizens with college degrees).[61]

Among those volunteering for military service today, whites
make up 73.1 percent—in line with their percentage of the population (75.6 percent). Blacks represent 13 percent of those enlisting
and 13 percent of the population as a whole. The areas of the country with the highest concentration of African-Americans account
for 14.6 percent of the adult population but only 14.1 percent of
new recruits. Recruiting data for 2005, for example, shows that
only two recruits signed up from Congressman Rangel's Harlem
district.[62] This disproves claims that the military specifically targets
minority neighborhoods—or if they are targeting such neighborhoods, they aren't finding commensurate numbers of applicants.
Hispanic enlistees make up 13.9 percent of those who join (compared to 14.2 percent of their peer population).[63]

What about the notion that minorities bear a disproportionate burden of fatalities in war? This leftist refrain is as inaccurate today as it was during Vietnam. The truth, then and now, is that the troops most likely to die in combat are white. Official casualty statistics for Operations Iraqi Freedom and Enduring Freedom report that as of March 24, 2007, white soldiers represented 74.9 percent of those killed in the war, Hispanic or Latino soldiers suffered 10.5 percent of the fatalities, and blacks 9.5 percent of U.S. fatalities.[64]

Whites serve in the combat units, in special operations units, and as pilots in higher percentages than their population and are thus more likely to confront the enemy. Blacks serve disproportionately in the support areas, such as administration, supply, and medical and dental units. Although blacks represent about 21 percent of the enlisted forces and 8 percent of officers, they constitute only 9 percent of infantry, or frontline, troops.[65]

The same was true during the Gulf War in 1991. Fully 86 percent of those who died in the Persian Gulf were white; 12.5 percent were black, at a time when African-Americans made up 13.1 percent of the population. The facts don't quite jibe with what the Reverend Jesse Jackson told a largely black audience on the eve of the Gulf War: "When that war breaks out, our youth will burn first."[66]

Ah, but facts are irrelevant when a myth furthers the Left's political agenda. Inaccurate as the claim is, the contention that minorities are sent to front lines as "cannon fodder" and incur a disproportionate burden of combat fatalities remains a staple for race-baiters and the antimilitary. Sometimes, though, leftists have to contort themselves into new positions to keep attacking the military. Today, many on the Left are clamoring for the very thing they denounced as a great evil during Vietnam: the draft. Yes, they've done a 180. In 2004, Congressman Rangel and fourteen of his liberal colleagues in the House went so far as to introduce legislation calling for reinstatement of military conscription.

But wait, wasn't it the draft that unfairly targeted the poor and minorities? Never mind. Rangel and Company didn't call for a draft out of a noble desire to secure victory against Islamofascism, needless to say; it was simply to denounce the way the military supposedly preyed on minorities and the underprivileged in recruiting. After all, the Left's ideology requires victims.

"WHY THEY FIGHT"

Whether or not the Left is willing to accept this reality, today's military is built completely from willing and capable volunteers. Our nation is fortunate that this is true. Indeed, even in the face of decades of efforts by the Left to reduce and denigrate the U.S. military, our Army, Navy, Air Force, Marines, and Coast Guard remain the most capable and motivated force the world has ever known.

Given that so many antiwar activists protested Vietnam because they didn't want to put their own butts on the line, it's not surprising that today they can't conceive of someone deciding to join the military of his or her own free will. But it's true, our soldiers, seamen, airmen, and Marines join because they want to. They join the military for many reasons—adventure, education, career opportunities, and, yes, patriotism. They don't do it for the money, or fame; there isn't enough money in the U.S. budget to compensate military members for their family's sacrifices, their long and arduous duties, their frequent and difficult geographic relocations, and a substantially increased likelihood of injury or death. Nor are they coerced into service or forced to join because they have no other alternative.

They come from a generation that trusts the institution of the military, quite unlike the Baby Boomer generation that spawned the New Left. A post-Vietnam 1975 Harris Poll reported that only 20 percent of people within the ages 18 to 29 had a great deal of confidence in the military.[67] In contrast, a recent poll by the Harvard University Institute of Politics found that 70 percent of college undergraduates trust the military to do the right thing either all or most of the time.[68]

In October 2004, the Annenberg Public Policy Center conducted a survey of the attitudes of military members. To the question, "What was your primary reason for joining the military?" 36 percent of all respondents said "serving the country," 28 percent replied for "the benefits," and only 4 percent answered for "job skills training." When the question was asked of officers and senior enlisted only (those who had chosen to continue beyond the initial enlistments), almost half of all officers joined to "serve the country" and 37 percent of noncommissioned officers agreed.[69]

Army Sergeant Joe Skelly, 411th Civil Affairs Battalion, was a professor of history and political science at the College of Mount Saint Vincent in New York City. Driving to work on the morning of September 11, 2001, Skelly heard the attacks unfold over the radio. "I knew immediately it was a terror attack and I started screaming that we had to take action," Skelly told me. "When I reached the campus I told a colleague, 'We're at war and we will win.' "[70] Professor Skelly drove to the nearest Army recruiter, enlisted in the National Guard, and became Sergeant Skelly.

Marine Corps Corporal Matt Sanchez, a junior at Columbia University, agreed. "I joined the Corps not because I couldn't make it elsewhere or because I needed money to go to school. No signing bonus was going to turn me into a soldier. I became a Marine because I wanted to be among the best, just as I applied to Columbia because I wanted to be among the brightest. I knew both required a high price."[71]

Army Specialist Christopher Arnold was a student at Rutgers University when the fateful attacks occurred. "I joined the military because of 9/11," Arnold told me. "I needed to make a difference. It's great to sit in a liberal academic classroom and debate the issues. It's altogether different to get involved and do something about it. I wanted to get involved and do something about it."[72]

Matt Pottinger, a journalist for the *Wall Street Journal,*

explained his reasons for leaving his civilian career to join the Marines: "I came across a video of an American in Iraq being beheaded by Abu Musab al-Zarqawi. . . . At first I admit I felt a touch of the terror they wanted me to feel, but then I felt the anger they didn't. We often talk about how our policies are radicalizing young men in the Middle East to become our enemies, but rarely do we talk about how their actions are radicalizing us. In a brief moment of revulsion, sitting there in that living room, I became their blowback."[73]

For many in the armed forces, their reasons for joining evolve into reasons to stay. Initial training in the armed forces emphasizes the virtues of courage, honor, duty, discipline, loyalty, and adherence to a professional code of conduct, all of which can have a profound impact on individuals. "Even if you don't have it when you enlist," explained Army Sergeant Kevin Blanchard, "they breed it into you to be a better person. When you go home you see how you're different than the people you grew up with."[74]

Once they enter, they stay and they fight because they form a bond with the other members of their unit. They become, as Shakespeare's Henry V put it, a "band of brothers." It sounds trite, but nothing could be more true. The bonds of trust between soldiers, sailors, airmen, and Marines take months of shared experiences to develop. It's the trust that calms you when you're in the midst of a firefight or flying aircraft in formation through bad weather, wings just feet apart from the other planes. It's a bond that defies description, a kinship and an understanding that only those with common experiences and common losses can truly understand.

U.S. Army First Sergeant Jeff Nuding explained it this way from his post in northern Iraq:

I [had] never fully understood the devotion expressed by survivors of past wars and conflicts. I must have thought somehow that such attachment of sentiment had to have something to do with something unique about the individuals or the units, or even the war. The Greatest Generation was great, wasn't it, because of the depth of their sacrifice or magnitude of their struggle or the great consequence of their triumph?

I don't think that anymore. I think I now understand the bond that veterans speak of, the bond of common experience, of course, but a bond of common sacrifice and loss as well. We have shed blood here. We leave a piece of the whole here. Innocence lost, some scarring in a place that had for most of us not known wound before. But we will never share with others outside, that connection to the past that does not travel with us forward in time. There are memories that will stay locked in OIF III [Operation Iraqi Freedom], in 2005, in the Month of June, in the sweltering heat of the Iraqi summer.[75]

When I spoke with soldiers and Marines in Iraq during the summer of 2005, I asked them what kept them going in the difficult combat conditions they faced. The most frequent response was "supporting my friends" and "protecting each other." One young soldier told me, "Sir, I'm fighting for my buddies and my buddies are fighting for me." Another described the intense relationship he felt for his fellow soldiers: "The guy next to you means more to you than anybody. He's got your back and you've got his. It has to work that way. And I know that if I mess up he'll get hurt . . . and that isn't going to happen."[76]

Marine Corporal Michael Pinkney looked around at the dust and deprivation in Iraq and said, "I don't want to be anywhere else but Iraq. . . . This is what manhood is all about. I don't mean macho shit either. I mean moral character."[77]

Staff Sergeant Jamie McIntyre of Queens, New York, told

American Enterprise magazine, "I look at faces and see fellow human beings, and I say, 'O.K. This is the sacrifice I have to make to bring them freedom.' That's why I joined the military. Not for the college money, for doing what's right. Fighting under our flag. That's what our flag stands for. I believe in that stuff. Yeah, we might lose American soldiers, but they are going to lose a society, lose a people. You've got to look at the bigger picture. I've lost friends, and it hurts. It definitely hurts. But that's even more reason why I say stay. It's something that has to be done. If we don't do it, who will?"[78]

In 2003, the Strategic Studies Institute at the U.S. Army War College at Carlyle Barracks, Pennsylvania, commissioned a study titled "Why They Fight" to examine the motivating factors of troops in combat. Interviewing members of Army and Marine units in the Baghdad and Al Hillah areas of Iraq, the researchers asked, "In your combat experience, what was most important to you in making you want to keep going and do as well as you could?"

One soldier stated, "I know that as far as myself, sir, I take my squad mates' lives more important than my own." Another spoke to the profound bonds he formed with his fellow soldiers: "That person means more to you than anybody. You will die if he dies. That is why I think that we protect each other in any situation. I know that if he dies and it was my fault, it would be worse than death to me." Speaking of the trust involved, an infantryman said, "You have got to trust them more than your mother, your father, or girlfriend, or your wife, or anybody. It becomes almost like your guardian angel."[79]

The all-volunteer force has produced a military that is also greatly motivated by compassion and patriotism. Soldiers understand that they are members of a values-based institution and not shift workers punching a time clock. They trust one another and their leaders, and understand the moral aspects of war.

This is how one soldier explained his motivations to "Why They Fight" researchers: "Liberating those people. Liberating Iraq.

Seeing them free. They were repressed for, I don't know how many years, 30 something years. Just knowing that they are free now. Knowing that is awesome to me."[80]

Another soldier related, "There were good times when we see the people . . . how we liberated them. That lifted up our morale. Seeing the little children. Smiling faces. Seeing a woman and man who were just smiling and cheering 'Good! Good! Good! Freedom good!' . . . That lifted us up and kept us going. We knew we were doing a positive thing."[81]

Still another said, "It may be a cornball answer, but believe me, I'm not into all that, but just actually seeing some of them waving and shooting thumbs up. They are like, 'We love you America!' . . . I am not like a very emotional person, but the kids come up to you, they give you a hug. One lady came up to one of our soldiers and tried to give him the baby so that the baby could give him a kiss. It was like, 'Whoa!!' It was a heartfelt moment for me."[82]

Marine Corps Lieutenant Brian Donlon described his service thusly. "Reflecting on what I have seen here in Iraq, the overwhelming emotion I feel is of pride, not in myself or even in my Marines, but in being an American. Patriotic sentiments tend to gravitate between cliché and taboo in the sensibilities of popular culture, but if I was not defined before as a 'patriot,' I am now. I am very proud to have been a small part of this effort and to come from a nation where not only could such an effort be sustained but whose aim was the betterment of another people a world away. . . . For all the insinuations of imperialism, corporate benefit and hawkish war-mongering, the most dramatic moments I witnessed here revolved around an election, not an exploitation. What other nation would spend such sums to give a people so far away self-determination?"[83]

Therein lay the answer. They do it because for them duty, honor, country, commitment, courage, and loyalty still have a home. For them service comes before self.

When was the last time you heard any of those qualities used to describe anybody in academia, Hollywood, the Democratic Party, or the media?

It's a culture the Left simply doesn't understand, certainly doesn't respect, and definitely wants eradicated. Former Democratic representative Pat Schroeder captured the Left's disdain for the armed forces years ago when she excitedly described problems the services were experiencing as "the sound of a culture cracking."[84]

She had it exactly wrong—it's not the military culture that's cracking.

THREE

———

THE LEFT'S MADRASSAS

The only true heroes are those who find ways that help defeat
the U.S. military.

> —Nicholas De Genova,
> professor of anthropology,
> Columbia University

At Saddleback College in Mission Viejo, California, Marco
Martinez is majoring in psychology. But he is not an ordinary
student. Marine Sergeant Marco Martinez is a genuine American
hero who proudly served his nation in Iraq. A veteran of Operation Iraqi Freedom and the 2nd Battalion, 5th Marines, he was
awarded the Navy Cross—second only to the Congressional Medal
of Honor as the nation's most distinguished honor—for gallantry
and courage under fire during the Battle of al Tarmiya.

On April 12, 2003, then-Corporal Martinez and his platoon of
forty-two Marines headed north from Baghdad, conducting a re-
connaissance mission on the outskirts of the town of al Tarmiya.
As the vehicles crossed a bridge, they entered into an ambush by

Iraqi Republican Guard and fedayeen troops. It was a textbook trap. Enemy gunners were stationed on both sides of the road and they had the Marines right where they wanted them—squarely in the middle of the "kill zone."

Enemy fire wounded several Marines, including Martinez's squad leader. Realizing that his leader was down, Corporal Martinez quickly assumed command of the squad. Another Marine was shot in both legs, his spine severed. In the face of intense fire emanating from a nearby garden shed, Martinez used his body as a shield to allow the wounded Marine to be evacuated.

Then, armed only with a rifle and a single hand grenade, Martinez turned his sights on the enemy, mounting a 20-meter charge directly into the gunfire. Bullets pinged off his protective vest. Reaching the wall of the terrorist hideout, Martinez unpinned the grenade and lobbed it through a window, killing four enemy soldiers. When asked later if he was afraid, Martinez said quietly, "There's really no time for fear."[1]

Sergeant Martinez personifies the American dream. He'll be the first male in his family to graduate from college and is the first Hispanic since Vietnam to earn the Navy Cross. In the United States, Sergeant Martinez's accomplishments should engender public adulation and gratitude particularly from the Left, which pretends to champion minority rights and accomplishments.

In the netherworld of American academia, however, there is no appreciation for the dream or for the uniform—only vitriol and condemnation. Martinez explained the reception he received to National Review Online: "A woman on campus had apparently learned I might be a Marine. When I told her I was, she said, 'you're a disgusting human being and I hope you rot in hell!'"[2]

The traditional values—duty, honor, country—that make America's military the greatest and most compassionate in the history of the world are not only unwelcome on the nation's campuses, they are openly disdained. Our institutions of higher learning have become occupied territory, hotbeds of anti-Americanism where our youth is indoctrinated, patriotism scorned, military service reviled, and the notion of heroism ridiculed.

Sergeant Martinez has risen above all these shots. Bullets have more impact. With characteristic Marine humility he said, "There are a lot of people who don't appreciate military service in college. If someone asks me about it, and I think that they're not too liberal, I might tell them I was in Iraq. But I don't tell them the full extent of it or anything about the Navy Cross."[3]

MILITARY-FREE ZONES

Nowhere in our culture is the anti-American and antimilitary movement more unabashedly embraced than in the nation's educational system—universities, colleges, high schools, elementary levels, and, yes, even preschools. Just as jihadists have successfully institutionalized their extreme Islamist and anti-Westernism doctrine in madrassas, so too have America's academics seized the educational system as a platform for fomenting their radical ideologies.

This isn't a recent development. Germany's universities were among the first institutions to support Adolf Hitler's policies in the 1930s. In the face of the spreading Nazi aggression, England's renowned debating society the Oxford Union resolved "not to defend King and country." The inevitable result of academia's shortsighted and misguided perspective was world war and the deaths of tens of millions.

In this country, the campus unrest of the 1960s spurred the opposition to the Vietnam War and led to American withdrawal from Vietnam—the result of which was the deaths of 2.5 million people. Today, blind to the repeated lessons of history, educational institutions propound the message that America is imperialist, its leaders are warmongers, and the U.S. military is evil.

It wasn't always this way. For most of this nation's history America's intellectuals abandoned classrooms and filled our nation's ranks to fight for liberty and justice. It was understood that to be a soldier was to be a good citizen. A statue of Nathan Hale stands in front of the oldest building at Yale University as a reminder of the role educational institutions once played in our nation's defense. Hale, a member of Yale's class of 1773, served as a captain in George Washington's Continental Army during the Revolutionary War. Captured by British General William Howe and hanged at the age of twenty, Hale is remembered for his inspiring final words: "I only regret that I have but one life to lose for my country."

Thomas Jefferson, arguing that "the good sense of the people is the strongest army our government can ever have," proposed that military training be incorporated into the curricula of colleges and universities. Congress eventually created a system of collegiate military training at land-grant colleges when it passed the National Defense Act of 1916, on the eve of America's entry into World War I. Fearful of being left out of the patriotic response, Ivy League schools petitioned to be included.

Our most prestigious colleges embraced Reserve Officer Training Corps (ROTC) detachments, which produced the overwhelming majority of America's officers. Columbia University became one of the first to host an ROTC program in 1916. Harvard and Yale established their programs in 1917, Princeton in 1919; by 1955 every Ivy League school hosted its own detachment. During World War I, World War II, and the Korean War, institutions such as Columbia, Harvard, Yale, and Princeton were vital training grounds for military officers.

But we're very far removed from those days. The mutually beneficial marriage of the military and education ruptured in the 1960s, when the New Left emerged. In the aftermath of their successful campaign to twist Vietnam from military victory into humiliating international defeat, these antiwar activists didn't go away. They pursued advanced degrees, became tenured, and hired like-minded people in what German radical Rudi Dutschke termed the "long march through the institutions."[4]

New leftist leader and current Columbia University professor Todd Gitlin confessed, "All that was left to the Left was to unearth righteous traditions and cultivate them in universities. The much-mocked 'political correctness' of the next academic generations was a consolation prize. We lost—we squandered the politics— but won the textbooks."[5] Harvard University English professor Robert Brustein noted, "The radical students who once occupied university buildings over the Vietnam War . . . are now officially occupying university offices as professors, administrators, deans and even presidents."[6]

And as they did, they increasingly viewed themselves not as educators whose mission was to *enhance* society but as proponents of an adversary culture whose goal was to *change* it.

The statistics reveal just how ideologically homogeneous our campuses are today. To say that college faculties are largely liberal is hardly news, but the uniformity of views in an institution preaching diversity and the healthy debate of ideas is simply staggering, as study after study reveals.

In an academic review of more than 180 colleges and universities and 1,600 faculty members, researchers found that liberals outnumbered conservatives by a 5-to-1 ratio.[7] Another study revealed that 72 percent of professors at American universities consider themselves "liberal," while only 15 percent consider themselves "conservative"; in elite institutions the disparity is even greater, with 87 percent professing to be liberal and only 13 percent conservative. "What's most striking is how few conservatives there are in any field," the report concluded.[8]

A separate study focusing specifically on political party affiliation discovered the ratio of college professors claiming to be

Democrats has increased significantly since the Vietnam era. In 1970, the proportion of professors who were Democrats was 3 out of 5; today that figure is 8 out of 9. More troubling, the researchers noted that Republicans and conservatives were being "sorted out" of academic positions.[9]

Another survey devoted to the political bias at 32 elite colleges and universities found the overall ratio of Democrats to Republicans was 10 to 1. At Brown, the ratio was 30 to 1, at Columbia and Yale 14 to 1, at Pennsylvania, UCLA, and Berkeley 12 to 1. At four elite schools, including the Massachusetts Institute of Technology, not a single Republican was found on the faculty.[10]

This overwhelming disparity exists not only at the more prestigious schools. At the University of California–Santa Barbara, 97 percent of the professors are Democrats; at the University of Colorado, a public university in a conservative state, 94 percent of the liberal arts faculty are Democrats; and at the University of North Carolina, 91 percent of the faculty are registered Democrats.[11]

Can you imagine the hysterical squawking from the Left if the tables were turned? If political ideology were an ethnicity, a gender, a sexual orientation, or a physical handicap, liberals would be screaming for "affirmative action." But instead we are left with liberal orthodoxy on America's campuses, which Professor William Forstchen of Montreat College in North Carolina aptly summed up by saying, "Freedom of Speech is a river that moves in only one direction at most of our universities . . . downhill and to the left."[12]

ROTC: A FOUR-LETTER WORD

As the Left marched through higher learning, they went to enormous lengths to guarantee that campuses remained patriotism-free. Two key elements of the effort to subvert America's armed forces were to disband and outlaw ROTC units at the elite schools and to prohibit on-campus visits from military recruiters. The once vibrant and thriving conduit for military officers was closed.

Columbia University, which at one time produced as many officers as the Naval Academy, hasn't allowed a U.S. military presence on its campus since 1969. That year, Students for a Democratic Society (SDS) launched major antiwar protests at Columbia, seized school buildings, and tossed Molotov cocktails into the ROTC offices. Soon thereafter, university faculty banished all ROTC from campus, and the prohibition has stood ever since. So bitter is the disdain for military service that even if Columbia students choose to take ROTC classes elsewhere (which a handful do at Fordham University and Manhattan College), the university prohibits their transcripts from reflecting participation or credit.

Apparently, though, the military is the only group Columbia refuses to embrace, as left-wing student associations such as Amnesty International, the American Civil Liberties Union (ACLU), the Columbia Anti-War Coalition, the International Socialist Organization, the Campaign to End the Death Penalty, Everyone Allied Against Homophobia, and the Columbia University Greens are allowed to champion their causes.

A recent victim of the antimilitary bigotry and abuse on campus, Columbia University student (and Marine Corps reservist) Matt Sanchez recalled,

> I was talking with friends when a group of students gathered in mass and started to yell, "Get off our campus! The military exploits minorities!" they chanted in a frenzy.
>
> It does? "Hey," I replied, "I'm a minority; I joined the military, and I don't think I'm being exploited."
>
> "That's because you're stupid—too stupid to realize you're being used as cannon fodder."

What disturbed me was the odd disconnect between Columbia University, an elite institution of higher learning, and
the Marine Corps, an elite branch of the military. The group
I had offended just wanted a poster boy. So they printed a
flier of me next to a dead Iraqi kid and a homeless veteran
and wrote "Victim?" next to it.

The university has chalked it up to free speech. All points
of view are welcome at Columbia, from Venezuelan presidents to voices from vaginas. Unless you're in the military.[13]

Similar disdain for military service exists at other elite institutions, including Harvard, Yale, Stanford, Brown, and Dart-
mouth—none of which, incidentally, have any problem accepting
millions of dollars annually in Department of Defense research
monies. In 1969, the Harvard and Yale faculties sided with the
radical Left and withdrew all curricular and academic status from
ROTC. Yale students who want a military education must rise
early and travel 70 miles to the University of Connecticut for Air
Force ROTC or 23 miles to Sacred Heart for Army training.

While president of Harvard, Lawrence Summers supported
reinstating ROTC on his campus. Military service, the former
treasury secretary said, was "vitally important to the freedom that
makes possible institutions like Harvard."[14] In a devotion his peers
must have found disturbing, he delivered commencement addresses for Harvard's few graduating military cadets. Of course,
Summers didn't last long at the university; Harvard's entrenched
lefties would not stand for his traditional views on this and many
other issues.

The double standards these bastions of "inclusion" practice
can be truly appalling. While continuing to ban ROTC, Harvard
had no qualms about inviting the former president of the Islamic
Republic of Iran, Hojat al-Islam wa al-Moslemeen Sayyed Mu-
hammad Khatami, to its campus in 2006. Khatami is a follower of
the late Ayatollah Ruhollah Khomeini, who harbored the terrorists

responsible for murdering nineteen U.S. servicemen at Khobar Towers in 1996, and is charged with murdering more than 1,300 of Iran's citizens during his rule.

Yale, meanwhile, continues to exclude its students from a military curriculum, but it has admitted Sayed Rahmatullah Hashemi—a former senior official in Afghanistan's Taliban government, under which homosexuals and women were beaten and murdered—as a student. Hashemi's transcript boasted only a fourth-grade education.

Today, students and faculty base their protest of military presence on campus on Washington's "don't ask, don't tell" policy, which prohibits openly gay lifestyles in the uniformed ranks. In reality, that's a smokescreen not-so-artfully concealing an underlying institutional hatred of all things military.

In 2005, Columbia's university senate—composed of administration, faculty, and students—revisited whether or not to restore ROTC on campus. The vote was 53–10 to retain the ban, with President Lee Bollinger among those choosing to deny interested students the opportunity to join our military during wartime. In a passionate argument against allowing the military to return, Columbia provost Alan Brinkley equated the right of gays to openly practice their lifestyle in the military to black Americans' long march for equality. "Would we agree to an organization on campus," Brinkley asked, that allowed "African-Americans to join this organization only if they pass for white? . . . Is there a difference? Does the moral weight of the demands by gays and lesbians have less moral weight than demands by any other minority?" He received long applause from the audience.[15]

Brinkley's argument greatly obfuscates the facts. Legislation prohibiting the open practice of alternative sexual lifestyles in the services didn't come along until 1993—and then under the auspices of the liberal Clinton administration—which doesn't nearly explain the intervening twenty-four years during which ROTC was excluded from elite campuses. Moreover, the "don't ask, don't tell" policy is a federal law, not a Defense Department policy, and one that the U.S. Congress could alter if it so desired. Finally, ROTC students are not *in* the military and are not subject to the legal constraints of active duty. They are commissioned upon graduation.

If the leftist aristocrats were genuinely interested in the plight of gays, they might be forced to acknowledge that since 2001 the U.S. military has ousted two regimes under which homosexuals were stoned for sport and gay sex was punishable by death. And Columbia University might be forced to explain how it can bar the U.S. military from campus but unscrupulously accept $200,000 toward an endowment for Middle Eastern studies from the United Arab Emirates, where homosexuality is similarly punishable by death.

If it weren't the rights of gays, there'd be another issue the academy's disaffected Left would quickly rally around to denounce our armed forces. Indeed, the real reason academic elites protest any military presence on their campuses has nothing to do with the human rights of gays or the pursuit of academic freedom. They have made their hatred for the military abundantly clear.

Barton Bernstein, a professor of history at Stanford, spoke for many ivory tower elites when he condemned ROTC for "preparing students for war and training them to kill, and that is fundamentally unacceptable at a university."[16] The academic senate at the University of California–Santa Barbara launched a campaign opposing ROTC based on their beliefs that "the war system in which we are all so deeply involved has become too destructive to tolerate any longer."[17] Protesters vandalized the ROTC offices at the University of North Carolina and North Carolina State with red paint and slogans reading "We won't fight your wars" and "Army ROTC trains murderers; resist acts of war."

Student Nick Rosenthal revealed the real justification for the institutional bigotry and elitist arrogance in an op-ed he wrote for the *Columbia Spectator* titled "ROTC, You Are (Still) Not Wanted Here." "Joining the military is flushing your education down the toilet," concluded Rosenthal. "We do not want a military presence on this campus, and we do not wish to see our school assisting the U.S. military in any way. By accepting ROTC on campus, Columbia would be encouraging some of its students not to be great thinkers but to be warriors whose purpose is to kill."[18]

At the University of Washington, the student senate met to consider erecting a memorial statue of graduate and World War II legendary hero Colonel Gregory "Pappy" Boyington. The resolution recognizing the Medal of Honor winner was rejected because, as student Jill Edwards reasoned, they didn't believe "a member of the Marine Corps was an example of the sort of person U.W. wanted to produce."[19]

So much for diversity.

"HEY, RECRUITERS, GO AWAY!"

Military recruiting efforts at universities fare no better than ROTC programs. Once encouraged to interview prospective officers, military recruiters over the past few decades have been prohibited from even setting foot on campuses.

In January 2005, hundreds of students at Seattle Central Community College interrupted a campus job fair by throwing water bottles, newspapers, and insults, forcing military recruiters to flee under security escort. "We do not want the military in our schools asking our friends and family to fight for a war that is wrong," student Nicole Thomas said. "We want recruiters out of our schools."[20]

On March 9, 2005, more than one hundred students at San Francisco State University protested Air Force and Army recruiters who were handing out literature. "Our military is racist, homophobic, sexist and screwing people," said student Michael

Hoffman. Student Sarah Ballinger concluded that the military was "a discriminatory organization that is taking our brothers and sisters and classmates to a war for oil and empire."[21]

Writing in Cornell's student newspaper, *The Sun*, Professors Moncrieff Cochran and William Trochim, along with students Patrick Young and Bekah Ward, argued their opposition to allowing military recruiters on campus by stating that "they are selling a career in killing."[22]

At the University of California–Berkeley's job fair in April 2005, members of the Berkeley Stop the War Coalition attempted to interdict military recruiters, carrying signs that read "Get the Military off UC" and "US Out of Berkeley" (although, having lived near there for a time in the 1990s, I can confirm that we were removed a long time ago).[23]

In April 2005 and 2006, hundreds of protesters stormed the campus job fair at the University of California–Santa Cruz, shouting, banging on windows, and demanding that military recruiters, leave. They chanted, "Racist, Sexist, Anti-Gay. Hey, recruiters, go away!" and "Whose campus? Our campus!" They carried signs and banners proclaiming, "Military Off Our Campus," "Destroy the War Machine," and "F*** the Army!" Recruiters reported that the tires of their cars were slashed. On both occasions, police were called in to defuse the situation.[24]

THE SOLOMON BATTLES

The rare voices of reason on elite campuses have learned how hard it is to combat the antimilitary bias on campuses. (Just ask Larry Summers.) The U.S. Congress has learned the same lesson.

In the mid-1990s, the Republican Congress decided to try to lift academia's ban on the military. Congressman Gerald Solomon of New York proposed, and Congress passed, an amendment designed to stop taxpayer subsidization of the anti-

American and antimilitary agenda on university campuses. The original version of the Solomon Amendment denied Department of Defense funding to schools if they refused access to military recruiters.

Not surprisingly, however, the Clinton administration and Janet Reno's Justice Department ignored the Solomon Amendment. Consistent with the Clintons' loathing of the military, the government did nothing to enforce the amendment or to compel the universities to allow recruiters on campus.

In 1996, Congress attempted to up the ante by adding the potential funding of the Departments of Labor, Education, and Health and Human Resources to the law. Still, the Defense Department did little to enforce the statute, as it reeled from the devastating budget cuts and the numbing malaise of the Clinton years.

Things changed after the Bush administration came in and, even more important, after 9/11. Facing a long, global campaign against terror, the Pentagon in the spring of 2002 began turning the screws on federally subsidized schools that continued to deny access to recruiters. The Air Force sent letters to dozen of law schools informing them that unless the prohibitions on military recruiters were lifted, the federal government would withdraw all funding. The administrations at these institutions relented . . . for a while. Apparently, even the ivory towers have their price. Yale, for example, receives approximately $350 million in federal funding *annually.* Fearing the loss of all that cash, Yale permitted military recruiters to participate in their employment interviews. Harvard, given the choice either to permit the military on campus or to lose $300 million in federal funds, also opted for the money. In other words, "We have to let the buzz-cut warmongering barbarians visit, but we don't have to like it!"

What does any self-respecting left-wing group do when forced to accept results counter to its ideology? Sue, of course.

In October 2003, the Yale Student/Faculty Alliance for Military Equality and OutLAWS—an organization for lesbian, gay, bisexual, and transgender law students—filed a lawsuit against the government to stop the Solomon Amendment on the grounds that the Defense Department's "don't ask, don't tell" policy on sexual orientation violated the university's nondiscrimination policies. An amalgamation of law schools, professors, and student groups under the umbrella of the Forum for Academic and Institutional Rights (FAIR) charged that the Solomon Amendment violated free speech and the ability of schools to enforce their "antidiscrimination" policies. FAIR lawyer Josh Rosencrantz told *National Review Online,* "If the first amendment gives bigots the right to discriminate against gays then certainly it gives the right to right-minded academic institutions to discriminate against bigots."[25] Thirty-one law schools participated in the suit, including Georgetown, Boston College, George Washington, Stanford, and, not surprisingly, Harvard.

In short, instead of working to close the gap between the academy and the military, academia sought to widen it.

Congress strengthened the Solomon Amendment in March 2004 by explicitly requiring institutions to afford military recruiters the same access as recruiters from any other employer—corporations such as Microsoft, Ford, and AT&T. But in December of that year a federal court rendered the change moot. The Third U.S. Circuit Court of Appeals ruled the Solomon Amendment unconstitutional.

Immediately, Harvard and others announced that they were sending military recruiters packing. So discrimination against homosexuals was unacceptable. But discrimination against the *military*? Apparently that was just fine.

The Democratic side of the U.S. Congress colluded with these radical academics and judges legislating from the bench. Although on February 2, 2005, the House of Representatives voted to uphold the Solomon Amendment, eighty-four members of the

House voted against the resolution, which, during a time of war, qualifies at a minimum as shameful abandonment of our men and women in uniform and a dangerous threat to our ability to field a talented officer corps in the future. Among those who voted "nay" (all Democrats and one Independent) were Nancy Pelosi (now the speaker of the House), Charles Rangel, John Conyers, Rahm Emanuel, Barney Frank, Maurice Hinchey, Sheila Jackson Lee, Dennis Kucinich, Jerry Nadler, and Henry Waxman.

It's interesting to note that Rangel and others on that list have beaten the tired drum that our military is made up only of the sons and daughters of the poor and oppressed. But when the military wanted access to elite college campuses—where, ostensibly, the sons and daughters of the rich reside—they voted no.

But the reprieve was short-lived for Harvard and the other liberal elite universities. In March 2006, the U.S. Supreme Court unanimously overturned the lower court's ruling, showing that America's law professors were incapable of properly interpreting the clear language of the First Amendment. Chief Justice John Roberts wrote in the decision, "A military recruiter's mere presence on campus does not violate a law school's right to associate, regardless of how repugnant the law school considers the recruiter's message. . . . The Solomon Amendment neither limits what law schools may say nor requires them to say anything."[26]

So, for now at least, the law stands. But let there be no doubt, academia's decades-old war against the U.S. military will continue. The left-wing radicals who rule the academy will see to that.

THE AYATOLLAHS OF HATE

The ideological homogeneity on America's campuses allows radical leftists to flourish. One of the most powerful messages these intellectual radicals propagate is that the U.S. military is evil and that American leaders are warmongers.

Probably the most visible and infamous of the hate-America radicals is MIT professor Noam Chomsky. It's impossible to understate Chomsky's impact on the Left. David Barsamian, who hosts the show *Alternative Radio*, refers to him as "our rabbi, our preacher, our rinpoche, our pundit, our imam, our sensei."[27] Chomsky is a rock star, almost literally. Popular groups such as Pearl Jam, U2, and Rage Against the Machine quote Chomsky-isms during their concerts. Hollywood's award-winning film *Good Will Hunting* featured actor Matt Damon lecturing fellow college students with a fiery recitation of Chomsky on the evils of American imperialism. Venezuela's tyrannical leader Hugo Chavez considers Chomsky his favorite American writer and even displayed a copy of the professor's book *Hegemony or Survival* when addressing the United Nations in 2006. While denouncing President George Bush as an "imperialist, fascist, assassin, genocidal" and "the devil," Chavez was absolutely Chomsky-like.[28]

The *New York Times* called Chomsky "arguably the most important intellectual alive," Britain's *The Guardian* declared that he "ranks with Marx, Shakespeare, and the Bible as one of the ten most quoted sources in the humanities—and is the only writer among them still alive,"[29] and *The New Yorker* proclaimed him "one of the greatest minds of the 20th century."[30] But David Horowitz of the Freedom Center described Chomsky more accurately: "without question, the most devious, the most dishonest, and—in this hour of his nation's grave crisis—the most treacherous intellect in America . . . the leader of a secular religious cult, the ayatollah of anti-American hate."[31]

As a professor of linguistics, Chomsky was just a stilted academic until he made the transition from campus intellectual to radical leftist in the mid-1960s. In articles published in the *New York Review of Books* and other publications over the past forty years, he has fiercely criticized America's involvement in the Vietnam War and the Cold War, and likened the United States to Nazi

Germany. In his book *9/11,* he declared the United States to be one of the world's "leading terrorist states."[32]

Very early on, the U.S. military became a particular target of his ire. Chomsky called the Pentagon "the most hideous institution on this earth" and suggested that our men in uniform "constitutes a menace to human life."[33]

The New Left adopted him during the 1960s as one of its leading spokesmen. Chomsky's words and actions allied him with fellow radicals Jane Fonda, Tom Hayden, Susan Sontag, John Kerry, and Ramsey Clark—all of whom conspired against America during the Vietnam War. Like many of his cohorts, Chomsky illegally visited Hanoi. After his visit there in April 1970, he produced a propaganda broadcast on behalf of the Communists in which he praised our enemy's "liberty and justice" at a time when the North Vietnamese were torturing and killing American prisoners of war. According to his own account of his visit, he "sang songs, patriotic and sentimental, and declaimed poems" with his hosts.[34]

The seriousness of these actions cannot be underestimated: Chomsky, like his fellow turncoats, aided and abetted America's enemy at a time of war.

Chomsky was also smitten with Cambodia, its ruthless leader Pol Pot, and the Khmer Rouge. When later confronted with the realities of the murderous regimes of both postwar Vietnam and Pol Pot's Cambodia (2.5 million were murdered after the United States withdrew from the region), Chomsky blamed a failed rice crop and ultimately the United States.[35]

For Chomsky and his minions, it's *always* America's fault.

Indeed, in his view the "major policy goal" of the United States "has been to maximize repression and suffering in the countries that were devastated by our violence." He also has said that "there's a very solid case for impeaching every American president since the Second World War," since "they've all been either outright war criminals or involved in serious war crimes."[36]

Chomsky fell out of the public eye with the collapse of the Soviet Union, a nation he had often championed. He reemerged with the attacks of 9/11. The day after the attacks, with the nation shocked and grieving, he railed that America had had it coming. Over the past two centuries, Chomsky claimed, "the U.S. annihilated the indigenous population (millions of people), conquered half of Mexico, intervened violently in the surrounding region, conquered Hawaii and the Philippines (killing hundreds of thousands of Filipinos), and in the past half century, particularly, extended its resort to force throughout much of the world. The number of victims is colossal."[37] In other words, the attacks on America were a justified response to America's past "transgressions"—a view identical to that of Osama bin Laden.

In October 2001, just a few days into U.S. military intervention in Afghanistan, Chomsky argued that America was conducting a "silent genocide" against the people of Afghanistan. Chomsky wildly (and incorrectly) predicted that the U.S. military response would lead to the starvation of 3 to 4 million Afghans.

Chomsky has not eased off in the years since the 9/11 attacks. In fact, in May 2006 he traveled to Lebanon and visited the headquarters of the terror organization Hezbollah. Al-Manar, Hezbollah's television network, trumpeted the visit from the famous U.S. intellectual, who declared once again that America is "one of the leading terrorist states."[38]

Noam Chomsky's leftist soul mate is Boston University political science professor Howard Zinn. The source for much of the leftist reinterpretation of history is Zinn's radical text *A People's History of the United States.*

Zinn writes from an unabashedly Marxist point of view and explains virtually every major historical event as driven by greed. When Christopher Columbus discovered the New World, it was solely for "slaves and gold"; the Revolutionary War was the result of the tyrannical profiteering of the Founding Fathers; the Civil War was about "money and profit, not the movement against slavery"; World War I was precipitated because "American capitalism needed an international rivalry"; World War II was caused not by Nazism and Pearl Harbor but by American businessmen and diplomats seeking to expand their empire and economic reach.[39]

Amazingly, this claptrap propaganda is one of the bestselling history books of all time and has been required reading in many high school and college history courses for the past quarter century. The academy has given the book this welcome reception in spite of the fact that it is based totally on Zinn's personal Marxist worldview and not on actual American history. Zinn admits as much. "Objectivity is impossible," Zinn wrote, "and it is also undesirable. . . . I wanted my writing of history, and my teaching of history to be a part of social struggle."[40]

Like Chomsky, Zinn detests the U.S. military. "The use of military power abroad, in the history of this country, has not been for moral purposes, but to expand economic, political, and military power," Zinn has said. "I think the real objectives have to do with the control of Mideast oil, and with the expansion of military bases to even more countries in the world . . . and with the political advantages seen by a 'war on terrorism' which is used to rally the public behind the president."[41] And, "[I]t is safe to say that since World War II, there has not been a more warlike nation in the world than the United States."[42]

In a column he wrote for *The Guardian*, Zinn exported his hatred overseas. "It is not only Iraq that is occupied," Zinn contended. "America is too. The U.S. is in the grip of a president surrounded by thugs in suits. . . . And then the largest lie, that everything the U.S. does is to be pardoned because we are engaged in a 'war on terrorism,' ignoring the fact that the war is itself terrorism."[43]

Unlike Chomsky and Zinn, University of Colorado professor Ward Churchill was virtually unknown before September 11. But he became a leftist icon immediately following the terrorist attacks.

Soon after 9/11, he wrote a paper titled " 'Some People Push

Back': On the Justice of Roosting Chickens," with the thesis that the World Trade Center and Pentagon were legitimate terrorist targets given American imperialism and "Christian aggression" toward Islam. In the essay, which he eventually turned into a book, he called Americans killed on September 11 "little Eichmanns," equating the murdered victims in New York with Nazi maniac Adolf Eichmann, who masterminded the extermination of 6 million Jews during the Holocaust.[44] It is indicative of the welcoming reception for America haters on our campuses that Churchill has subsequently been invited to speak at more than forty academic institutions.

Churchill is Chomsky-like in his penchant for bile and contempt and in his egocentric pursuit of attention. Lamenting that the attacks in New York and Washington had proven "insufficient to accomplish its purpose," Churchill concluded, "What the hell? It was worth a try." On another occasion he stated, "One of the things I've suggested is that it may be that more 9/11s are necessary. This seems like such a no-brainer that I hate to frame it in terms of actual transformation of consciousness."[45]

Churchill went so far as to champion the bravery of the 9/11 terrorists over that of U.S. Air Force pilots. "The men who flew the missions against the WTC and Pentagon were not 'cowards,' " Churchill wrote. "That distinction properly belongs to the 'firm-jawed lads' who delighted in flying stealth aircraft through the undefended airspace of Baghdad, dropping payload after payload of bombs on anyone unfortunate enough to be below—including tens of thousands of genuinely innocent civilians—while themselves incurring all the risk one might expect during a visit to the local video arcade."[46]

Oh, I know a few "firm-jawed lads" I'd be happy to introduce the good professor to.

At an antimilitary forum in Oregon in the summer of 2005, Churchill spoke out about the practice of "fragging" U.S. military officers; fragging is the killing of an officer by a subordinate. "Conscientious objection removes a given piece of cannon fodder from the fray," he said. "Fragging an officer has a much more impactful effect." When an audience member expressed concern about how such practice would affect the murdered officer's family, Churchill replied, "How do you feel about Adolf Eichmann's family?"[47]

Churchill is not only a traitor but also a fraud and a liar. The professor and former department head of "ethnic studies" has a BA and an MA in communications from Sangamon State (now the University of Illinois at Springfield), which was at that time an "experimental" school for aspiring radicals. His academic expertise upon graduation was as a graphic "artist" and not in any way associated with the academic pursuit of ethnicity.[48]

Churchill received tenured professorship at the University of Colorado by claiming he was a member of the Keetoowah Cherokee tribe. He has stated, "Although I'm best known by my colonial name, Ward Churchill, the name I prefer best is Kenis, an Ojibwe name bestowed by my [Native American] wife's uncle."[49]

It turns out that "Kenis" lied. He has no Native American ancestry. Churchill's tribal membership was in fact honorary (Bill Clinton received such a membership as well) and has since been revoked by some really upset Keetoowahs.[50]

The University of Colorado chancellor and student union recommended that the anti-American radical be dismissed for plagiarism, fabrications, and misuse of others' works. At this writing, Churchill's case is under appeal.

"YOU ARE A DISGRACE TO THIS COUNTRY"

It would be comforting to think that Chomsky, Zinn, and Churchill, hateful and dangerous as they may be, are anomalies.

Sadly, there are thousands of members of the intellectual elite just like them. They are representative of a generation of radicals who have dominated the academy over the past four decades seeking to oppose America at every turn.

It is no surprise that radicals like Chomsky, Zinn, and Churchill thrive in an environment in which liberals dominate. And it's no surprise that conservatives are utterly scorned in a world in which right-leaning thinkers are practically nonexistent.

University of Hawaii administrator Mark Burch is representative of the view from the academic Left. Responding to a mass e-mail sent to hundreds of educators in October 2005 requesting feedback on a study documenting liberal bias in law and journalism schools, Burch replied, "There is a simple explanation for the preponderance of liberals at institutions of higher learning. Liberals are smart and conservatives are stupid. . . . If you want me to stop humiliating you with my superior intellect, stop sending me this crap."[51] Burch's superior intellect apparently wasn't enough to prevent him from hitting the "send" button on his unprofessional screed, which found its way to this author.

Given the contempt in which conservatives and conservative ideas are held, is it any wonder that the traditional concepts of patriotism, honor, courage, and commitment are disparaged? Is it any wonder military service is demeaned and denigrated?

Consider the extreme and subversive comments we hear again and again from leading academics.

In the spring of 2003, Columbia University held an antiwar "teach-in." If Noam Chomsky is the Ayatollah for the Hate America set, Columbia is the Grand Mosque. During the six-hour-long hatefest, thirty leading faculty members took turns attacking America, to the roaring delight of 3,000 students. It was a clear glimpse into the psychosis of the American Left—not only in what was said but in the dripping emotional hatred with which it was said.

Nicholas De Genova, an anthropology professor, declared that "the only true heroes are those who find ways that help defeat the U.S. military" and "I personally would like to see a million Mogadishus."[52] In Mogadishu, Somalia, in 1993, the forces of Mohammad Farah Aideed, a warlord supported by al Qaeda, ambushed and killed eighteen American soldiers and dragged their bodies through the streets. (This was the horrible event documented in *Black Hawk Down*.)

Not only was De Genova allowed to retain his position in the aftermath of his hateful rhetoric, he was rewarded with a graduate lecture.

Columbia's late Middle East Studies professor Edward Said, a former member of the governing council of the Palestine Liberation Organization (PLO), called the U.S. policy in Iraq the "grotesque" work of a "small cabal" of unelected, warmongering imperialists lusting for "oil and hegemony" and carrying the banner of an "avenging Judeo-Christian god of war." America was guilty, he said, of "reducing whole peoples, countries and even continents to ruin by nothing short of holocaust."

When Said passed away in late 2003, Columbia created the Edward Said Chair in Middle Eastern Studies with $200,000 in support from the United Arab Emirates.[53] The school promptly hired another former PLO activist, Rashid Khalidi, to replace Said. Khalidi blames the horrors of 9/11 on U.S. aggression toward the Middle East and support for Israel, not on Muslim extremism.

Yet another Columbia professor, Todd Gitlin, a radical holdover from the 1960s, framed the Left's contempt more succinctly: "You can hate your country in such a way that the hatred becomes fundamental, a hatred so clear and intense came to feel like a cleansing flame."[54]

And the Left's hatred extends far beyond Columbia University. Not long after 9/11, University of New Mexico history professor Richard A. Berthold told his class, "Anyone who can blow up the Pentagon has my vote."[55] Robert Jensen, a professor at the University of Texas, wrote an op-ed for the *Austin American-Statesman* in December 2004, as the U.S. Marines were engaged in the Battle for Fallujah, the most intense urban warfare since the Battle of Hue, Vietnam. Jensen wrote, "The United States has lost the war in Iraq, and that's a good thing. . . . I welcome the U.S. defeat, for a simple reason: It isn't the defeat of the United States—its people or their ideals—but of that empire. And it's essential the American empire be defeated and dismantled."[56]

Berkeley guest lecturer Hatem Bazian called for violent revolution in America. At an antiwar rally in April 2004, Bazian screamed, "Are you angry? (Yeah!) Are you angry? (Yeah!) Are you angry? (Yeah!) Well, we've been watching intifada in Palestine, we've been watching an uprising in Iraq, and the question is that what are we doing? How come we don't have an intifada in this country? . . . It's about time that we have an intifada in this country that changes fundamentally the political dynamics in here. And we know every—they're gonna say some Palestinian being too radical—well, you haven't seen radicalism yet!"[57]

In several instances college professors have directed their hatred more specifically at the U.S. military. In the fall of 2002, Cadet Robert Kurpiel, an aspiring officer candidate in his first year at the Air Force Academy, sent a mass e-mail to professors across the country asking for advice in organizing a political debate on his campus. Here's Cadet Kurpiel's e-mail:

Dear Sir or Ma'am:

The Air Force Academy is going to be having our annual Academy Assembly. This is a forum for mainly but not only Political Science majors, discussing very important issues dealing with politics.

Right now we are in the planning stage for advertising and

we would appreciate your help in the follow areas. Do you know of or have any methods or ways for inter-school advertising and/or communications? What would be the best way for us to advertise at your school whether it is sending you the fliers and you making copies or by perhaps putting an advertisement in your local publication? We would appreciate your input and the cost of what you recommend. Thank you for your time and consideration.

Very Respectfully,
Cadet Robert Kurpiel[58]

Saint Xavier University professor Peter Kirstein replied. Most adults in positions of authority would have encouraged the young man in his academic pursuits and willingly offered assistance to one of America's premier military academies. In this instance, however, the cadet proved to be more mature than the professor. Kirstein responded by calling the cadet a "baby killer" and a "disgrace to this country." Here's the professor's e-mail:

From: Peter Kirstein
Sent: Thursday, October 31, 2002 1:46 PM
To: Kurpiel Robert C4C CS26
Subject: Re: Academy Assembly

You are a disgrace to this country and I am furious you would even think I would support you and your aggressive baby killing tactics of collateral damage. Help you recruit. Who, top guns to reign [sic] death and destruction upon nonwhite peoples throughout the world? Are you serious sir? Resign your commission and serve your country with honour [sic].

No war, no air force cowards who bomb countries without

AAA [antiaircraft artillery], without possibility of retaliation. You are worse than the snipers. You are imperialists who are turning the whole damn world against us. September 11 can be blamed in part for what you and your cohorts have done to Palestinians, the VC, the Serbs, a retreating army at Basra.

You are unworthy of my support.

> Peter N. Kirstein
> Professor of History
> Saint Xavier University[59]

This professor appears unworthy of his paycheck. Kirstein's elitist enmity is frightening, and his ignorance of all things military is stunning. For starters, a first-year academy cadet is four years from graduating and commissioning as an officer; he can't *resign* a commission he hasn't received. He's a cadet pursuing a degree at a demanding educational institution whose entry standards are far superior to those of most major academic institutions (and I graciously include Saint Xavier).

Kirstein later acknowledged that he had "crossed the line," but with Clintonesque obfuscation. He was protesting, he said, "a military institution that trains its students to kill other human beings with high-tech, invulnerable flying machines. . . . The militarization of American society and its incessant military crusades pose a greater threat to our freedoms than the putative enemies that we slaughter on the battlefield or even worse in their homes or hospitals in distant lands."[60]

When the local chapter of the Young America's Foundation (YAF) invited a decorated Iraq War veteran to speak at Warren County Community College in New Jersey in 2005, English professor John Daly responded by attacking the freshman student who'd invited the guest lecturer. In an e-mail the professor sent to the student, Daly advocated the fragging of military officers:

I am asking my students to boycott your event. I am also going to ask others to boycott it. Your literature and signs in the entrance lobby look like fascist propaganda and is [*sic*] extremely offensive. . . . I will continue to expose your right-wing anti-people politics until groups like yours won't dare show their face on a college campus. Real freedom will come when soldiers in Iraq turn their guns on their superiors and fight for just causes and for people's needs.[61]

"SURE, WE'LL HOST THE INTIFADA"

The situation on our campuses has deteriorated to the point where professors spewing rancor and invective aren't the only threat. Convicted terrorists and other avowed enemies of the United States have maneuvered their way into key positions at our nation's universities and are indoctrinating America's youth. Do you know who's teaching your children?

Laura Whitehorn, for example, received invitations to speak at Duke University, Cornell University, Brown University, and Vassar College, to name a few. During the 1960s, Whitehorn was a member of SDS as it evolved into the radical splinter group the Weather Underground (also known as the Weathermen), America's first terror cult. In the 1980s, she was a member of a domestic terror cell that emerged from the eventual collapse of the Weathermen, the May 19 Communist Organization, and carried out bombings at the National War College, the Washington Navy Yard, and the U.S. Capitol Building.

Whitehorn was convicted for her involvement in the attack on the Capitol, which she said was done to protest the U.S. liberation of Grenada, and served fourteen years in federal prison. She makes no apologies for her traitorous attacks, saying, "I'm unrepentant. I'm proud of my motives. . . . I don't really even care that much whether people think I'm a terrorist or not."[62]

Duke University (nice basketball school, not so noted for its patriotism) released a press kit promoting the speech that praised her
as a "political prisoner" and a "champion of human rights."

In 2005, Hamilton College hired domestic terrorist Susan
Rosenberg to teach a course titled "Resistance Memoirs: Writing,
Identity, and Change." Rosenberg was involved with several terrorist groups in the 1970s and early 1980s, including the Black
Liberation Army, the Weather Underground, and The Family. In
1984 she was sentenced to fifty-eight years in prison after being
arrested for possessing weapons and 700 pounds of explosives
along with false identification papers. She was also indicted for
her involvement in the October 1981 Brinks armored car robbery
in Nyack, New York, in which two policemen and an armed guard
were murdered. "Long live the armed struggle!" she exclaimed
upon her arrest.[63] Rosenberg, who advocates the violent over-
throw of the U.S. government and has referred to herself as a
"revolutionary guerrilla," saw her prison sentence commuted—
forty-two years early—by President Bill Clinton in his final few
hours in the White House.

Neither Rosenberg's domestic terrorist past nor her weak
qualifications (she received her master's degree by taking corre-
spondence courses behind bars) deterred Hamilton College from
offering her the position, although she was forced to withdraw
from the position after her past was exposed and the school faced
withering public opposition.

Another anti-American terrorist profiting from academia's
radical bent is Bill Ayers, the Osama bin Laden of the Weather
Underground. Under his supervision, the Weathermen declared
war on "AmeriKKKa" (always with capitalized "KKK") in 1969
and bombed the U.S. Capitol, the Pentagon, the National Guard
offices in Washington, D.C., and the New York City police headquarters. In 1970, three members of Ayers's terror cell blew themselves up as they were preparing a bomb that they had planned to
detonate at an Army recruit social dance in Fort Dix, New Jersey.

In all, Ayers and the Weather Underground were responsible for thirty bombings of U.S. government, security, and military facilities. In his memoirs Ayers described his radical glee when he bombed the Pentagon: "Everything was absolutely ideal. . . . The sky was blue. The birds were singing. And the bastards were finally going to get what was coming to them."[64]

Today, unbelievably, as the distinguished professor of early childhood education at the University of Illinois–Chicago, Ayers is teaching the teachers who are educating America's children. "I don't regret setting bombs," Ayers said in a *New York Times* article (ironically appearing on September 11, 2001, as other terrorists attacked America). "I feel we didn't do enough." When reflecting on whether or not he would use bombs against the United States in the future, Ayers wrote, "I can't imagine entirely dismissing the possibility."[65]

Only five days after the 9/11 attacks, with the nation in deep grief, the *New York Times* again featured a fawning profile of Ayers in which he said of the United States, "What a country. It makes me want to puke."[66]

As a father of three young children, I can't imagine Bill Ayers teaching my kids or the teachers of my kids. Quite the opposite, in fact; I insist that he and his disciples do not.

Ayers's wife is former Weathermen comrade Bernardine Dohrn, who spent time on the FBI's Ten Most Wanted List and was named by J. Edgar Hoover as "the most dangerous woman in America—La Pasionara of the lunatic left."[67] In a 1969 meeting in Flint, Michigan, that the Weather Underground dubbed the War Council, Dohrn celebrated the Charles Manson Family's gruesome Hollywood murder of pregnant actress Sharon Tate by holding her fingers as if to simulate a fork and said, "Dig it. First they killed those pigs, then they ate dinner in the same room with them. They even shoved a fork into the victim's stomach! Wild!"[68]

Today this terrorist, who evaded prosecution for her crimes by going underground, is a professor of law at Northwestern

University. More appallingly, she is the director of Northwestern's Legal Clinic's Children and Family Justice Center.

The University of California–Santa Cruz has employed its own leftist icon with a violent past. Communist radical and former Black Panther Angela Davis was one of the higher-profile domestic terrorists in the late sixties and seventies yet currently holds a position as a tenured professor in the "history of social consciousness." She is a strong opponent of the military and America's involvement in the War on Terror and is frequently called on to speak at antiwar rallies across the country.

In 1970, Davis was involved in a plot to free her imprisoned Panther boyfriend George Jackson in which a Marin County, California, courtroom was seized and hostages taken. In the ensuing gun battle, Judge Harold Haley's head was severed by a blast from a sawed-off shotgun belonging to Davis. Three others were killed. More than twenty witnesses implicated her in the plot.

Davis fled California using aliases until she was captured by the FBI in New York City. In the ensuing trial, Davis chose to act as her own attorney, exempting her from cross-examination; a friendly jury eventually acquitted her. Davis, once the protégée of American Communist Party leader Herbert Aptheker, received the International Lenin Peace Prize from the Soviet Union and remained a party member until 1991.

THE INDOCTRINATION STARTS EARLY

The antimilitary, anti-American sentiment of educators and educational institutions is not limited to higher learning. It has infected the nation's high schools and elementary schools as well.

In March 2005, Major Terry Thomas, U.S. Marine Corps, was invited by West Seattle High School in Washington to participate in a panel discussion on the Iraq War. As he entered the student assembly, Major Thomas was appalled at what he saw. He had walked into an antimilitary "guerrilla theater" being performed by faculty, students, and parents.

He recounted the incident in a letter to the Seattle school board. "As I stood there in my Marine Corps Dress Blue uniform," he wrote, "there before me stood numerous kids running around in sloppily dressed and ill-fitted helmets and military fatigues with utter disrespect for the symbols and uniforms of the U.S. military. The walls were covered in camouflaged netting and the stage was covered with approximately twenty white, life-sized cutout patterns in the shape of dead women and children, all of which were splattered in red paint to depict human blood. Onstage, children were kneeling and weeping while dressed in ill-fitted Arabic headdresses with white-faced masks similarly covered in red paint to depict human blood. At a podium, children were reading a monologue of how U.S. troops were killing civilians and shooting at women and children. Moreover, several grown adults were standing on stage in bright orange jumpsuits, with black bags on and off their heads, some bound and tied, and some banging symbols and gongs in a crude depiction of what I believe were their efforts to depict victims of the Abu Ghraib prisoner abuse episode."[69]

Nadine Gulit of Operation Support Our Troops also witnessed the outrageous scene, having been asked by the organizers to arrange the military speakers. "As I walked into the theater there was a young girl wearing a mask and crawling on the floor," Gulit told the Seattle school board. "And, over the loudspeaker [someone] was denouncing our military, saying 'Americans are killing my family!' " According to the *Seattle Post-Intelligencer,* Gulit watched as a "student dressed as a grieving Iraqi woman knelt near a bloody body while, over a microphone, a narrator wailed the story of civilians shot, kicked and beaten by American soldiers."[70]

Major Thomas wouldn't stand for this treatment. In his letter to the school board he wrote, "I have served my country honorably for nearly 13 years all around this globe. I have fought on the battlefield in Iraq, lost good friends dead and wounded in this conflict and I will not sit back and allow our Seattle school district to shame or sully the name, reputation and good name of our military and our returning veterans. I will not tolerate an ill-administered school bureaucracy that seeks to sanction, condone, advocate or chaperon a vile position that America's military men and women are somehow blood thirsty, indiscriminate murderers, executioners and war criminals."[71]

Unfortunately, that vile position is now the standard in our nation's educational institutions.

The San Francisco Board of Education voted in November 2006 to end ninety years of Junior Reserve Officer Training Corps (JROTC) in its high schools. More than 1,600 San Francisco students were enrolled in the program at the time, many of them from the more depressed neighborhoods of the city. "We don't want the military ruining our civilian institutions," said Sandra Schwartz, a representative from the radical leftist pacifist organization American Friends Service Committee. Board of Education member Dan Kelly justified his vote by saying that JROTC was "basically a branding program or recruiting program for the military."[72]

In fact, it's nothing of the sort. The school board's action is simply another case of antimilitary bigotry, this time at the high school level. JROTC is not a recruiting tool of the military, and the majority of students participating do not eventually join the military. What the program does is provide life skills and leadership education. In this case, San Francisco's school system chose to place its leftist ideology over the future of its high school students.

Illustrative of the city's scorn for the military and reckless disregard for the education of its children is the "history" textbook titled *Addicted to War,* which is part of the school system's curriculum. Written by Joel Andreas, this self-described "illustrated exposé" is endorsed by Noam Chomsky, Howard Zinn, Cindy Sheehan, former U.S. attorney general and radical activist Ramsey Clark, and actors Martin Sheen, Susan Sarandon, and Woody Harrelson.

On the book's table of contents page, a black soldier is depicted holding up the "black power" salute and a white soldier is flashing the peace sign with FTA (symbolizing the Vietnam-era war protester's phrase "F*** the Army") written across his helmet. Among the many assertions contained in the text are the claims that the Pentagon trains allies to conduct "torture and summary executions," the American military buries dead civilians in "garbage bags and . . . mass graves," and "the most dangerous characters of all (are) the military recruiters."[73]

Radical historian Zinn concludes that "*Addicted to War* is a witty and devastating portrait of U.S. military policy, a fine example of art serving society."[74]

Another example of the leftist antimilitary reach into schools is the textbook *Rethinking Mathematics: Teaching Social Justice by the Numbers,* edited by Eric Gutstein and Bob Peterson and distributed by the radical teachers' group Rethinking Schools. In its "math book," this leftist organization bases its curriculum on issues such as racial profiling, sweatshops, multicultural math, and the war in Iraq. Using figures, statements, and "teaching suggestions" from antimilitary groups such as the War Resisters League, the National Priorities Project, and Global Exchange, the authors write, "Thanks to the U.S. government's addiction to military spending, students have an endless stream of large numbers to study," and "The growth in the military budget comes as schools face massive budget cuts. Teaching about these matters provides students an opportunity to improve their understanding of large numbers and, more importantly, to understand the power of math in debates about the future of our communities and world."[75] The book also suggests a project in which students are asked to compare the cost of one stealth bomber to the cost of four-year scholarships at out-of-state prestigious universities for inner-city high school graduates.

The antimilitary lessons reach down even into our preschools. *That's Not Fair!: A Teacher's Guide to Activism with Young Children,* a manual for preschool teachers endorsed by the national organization of early childhood educators, offers a story illustrating how to discuss the military with preschoolers. Coauthor Ann Pelo writes that, while on a visit to a park, her students noticed the Navy's Blue Angels aerobatic demonstration team flying overhead. Pelo saw an opportunity to indoctrinate the youngsters. "Those are Navy airplanes," she told them. "They're built for war, but right now, there is no war, so the pilots learn how to do fancy tricks in their planes."

The following day, she asked the children to "communicate their feelings about the Blue Angels." In *That's Not Fair!* Pelo proudly recounts the results: "They drew pictures of planes with X's through them: 'This is a crossed-off bombing plane.' They drew bomb factories labeled: 'No.' " Other kids wrote, "Respect our words, Blue Angels. Respect kids' words. Don't kill people." And, "If you blow up our city, we won't be happy about it. And our whole city will be destroyed. And if you blow up my favorite library, I won't be happy because there are some good books there that I haven't read yet."[76]

The Left's indoctrination of America's youth starts early.

"NOTHING WORTH DYING FOR"

The intellectuals who preach that the U.S. military is the true evil in this world fail to realize that it's this very military that affords them the freedom to spout their radical views. Sometimes it takes the soldiers themselves to provide a reality check to these coddled, insulated left-wingers. Marc Fencil, a senior majoring in political science, criminology, and Spanish at Ohio University and serving as a Marine in Iraq, penned an open letter to his classmates published in the campus newspaper after he heard that antiwar protesters had staged a "die-in" at his school. Fencil wrote:

It's a shame that I'm here in Iraq with the Marines right now and not back at Ohio University completing my senior year and joining in blissful ignorance with the enlightened, war-seasoned protesters who participated in the recent "die-in." . . . This is an open invitation for you to cut your hair, take a shower, get in shape and come on over! If Michael Moore can shave and lose enough weight to fit into a pair of camouflage utilities, then he can come too! . . .

I know you think that nothing, even a world free of terror for one's children, is worth dying for, but bear with me here. . . . When it's all over, I promise you can go back to your coffee houses and preach about social justice and peace while you continue to live outside of reality. . . .

If you decide to decline my offer, then at least you should sleep well tonight knowing that men wearing black face-masks and carrying AK-47s yelling "Allahu Akbar" over here are proud of you and are forever indebted to you for advancing their cause of terror. While you ponder this, I'll get back to the real "die-in" over here. I don't mind.[77]

FOUR

STEALING THEIR HONOR

If our intended goal in this age is the establishment of a caliphate in the manner of the Prophet and if we expect to establish its state predominantly . . . I say to you: that we are in a battle and that more than half of this battle is taking place in the battlefield of the media.

—Letter from Ayman al-Zawahiri
to Abu Musab al-Zarqawi,
July 9, 2005

On February 27, 1968, for the first time in America's history the mass media, not the military, determined the outcome of a war. The Vietcong and North Vietnamese armies launched surprise attacks coinciding with the Lunar New Year in what would become known as the Tet Offensive. The Communist forces targeted 36 of 44 provincial capitals and 70 other towns and military installations across South Vietnam during a time previously announced to be a cease-fire.

Walter Cronkite—"Uncle Walter," the "most trusted man in

America"—visited Saigon during the fighting and returned to the United States to declare that while the war was not yet lost, it could not be won. Speaking to America, Cronkite opined:

> To say that we are closer to victory today is to believe, in the face of the evidence, the optimists who have been wrong in the past. To suggest we are on the edge of defeat is to yield to unreasonable pessimism. To say that we are mired in stalemate seems the only realistic, yet unsatisfactory, conclusion. . . . It seems increasingly clear to this reporter that the only rational way out will be to negotiate, not as victors.[1]

Everyone in America watched the CBS Evening News, and if Cronkite said it, it must be true. The nation believed him. Cronkite and the CBS executives assumed—incorrectly, as it would turn out—that the American military could do no better than a negotiated withdrawal and had suffered the first great loss of the Cold War. As a result of the media's overwhelmingly negative spin, President Lyndon Johnson was convinced not to seek reelection, famously muttering to an aide, "If I've lost Cronkite, I've lost America."[2]

Each evening Cronkite signed off his broadcasts with "And that's the way it is." Only—at the expense of the United States, its military, and the lives of millions of Vietnamese and Cambodians—in reality that's the way it wasn't.

The Tet Offensive was, in fact, a complete military victory for the U.S. and South Vietnamese armies and an unmitigated disaster for the Communist North. Nobody in the media bothered to ask the military, however. Not content with reporting the facts, Big Media chose to craft a different outcome. Despite achieving Pearl Harbor–like surprise, the enemy failed to seize a single city in its offensive. After suffering a series of initial blows and confusion, South Vietnamese and U.S. military responded quickly and decisively. Almost 50,000 of the 84,000 attacking troops were killed, while the United States suffered 1,100 fatalities and the South Vietnamese 2,300. North Vietnamese and Vietcong "death squads" executed more than 4,000 civilians but never achieved their strategic goal of generating a mass uprising in the South. The indigenous Vietcong were eliminated and the North Vietnamese were left incapable of fielding another significant military offensive for four years.

General Vo Nguyen Giap, commander of the North Vietnamese forces and the chief architect of the Tet Offensive, was so shaken by the losses that he considered seeking terms for his surrender. North Vietnamese Army Colonel Bui Tin concluded, "Our losses were staggering and a complete surprise. Our forces in the South were nearly wiped out. It took until 1971 to reestablish our presence."[3] Truong Nhu Tang, the minister of justice in the Vietcong's provisional government, concurred, saying, "Our losses were so immense we were unable to replace them with new recruits."[4]

But Cronkite and the American media portrayed it differently, and inaccurately. Western media elites filed their negative, rumor-laden reports from the safety of the bar at Saigon's Caravelle Hotel, creating the false impression of chaos and failure.

In a *Wall Street Journal* editorial shortly after the failed attacks, Joe Evans wrote, "We think the American people should be getting ready to accept, if they haven't already, the prospect that the whole Vietnam effort may be doomed; it may be falling apart beneath our feet. . . . Everyone had better be prepared for the bitter taste of a defeat beyond America's power to prevent."[5] NBC's Frank McGee agreed, declaring that "the war is being lost by the administration's definition" and that "it's futile to destroy Vietnam in the effort to save it."[6]

Former Marine Peter Braestrup, who covered Tet for the *Washington Post,* later acknowledged, "Rarely has contemporary crisis journalism turned out, in retrospect, to have veered so wildly from reality. . . . To have portrayed such a setback for one side as a defeat for the other—in a major crisis abroad—cannot be counted as a triumph for American journalism."[7]

The media's fallacious reports convinced U.S. leaders to turn against a war that was being won militarily. In the wake of the devastating defeat for the North Vietnamese and Vietcong, General William Westmoreland, commander of U.S. military operations in Vietnam, petitioned the Johnson administration to launch a major counteroffensive against the North to destroy the enemy's will to fight. American public opinion, though, had soured. Westmoreland's requests were denied. Instead of dealing a final blow to the enemy, the United States halted the highly effective bombing campaign in the North.

Ho Chi Minh's North Vietnamese leaders were both shocked and pleased at the American response following their overwhelming loss. Bui Tin, who ultimately received South Vietnam's unconditional surrender, directly attributed the Communist triumph over U.S. forces to the efforts of the American antiwar movement and a complicit media. "Every day our leadership would listen to world news over the radio at 9 A.M. to follow the growth of the American antiwar movement," said Tin. "Visits to Hanoi by people like Jane Fonda . . . gave us confidence that we should hold on in the face of battlefield reverses." He added that "through dissent and protest," the United States "lost the ability to mobilize a will to win."[8] General Giap said, "We were not strong enough to drive out a half-million American troops, but that wasn't our aim. Our intention was to break the will of the American government to continue the war."[9]

The plan worked. As the eminent military historian John Keegan concluded, "The Vietnam war was not lost on the battlefield, but in the media's treatment of news from the front line."[10]

More significantly, the manner in which Cronkite and his fellow journalists grossly misrepresented the Tet Offensive and the rest of the Vietnam conflict dramatically harmed America's ability to fight other wars.

For the first time in the nation's history, we ran. In doing so, we turned our back on a faithful ally and our word. America's capacity to successfully prosecute wars would henceforth be called into question, and the media would always view the use of military force through the prism of Vietnam. For the media, the ghosts of Tet would appear again and again in places such as Grenada, Panama, Somalia, Bosnia, Kosovo, Afghanistan, and Iraq. America's current war with Islamofascism is undermined because of it.

Al Qaeda leaders and other Islamofascist enemies understand these lessons well. They are scholars of history if nothing else.

In a July 2005 letter, al Qaeda's number-two leader, Ayman al-Zawahiri, told the foremost terrorist in Iraq at the time, Abu Musab al-Zarqawi, "The aftermath of the collapse of American power in Vietnam—and how they ran and left their agents—is noteworthy."[11]

In late 2006, speaking with Al Jazeera TV, Hezbollah leader Hassan Nasrallah boasted that the Americans "will leave the Middle East, and the Arab and Islamic worlds, like they left Vietnam. I advise all those who place their trust in the Americans to learn the lesson of Vietnam, and to learn the lesson of the South Lebanese Army with the Israelis, and to know that when the Americans lose this war—and lose it they will, Allah willing—they will abandon them to their fate, just like they did to all those who placed their trust in them throughout history."[12]

To ensure that the American "infidels" suffer a fate similar to what they experienced in Vietnam, Islamofascist terrorists have made manipulation of the media a key part of their strategy. Zawahiri, for example, reminded Zarqawi that "more than half of this battle is taking place in the battlefield of the media."[13]

Want to know how shrewdly the terrorists use the media to try to show they are defeating the "infidels"? Consider this story that Air Force Major Eric Egland told me from Iraq:

One morning, the Iraqi police guarding the bridge noticed an abandoned car near their checkpoint. Upon investigation, they found that it was filled with explosives. After safely moving the dozens of innocent civilians who would likely have otherwise been killed by a blast, the police neutralized the car bomb.

Within minutes, a television camera crew emerged from the abandoned building. When the Iraqi police questioned them, they simply showed their Al Jazeera 'journalist' credentials, saying that they were filming the river and knew nothing of the car bomb. They then drove north toward the next bridge, where thirty minutes later a different car bomb detonated, killing Iraqi civilians. To the surprise of no one, the footage was aired on Al Jazeera that night. Obviously, the crew had at least been informed of the terrorist plans, and even back-up plans, and then actively supported terror against Iraqi civilians by filming and broadcasting it around the world.[14]

But the enemy does not use Al Jazeera only. The terrorists have found allies in the American media as well, just as the North Vietnamese found common cause with the U.S. media and anti-war movement nearly four decades ago. This is, in fact, a conscious strategy on the part of the Islamofascists, as made clear by a jihadist website. Under the heading "The Global Media: A Work Paper for Invading the US Media," the website states, "The people of jihad need to carry out a media war that is parallel to the military war and exert all possible efforts to wage it successfully. This is because we can observe the effect that the media have on nations to make them either support or reject an issue." The website suggests that followers flood e-mail and video of their operations to "chat rooms," to "television channels," and to "famous U.S. authors who have public e-mail addresses . . . such as [Thomas] Friedman, [Noam] Chomsky, [Francis] Fukuyama, [Samuel] Huntington and others."[15]

The Islamofascists' media strategy is working. The antiwar leftists in this country are all too quick to compare this war (any war, really) to Vietnam, but they might end up being right in one respect: as in Vietnam, U.S. military successes could become irrelevant if our media's relentlessly negative reporting turns the American people against the war and robs our leaders of their will to see us through to victory. Tragically, that is already happening.

I've had a chance to see what's really occurring on the ground in the war against Islamofascists, and it's not what we usually hear reported. I've been to Iraq, spent time with hundreds of our soldiers over there, and witnessed the incredible work they're doing under the most difficult of conditions. And I can tell you for certain: The American people haven't heard the real story of the war, haven't heard the good news, and haven't received any balance or context. I can also tell you this: The inaccurate, biased reporting outrages our soldiers. This is a terrible abdication of responsibility on the part of our press.

The American media's war on the military can't go on.

AIDING AND ABETTING THE ENEMY

From the moment I enlisted in the Air Force, placed my right hand in the air, and swore allegiance to my nation "against all enemies foreign and domestic," I understood the potential for subversion. At that time, Cold War tensions with the Soviet Union were entering their fourth decade. What I didn't understand then was that the subversion of our military would come from our own Fourth Estate.

When the United States began military operations in the wake of the 9/11 attacks, the mainstream media wasted little time in launching their own war with America. From the beginning, the media's reporting of military operations in Iraq and Afghanistan has not been about the war. Journalists have made little effort to convey the complexities of combat or the nature of the Islamofascism threat.

For example, instead of calling the enemy what they are, *terrorists,* the mainstream media use euphemisms to avoid confronting the ugly truth. The *New York Times* refers to terrorists as "insurgents" or "perpetrators"; the Associated Press prefers "captors"; United Press International calls them "extremists"; the *Washington Post* says they are "fighters"; the *Chicago Tribune* considers them "militants"; and for National Public Radio, the mass-murdering beheaders are "assailants."[16] These self-righteous public watchdogs priding themselves on nuance are so oblivious to context.

In the past few years, too, we've heard the media make one dire prediction after another: brutal Afghan winters, hundreds of thousands of body bags, massive civilian casualties, uprisings across the Arab world, too many troops, not enough troops, streaming refugees, quagmires, and insufficient equipment for our soldiers. Time and again these predictions have been proven wrong, but we see nary a retraction or correction. The media just move on to the next topic, factual or not, that might (they hope) become this war's My Lai massacre. Failing to report the real story of what's happening on the ground, they insist on portraying the War on Terror as Vietnam Redux.

What might be most galling is the open hostility journalists show to our armed forces. The rancor was on display even before U.S. military operations began in Afghanistan in 2001. National Public Radio's senior foreign editor, Loren Jenkins, said he was sending out a team of reporters into the Middle East and that "the game of reporting is to smoke 'em out."

Who was he trying to "smoke out"? Osama bin Laden and al Qaeda? The Taliban?

No.

American troops.

Jenkins wanted his reporters to hunt down the locations of U.S. troops. And if they did uncover U.S. troop movements or secret operations? "You report it," Jenkins declared. Forget virtuous notions of protecting the national interest. Jenkins had no problem with the concept of reporting information that would damage the country during a time of war because, he said, "I don't represent the government. I represent history, information, what happened."[17]

Representing history must be a tremendous burden—how about *reporting* history? Typical of most media elites, his comments reveal a lack of national identity and confusion toward citizenship's obligations. America isn't his *nation,* it's only his *residence.*

Another major news executive made stunning accusations that U.S. soldiers had committed outrageous offenses. In November 2004, CNN news chief Eason Jordan told a group of journalists in Portugal that "at least ten journalists have been killed by the U.S. military, and according to reports I believe to be true, journalists have been arrested and tortured by U.S. forces."[18] Proving his careless words were more than a momentary lapse in judgment, he repeated the allegations a few months later during a panel at the World Economic Forum in Davos, Switzerland, saying that he "knew of about 12 journalists who had not only been killed by American troops, but had been targeted as a matter of policy."[19]

Jordan eventually resigned over the controversy his comments sparked. Perhaps he should have done so back in 2003 after acknowledging that his network had acted as a mouthpiece for Saddam Hussein. Over a period of ten years, Jordan's CNN withheld reporting the details of the tyrant's bestial behavior, murder, and torture in order to protect the network's "access" in Baghdad.

Linda Foley, the president of the Newspaper Guild, wouldn't

be upstaged by Jordan. A couple of months after Jordan's Davos comments, Foley said at a conference, "What outrages me as a representative of journalists is that there's not more outrage about the number, and the brutality, and the cavalier nature of the U.S. military toward the killing of journalists in Iraq. I think it's just a scandal. . . . It's not just U.S. journalists either, by the way. They target and kill journalists . . . uh, from other countries, particularly Arab countries like Al-, like Arab news services like Al Jazeera, for example. They actually target them and blow up their studios with impunity."[20]

Foley quickly came under attack for her irresponsible and libelous comments—and deservedly so.

Washington Post military affairs columnist and MSNBC news contributor William Arkin is another media representative whose enmity for and ignorance of American servicemen and women is shocking. In a column titled "The Troops Also Need to Support the American People," Arkin called our soldiers rapists and murderers, "mercenaries" who enjoy "obscene amenities."

"Through every Abu Ghraib and Haditha, through every rape and murder, the American public has indulged those in uniform, accepting that the incidents were the product of bad apples or even of some administration or command order," concludes Arkin. "So, we pay the soldiers a decent wage, take care of their families, provide them with housing and medical care and vast social support systems and ship obscene amenities into the war zone for them, we support them in every possible way. . . . The recent NBC report (voicing the military's concern for waning support in the war in Iraq) is just an ugly reminder of the price we pay for a mercenary—oops sorry, volunteer—force. . . ."[21]

Arkin's disdain for his nation and the military is also evident in a book he authored titled *Code Names: Deciphering U.S. Military Plans, Programs and Operations in the 9/11 World* in which he exposed highly classified military planes and code names for all the world to see. What sort of citizen intentionally undermines his nation and his military in the midst of war? Leftists in the media, that's who.

Another shocking example is veteran journalist Seymour Hersh, who characterizes the young men and women serving in Iraq as murderers. "In Vietnam, our soldiers came back and they were reviled as baby killers, in shame and humiliation," claimed Hersh. "It isn't happening now, but I will tell you, there has never been an (American) army as violent and murderous as our army has been in Iraq."[22]

Paul Whitefield, a columnist for the *Los Angeles Times,* took the opportunity to bash Vietnam vets as he bashed the Iraq war in an op ed piece he wrote recently. Suggesting that Vietnam vets should be called up to active duty and sent to Iraq, Whitefield wrote, "They're battle-hardened. Many already have post-traumatic stress disorder. Also, some have their own vehicles—Harleys mostly, which are cheap to run, make small targets, and are highly mobile. I'll even bet that lots of these guys still have guns (you know, just in case). . . . OK, some vets are a bit long in the tooth (or don't have teeth—because of Agent Orange?). Finally, these Vietnam War guys are hungry for revenge. After all, they fought in the only war the U.S. ever lost. And they didn't even get a parade. So this is their chance. We can throw them that big parade when they come marching home."[23]

Big media publications have also tried to cast American soldiers in the worst light possible. In May 2004, the *Boston Globe* published photos purportedly showing U.S. troops gang-raping Iraqi women. "The American people have a right and responsibility to see the pictures," said Boston city councilor Chuck Turner as he provided the images to the paper.[24] The photos, though, were quickly proven fraudulent. They had been lifted directly off of pornographic websites and submitted as authentic by Akbar Muhammed, a representative for the Nation of Islam. Three of the *Globe*'s editors, apparently eager to believe the worst of their military and equally unwilling to do the professional research necessary to confirm the photos' veracity, approved the images for publication.

Harper's Magazine in March 2005 featured a cover picture of seven Marine recruits in their T-shirts, shorts, and socks under the headline "AWOL in America: When Desertion Is the Only Option." Only problem: none of the recruits was a deserter. Lance Corporal Kyle Bridge, one of the Marines in the photo, was not amused. "It's kind of frustrating. Most people that see me, if they know me, they know I wouldn't go AWOL." But *Harper's* saw no problem with misrepresenting U.S. Marines during war. Giulia Melucci, *Harper's* vice president for public relations, denied any antimilitary bias and sniffed, "We are decorating pages."[25]

Sometimes it's not wild predictions or character assassination but hysterical pronouncements about a war supposedly gone horribly awry. Recall the first few days of America's incursion into Iraq and the thousands of ancient Iraqi artifacts that had supposedly been looted from Iraq's National Museum back in 2003. The *New York Times* reported that at least 50,000 artifacts were missing, prompting Robert Scheer of the left-wing magazine *The Nation* to shriek, "The complete, and by all accounts preventable, destruction of one of the world's most significant collections of antiquities is a fit metaphor for current U.S. foreign policy, which causes more serious damage through carelessness than calculation."[26]

In fact, the priceless collection wasn't stolen or destroyed; it had been moved to storage. Just a month later the acting governor of Iraq's Central Bank, Faleh Salman, revealed that the antiquities "were never lost. We knew all along that they were there."[27]

One of the most damaging attacks on the military and the nation's war effort by Big Media has been their largely invented, slanderous, and highly debilitating "torture narrative." They applied the narrative first to the Abu Ghraib prison incident, which in-

volved twelve American soldiers physically and verbally mistreat-
ing detained insurgents in Iraq. Located just outside of Baghdad,
Abu Ghraib had been the scene of murder, rape, and torture under
Saddam Hussein. But to the media the Americans' actions were far
more reprehensible. The press seized on Abu Ghraib as an example of all that was wrong with America, the Bush administration,
and the military—although all the instances of abuse by Americans occurred during a single night, the U.S. military had been
criminally investigating the case for almost a year by the time the
media picked up the story, and all twelve soldiers were subsequently convicted and imprisoned. For the media, Abu Ghraib became the equivalent of the Vietnam-era My Lai massacre.

The media tarred the Guantánamo Bay detention camp in
Cuba with the same brush, despite the fact that allegations of
abuse have been repeatedly proven false. Uncomfortable coercive
interrogation techniques such as reversed sleep patterns, isola-
tion, hot and cold temperatures, and loud music were corporately
interpreted as "torture" by the media elite, many of whom were
ignorant of the Geneva Conventions and lawfully allowable conditions for "enemy combatants."

The Media Research Center analyzed stories airing on the
major network evening news broadcasts from September 11,
2001, through the end of August 2006. Looking specifically at
ABC *World News Tonight,* the *CBS Evening News,* and *NBC
Nightly News* and their treatment of captured terrorists, the MRC
found 277 stories focusing on the U.S. military's detention center
at Guantánamo Bay. Of those, 105 stories highlighted allegations
that detainees were being mistreated or abused, and 100 stories
centered on the captured terrorists being owed additional rights
and privileges. By comparison, only 39 stories described the detainees as dangerous, and only 6 stories documented the fact that
released detainees returned to the war and committed additional
acts of terror. The predominant media portrayal of the inmates

captured on the battlefield was as "victims," and the oppressor was America.[28]

Another MRC study looked at the major evening news broadcasts from January 1, 2005, through September 30, 2005. Of almost 1,400 stories appearing on the ABC, CBS, and NBC evening news broadcasts, more than 60 percent focused on negative topics or presented a pessimistic analysis. That was four times as many as the number of stories focusing on positive accomplishments. And the trend grew more and more negative over time. While 79 stories emphasized alleged misconduct on the part of the U.S. military, a mere 8 reported the successful accomplishments of U.S. forces.[29]

When the nonpartisan Center for Media and Public Affairs studied evening news broadcasts, it discovered a similarly extreme predisposition to stress the negative. During the initial conventional war with Saddam, 51 percent of all news coverage was found to be negative. Six months after the conventional war ended, 77 percent of the reporting was negative. During the U.S. presidential campaign of 2004, 89 percent of the stories were negative, and by the spring of 2006, 94 percent of the press was negative.[30]

GOOD NEWS ISN'T "FIT TO PRINT"

When Hamid Karzai was sworn in as the president of Afghanistan in December 2004, capping off a highly successful U.S. military campaign and a historic move to democracy in a country the Left claimed was incapable of modernity or self-government, media elites revealed their intent: the New York Times buried the story on page A8; the Washington Post carried the story on A13; the Wall Street Journal mentioned the watershed event in the What's News column with one sentence—the same day that it devoted two sentences to violence along the Pakistani border that killed four soldiers.[31]

The Left and the media elite predicted disaster for democratic elections in Iraq as well and were similarly proven wrong. Australian blogger Arthur Chrenkoff took a look at the biased media coverage of Iraq on January 21, 2005, just nine days before the Iraqis' first-ever democratic elections.[32] Using the Google News search engine, Chrenkoff tallied the following negative stories:

- 1,992 stories about suicide bombings and other terror attacks

- 887 stories about abuse of Iraqi prisoners by British soldiers

- 761 stories reporting on the activities of and statements by terrorists in Iraq

- 357 stories about the antiwar movement and dropping public support for the war

- 216 stories about hostages being held in Iraq

- 182 stories about American soldiers killed or wounded in Iraq

- 121 stories about a possible American pullout from Iraq

- 107 stories about civilian deaths in Iraq

And that's just a sample of what Chrenkoff found. Now compare those with the positive stories he discovered:

- 73 stories about the return of Iraq's supposedly stolen antiquities

- 16 stories about success in the fight against terrorists

- 7 stories about positive developments relating to the upcoming Iraqi elections

As Chrenkoff's research suggests, the media simply aren't interested in the good news from Iraq and Afghanistan.

When Iraq's unprecedented new constitution was ratified by 79 percent of voters (in a turnout heavier than any American election) in October 2005, the *Washington Post* buried that story on page 13, and put this downbeat headline on it: "Sunnis Failed to Defeat Iraq Constitution: Arab Minority Came Close." The four top headlines on the front page of the *Post* that same day: "Military Has Lost 2,000 in Iraq," "The Toll: 2,000," "Bigger, Stronger, Homemade Bombs Now to Blame for Half of U.S. Deaths," and "Bush Aides Brace for Charges."[33]

Consider that on December 15, 2005, more than 11 million Iraqis went to the polls to choose a new government. It was a historic step in the Iraqis' march toward freedom: in less than three years the Iraqi people had moved from the tyrannical regime of Saddam Hussein to democracy. But the hot news in the United States that day wasn't the creation of the first democratic republic in 5,000 years in the birthplace of civilization. No, a movie named *Brokeback Mountain* featuring two male cowboys in love carried the day.

When the U.S. military tracked down and killed al Qaeda leader Abu Musab al-Zarqawi in Iraq in June 2006, the media quickly downplayed any significance. CNN's senior editor for Arab affairs Octavia Nasr claimed, "Some people say it will enrage the insurgency, others say it will hurt it pretty bad. But if you think about the different groups in Iraq, you have to think that Zarqawi's death is not going to be a big deal for them."

ABC's Diane Sawyer, while interviewing former Clinton adviser Richard Clarke, asked, "(Is) it any safer in Iraq and will the war end any sooner?" Clarke responded, "Well, unfortunately the answer is no. This man was a terrible man. He was a symbol of terrorism. He was the face of terrorism, the only real name we knew of an insurgent leader in Iraq. But he commanded only a few hundred people out of tens of thousands involved in the insurgency. And so, unfortunately for the loved ones of troops over in Iraq, this is not going to mean a big difference." Sawyer topped the piece with her own pronouncements as well, concluding, "So for overall terrorism against the U.S., it's, again, not a major effect."

CBS Evening News anchor Bob Schieffer, while interviewing news analyst Michael Scheuer, said, "It's my understanding you believe this might actually increase danger for U.S. troops." Scheuer replied, "I think that's probably the case, Bob." When Schieffer then asked Scheuer what significance, if any, Zarqawi's death might have, Scheuer replied, "Strategically, it's not very important."[34]

The idea that the war is going badly has become so ingrained that journalists often refuse to listen when soldiers actually get a chance to give the real story. For example, in August 2005 the *Today* show sent cohost Matt Lauer on an unannounced trip to Iraq to document just how bad things really were.

Interviewing a group of soldiers at Camp Liberty, Lauer said, "Talk to me a little bit about morale here. We've heard so much about the insurgent attacks, so much about the uncertainty as to when you folks are going to get to go home. How would you describe morale?"

Chief Warrant Officer Randy Kirgiss responded directly: "In my unit morale is pretty good. Every day we go out and do our missions and people are ready to execute their missions. They're excited to be here."

Lauer continued to hammer the poor-morale theme: "How much does that uncertainty of [not] knowing how long you're going to be here impact morale?"

This time Sergeant Jamie Wells responded—and, like Kirgiss, he politely but firmly indicated that Lauer's assumptions were mistaken. "Morale is always high," Wells said. "Soldiers know they have a mission. They like taking on new objectives and taking on the new challenges and training the Iraqi army."

But Lauer seemed intent on showing his viewers that morale was bad. "Don't get me wrong here," he said. "I think you are probably telling me the truth, but a lot of people at home are wondering how that could be possible with the conditions you're facing and with the attacks you're facing. What would you say to those people who are doubtful that morale could be that high?"

Captain Sherman Powell nailed the pompous host: "Well, sir, I tell you, if I got my news from the newspapers also, I'd be pretty depressed as well." With typical military tact, Powell indicted the elite media's slanted coverage and hotel-bound reporting: "Sir, I know it's hard to get out and get on the ground and report the news, and I understand that and I appreciate that fact. But for those who've actually had a chance to get out and go on patrols and meet the Iraqi Army and the Iraqi police and go on patrols with them, we are very satisfied with the way things are going here. And we are confident that if we're allowed to finish the job we started we'll be very proud of it and our country will be proud of us for doing it."[35]

If the American media want to honestly point the finger at those responsible for the deaths of 3,000 American soldiers in Iraq and Afghanistan and their proclaimed civil war doom, perhaps they should point it directly at themselves.

"WHAT LIBERAL MEDIA?"

It's no surprise that the media betray such a fierce bias against the War on Terror and the U.S. military, since journalists lean far to the Left. Many leftists still try to deny that liberal media bias exists. Those protestations, though, fly in the face of mountains of evidence revealing just how pervasive the bias is, from countless academic studies to voting preferences of media elites to personal testimonies from insiders such as Bernard Goldberg.

In a study published in 2001, Stanley Rothman, coauthor of the 1986 book *The Media Elite,* and political science professor Amy Black discovered that 91 percent of journalists voted for Democratic candidate Bill Clinton in 1992, which was virtually the same result found in a survey of Washington-based bureau chiefs and correspondents done by the Freedom Forum Poll. In a study published by the University of Connecticut Department of Public Policy, 68 percent of journalists reported voting for John Kerry in 2004, while just 25 percent said they voted for George W. Bush.[36]

And the bias is not defined only along lines of political party affiliation. The Pew Research Center discovered that 34 percent of national journalists admitted to being liberal and only 7 percent admitted to being conservative.[37] A December 2005 study published by UCLA found that eighteen of twenty major news outlets examined were "left of center" in their ideological approach. Among the most liberal outlets were the *CBS Evening News,* the *New York Times,* and the *Los Angeles Times.* The study's lead author said he was surprised by "just how pronounced" the media's leftward bias was.[38]

Some members of the media have acknowledged the slant. The late ABC News anchor Peter Jennings told CNN's Larry King in 2002, "Historically in the media, it has been more of a liberal persuasion for many years. . . . And so I think yes, on occasion, there is a liberal instinct in the media which we need to keep our eye on, if you will."[39] *Newsweek* Washington Bureau chief Evan Thomas went further, saying, "There is a liberal bias. It's demonstrable. You look at some statistics. About 85 percent of the reporters who cover the White House vote Democratic, they have for a long time. There is a, particularly at the networks, at the lower levels, among the editors and the so-called infrastructure, there is a liberal bias. There is a liberal bias at *Newsweek,* the magazine I work for—most of the people who work at *Newsweek* live on the Upper West Side in New York and they have a liberal bias."[40]

Newsweek political reporter Howard Fineman traces the bias to Vietnam and Cronkite. "The notion of a neutral, non-partisan mainstream press was, to me at least, worth holding on to. Now it's pretty much dead, at least as the public sees things. The seeds of its demise were sown with the best of intentions in the late 1960s, when the AMMP [American Mainstream Media Party] was founded in good measure by CBS. Old folks may remember the moment: Walter Cronkite stepped from behind the podium of presumed objectivity to become an outright foe of the war in Vietnam. . . . The problem was that, once the AMMP declared its existence by taking sides, there was no going back. A party was born."[41]

Terry Moran of ABC News has confessed to the media's disdain for the U.S. military, a contempt that he too traces to Vietnam. In 2005, Moran, then ABC's White House correspondent, told radio host Hugh Hewitt that there is "a deep antimilitary bias in the media, one that begins from the premise that the military must be lying, and that American projection of power around the world must be wrong. I think that that is a hangover from Vietnam, and I think it's very dangerous." Vietnam, of course, brought with it the so-called peace movement and the suspicion of any use of force that we still see today. Vietnam also brought us the glory days of the crusading, agenda-setting reporter.

While some media elites have acknowledged bias, many other reporters display no patience for criticism of their war coverage. For example, Newsweek's Michael Isikoff—who infamously reported the false charge that American interrogators at Guantánamo Bay had abused Korans—dismissed accusations of negative press coverage in Iraq. Appearing on MSNBC's Hardball on December 2, 2005, Isikoff scoffed, "Well, welcome to the news biz. That's the way it operates. We generally don't cover hospital and school openings. We cover bombings and, you know, mass suicides."[42]

Maybe if Isikoff realized how his beloved "news biz" affects our troops, he wouldn't so blithely dismiss criticisms of the war coverage.

NO HEROES FOR THE MEDIA

Particularly appalling are the media's bile and contempt for our soldiers' bravery and courage under fire. How can you fight a war and not have any heroes? If you depend on the media to inform you, you'd have to believe you can.

Soon after returning from his tour of duty in Iraq, Marine Captain Rory Quinn wrote of realizing "how petty or unimportant many of the seemingly pressing issues covered in the news media truly are. Compared to the shock of the instant, violent death of a squad-mate standing right next to me, or the excitement of a child looking at my uniform, the constant barrage of partisan politics, runaway brides and the activities of Paris Hilton seem utterly devoid of importance. I have marines slowly recuperating at hospitals in San Francisco, Washington, Bethesda and San Diego. Who is telling their stories?"[43]

Shamefully, not his country's media.

On April 4, 2005, Army Sergeant First Class Paul Smith became the first soldier in the War on Terror, and only the third since the Vietnam War, to receive the Medal of Honor, America's highest award for individual valor in combat. President George W. Bush honored Smith in a special White House ceremony.

The honor was granted posthumously, as Smith had sacrificed his life to save his troops in Iraq on April 4, 2003, just days into the U.S. invasion. On that day, Smith's unit was building a prisoner holding area when a hundred of Iraq's elite Republican Guards fell upon the Americans, pinning down Smith's men. The sergeant leapt into action, jumping behind a 50-caliber machine gun in the turret of a disabled vehicle. Smith alone held off over one hundred Iraqis, killing as many as fifty of Saddam Hussein's soldiers. While he fired on the Iraqis, he was shot in the head and killed. Through this last full measure of devotion, Smith saved more than one hundred American troops.[44]

In another time and in another America, Smith's bravery and sacrifice would have been heralded in the same way our nation hailed Sergeant York, Audie Murphy, or Billy Mitchell. But today's editors and producers were not so moved.

The *New York Times* saw fit to print more than fifty front-page, above-the-fold articles highlighting the Abu Ghraib transgressions, but on the day Sergeant Smith received his Medal of Honor posthumously, the best they could do for the American hero was a slot on page A16.[45]

Using the LexisNexis search engine, *American Enterprise* magazine conducted a comprehensive look at major U.S. media outlets to determine how many times Smith's Medal of Honor was mentioned. Over a period of two and a half months following his award, the media mentioned Sergeant Smith's accomplishments only ninety times, and many of those mentions came from press releases through military news outlets. To provide a point of comparison, the *American Enterprise* also investigated how many times media outlets mentioned court-martialed Abu Ghraib prison conspirator Lynndie England and the allegations of Koran abuse at Guantánamo (later proven to be false). The results: 5,159 mentions for England and 4,677 for the Koran story.[46]

The Lynndie England comparison is instructive. Think about the soldiers most identified with the Iraq War. Sergeant Smith, who certainly should be heralded, is not one them—but England is. Aside from England, the most prominent soldiers in the Iraq War have been Jessica Lynch, the female truck driver who was captured and held by Iraqi forces and eventually rescued by U.S. special operations forces, and whose supposed bravery in a firefight proved to be false; and Janis Karpinski, Lynndie England's commander in Iraq, who was removed from her position, demoted in rank, and forced to retire for her failure in leadership. So Big Media saw fit to trumpet a criminal, a victim, and a failure.

It is not as if there are no true heroes in the War on Terror. American soldiers have accomplished literally thousands of heroic and courageous acts in the War on Terror, as evidenced by the medals awarded: two Medals of Honor and thousands of Navy Crosses, Silver Stars, Bronze Stars, and Purple Hearts. It's just that typically we don't hear about these heroes.

In fact, according to a study by the Media Research Center, from September 2001 to June 2006 the total amount of time ABC, NBC, and CBS devoted to stories of American military heroism was fifty-two *minutes.* Fifty-two minutes in nearly five years! Yet in a period of only three *weeks* (May 17 through June 7, 2006), these same networks dedicated three and a half hours of coverage to unproven military misconduct in the incident at Haditha.[47]

CBS curmudgeon Andy Rooney perfectly captured Big Media's perspective on the U.S. military when he wrote, "Treating soldiers fighting their war as brave heroes is an old civilian trick designed to keep the soldiers at it. But you can be sure our soldiers in Iraq are not all brave heroes. . . . We pin medals on their chests to keep them going. . . . We should not bestow the mantle of heroism on all of them for simply being where we sent them."[48]

L.A. Times columnist Joel Stein also made the disdain crystal-clear: "I don't support our troops. . . . I'm not advocating that we spit on returning veterans like they did after the Vietnam War, but we shouldn't be celebrating people for doing something we don't think is a good idea. . . . Please, no parades."[49]

Why can't the mainstream media praise a soldier's extraordinary service? Why must they display such an appalling contempt for our fighting forces' bravery?

The short answer is that praising our armed forces for valor and exemplary conduct doesn't fit the template when you oppose everything the military represents.

THE SOLDIERS' PERSPECTIVE

In order to write this book I've interviewed literally hundreds of soldiers, sailors, airmen, and Marines. I traveled to Iraq and Kuwait in July 2005 specifically to speak with soldiers on the ground, and practically every week on my radio show I interview an active-duty soldier fighting in the War on Terror, whether it be in Iraq, Afghanistan, or the Horn of Africa. In virtually every conversation I ask this question: What are the greatest threats to you and America's success in Iraq and the War on Terror? And almost every single time, the response is the same: The terrorists and the media.

The media? Yes, the media. As one soldier put it to me, all the tactical victories in Iraq don't amount to anything when they are losing the strategic battle at home. The terrorists they can handle, but media bias makes their jobs much more difficult.

In one interview I conducted, Army First Sergeant Jeff Nuding said, "We daily see the gross distortions. We can't recognize the caricatures they scratch out, neither in our fellow soldiers, nor on the battleground. I know they claim to be objective but really they're nothing more than accomplices in the face of this evil."[50]

Similarly, Air Force Major Eric Egland told me, "The troops' number-one frustration has consistently been the media reporting." He cited a prime example: "The way the press mishandled Abu Ghraib and Guantánamo had a tremendous negative effect on us. It inflamed the Iraqis at a time when we were making great progress in their support and willingness to help."[51]

Army Sergeant Eddie Jeffers is also outraged at the media's blatant disregard for truth and context in their reporting of the War on Terror. "Terrorists cut the heads off of American citizens on the Internet . . . and there is no outrage," said Jeffers, "but an American soldier kills an Iraqi in the midst of battle, and there are investigations, and sometimes soldiers are even jailed . . . for doing their job.

"It is absolutely sickening to me to think our country has come to this," concluded Jeffers. "Why are we so obsessed with the bad news? Why will people stop at nothing to be against this war, no matter how much evidence of the good we've done is thrown in their face? When is the last time CNN or MSNBC or CBS reported the opening of schools and hospitals in Iraq? Or the leaders of terror cells being detained or killed? It's all happening, but people will not let up their hatred of President Bush. They will ignore the good news, because it just might show people that Bush was right."[52]

Plenty of other men in uniform have described the obstacles the American media put in their way. An Army soldier who blogs under the name Ma Deuce Gunner, for example, said, "The American soldier has 2 enemies: the terrorists who try to kill us, and all who stand for right, with bombs and bullets; and the press, who spew forth metaphorical, yet equally lethal, 'missiles' of word and thought at the American Fighting Man."[53]

Another, an airman in the Air Force, said, "The only thing that I get to see from the American people is what is portrayed on the news. The media, and the people that listen to what they say and believe it almost makes me more pissed off than the Iraqis that are over here shooting at us. At least when the Iraqis are shooting towards us, it is to our face, instead of like the traitors that call themselves Americans who stab us in the back."[54]

Upon returning from his tour of duty in Iraq, Army Captain Steve Alvarez wrote, "I don't think the charred skeletal remains of a vehicle-borne explosive device are the watermark of this war. The images I see back here [in U.S. media] are not the same indelible images I saw in Iraq—those of a resilient country making its way back from decades of oppression—helped by the many friendly nations that liberated them. . . . I remember the jubilation of my Iraqi friends as they showed off their ink-stained fingers, a badge of honor on their fingertips, indicating they had voted in their country's first democratic election in decades. I remember the Iraqi female military police soldiers who became pioneers for women in that region by joining the Iraqi military, clearing not just personal hurdles, but cultural ones. . . . Mostly, I remember the thousands of Iraqi and coalition troops that each day hunted the enemy and kept me safe. I remember the drivers and gunners on convoy, the pilots and crew chiefs in the sky, the sentries and tankers at the gates, and all of the warriors who were out there trying to make Iraq a better and safer place."[55]

Major General William McCoy, the on-scene commander for the U.S. Army Corps of Engineers, which is responsible for rebuilding Iraq, wrote, "I'm astounded at how distorted a good story can become and what agenda drives a paper to see only the bad side to the reconstruction effort here in Iraq. . . . Perhaps it's because some in the press don't want the American people to know the truth and prefer instead to only report the negative aspects of the news because 'it sells papers.' We deserve better from those who claim the protection of the Constitution we are fighting to support and defend."[56]

Referring specifically to CNN, a Marine in Iraq said, "They are complete misinformation artists—and I have seen firsthand how they warp and manipulate the 'truth' to fit their agenda. I have been on the scene and witnessed a situation with my own two eyes, while CNN was standing right next to me (Arwa Damon and Jennifer Eccleston have been our two offenders, by the way). Then, the story that I read on their website or saw on CNN International did not even remotely resemble the actual scene. The video had been altered, edited out of order, and the narration used in such a way to warp the situation and twist it into what they wanted it to be. It is amazing and despicable."[57]

An Army sergeant writing from Saudi Arabia noted, "As soldiers, we all understand that we may be asked to participate in wars (actions) that we (or our countrymen) don't agree with. The irresponsible journalism being practiced by organizations such as *Newsweek*, however, [is] just inexcusable. At this point, because of their actions, and failure to follow up on a claim [of Koran abuse at Guantánamo Bay] of that magnitude, they've set the process back in Afghanistan immensely. . . . I don't regret serving my country, not one bit, but to have everything I'm doing here undermined by irresponsible journalists leaves me disgusted and disappointed."[58]

INTREPID REPORTERS— BRAVING THE HOTEL BAR

The source of the problem is clear: Journalists often have no idea how the military works and even less inclination to learn. Big Media are on the other side of the cultural divide that separates the elites in this country from the military. As veteran *U.S. News & World Report* writer John Leo put it, "In all my years in journalism, I don't think I have met more than one or two reporters who have ever served in the military or who even had a friend in the armed forces. Most media hiring today is from universities where a military career is regarded as bizarre and almost any exercise of American power is considered wrongheaded or evil."[59] Remember, many of the universities to which Leo refers barred military recruiters for decades, and some of America's most prestigious journalism schools still do. The distance between the editorial room and the barracks is immense.

These days, it seems, reporters don't even look to report the ground truth. Real war reporting is dirty and dangerous work. But most American journalists don't provide real war reporting in Iraq. Instead, these denizens of the Baghdad news bureaus hole up in their hotel rooms, hang out at the hotel bar, or lounge by the pool and report the war from the safe confines of the Green Zone—the highly protected compound that houses the Coalition Provisional Authority, military headquarters, Iraq government officials, and civilian visitors.

It's called Hotel Bulletin Reporting. Iraq-based journalists file secondhand reports, getting their information from stringers and from surfing the Internet and talking with colleagues. Anyone with a cell phone and Internet access could do the same thing from anywhere. An AP reporter grumbled, "We live in a bubble. If we know one percent of what's going on in Iraq, we're lucky."[60]

When U.S. and coalition troops rolled into Iraq during the spring of 2003, there were approximately 770 journalists in the field and embedded with the forces. By October 2006, there were only nine: three from the Armed Forces' *Stars & Stripes* newspaper, one from the Armed Forces Network (AFN), one from a Polish radio station covering the Polish coalition forces, one from Italy's RAI television network covering the Italian troops, one an author gathering material for a project, one from the Associated Press, and one from the *Charlotte Observer*.

At the Department of Defense media briefings provided daily, Big Media "reporters" ignore the inputs as propaganda. If the military wants them to have the information, they figure, it must be either false or trumped-up. Instead they file sensational (read: negative) reports based on what they have gathered from Iraqi stringers, who have learned one very important lesson about American reporters: They pay more money for bad news—the bombs, the blood, and the death.

During Vietnam it was the Caravelle Hotel in Saigon; today it's the Al-Rashid or Palestine Hotel. The names have changed but the approach remains the same.

So a car bomb ignites near the Green Zone Gate or a missile flies overhead, and the American journalists hanging out at the Al-Rashid bar jump to. In a few minutes, stern-faced correspondents with perfect hair stand on their hotel balconies with smoke rising in the background and proclaim mayhem. And that becomes the war for that day. In a country the size of California, a single terror attack at the gates of the compound in Baghdad defines America's progress in the War on Terror.

In the summer of 2005 I had an opportunity to call out a so-called war correspondent for the lazy and inaccurate reporting in Iraq. On July 13, 2005, I appeared on MSNBC to debate NBC correspondent Richard Engel, who claimed to be the longest-serving war correspondent in Iraq. I asked Engel, "When was the last time NBC covered a story in Iraq that didn't involve a car bomb or terrorist attack of some sort?" Engel insisted, "Oh, we cover the other news stories all the time." To prove Engel's point, cohost Ron Reagan Jr. played a clip of Engel's Iraq reporting . . . on a car bombing![61]

You can't make this stuff up.

Engel's reporting of the war is symptomatic of the abject failure of the elite media. A typical example came on NBC's *Today* show on May 17, 2005, when, far from doing any original reporting, he aired three separate unsubstantiated rumors as fact.[62]

"There's one rumor spreading today in local newspapers," Engel said from Baghdad. "It's been on the local television and it was also broadcast on the Al Jazeera television network. It's that U.S. Marines, while raiding a mosque in Ramadi, kicked a Koran and then took it and spray-painted in black paint a cross right on top of the Koran."

He was watching Al Jazeera to get his information! That's the equivalent of Ernie Pyle researching his stories from the broadcasts of Tokyo Rose or Lord Haw-Haw.

Another rumor, Engel reported, "came out a couple of weeks ago [and] was in a local newspaper. It said that during a search of a woman's bag, U.S. soldiers with a team of dogs were sniffing through her bag. She had a Koran in her bag. The dog pulled the Muslim holy book out of the bag with its mouth and the soldiers started laughing."

The NBC newsman then cited a letter that a female terrorist suspect had written in an Iraqi newspaper. The woman, who had been detained at Abu Ghraib, claimed that "she was raped every

night by six American soldiers," Engel said. He did mention that
U.S. officials denied the claim, but he quickly added that "other
women came out and wrote similar claims in other newspapers,
and this does have repercussions on the ground."

Since there wasn't much evidence that Engel had done much
beyond read newspapers in his hotel, it's hard to trust his word
about what was really happening "on the ground" in Iraq.

When today's professional journalists never actually see the
war they claim to report on, is it any wonder that the coverage has
been so incredibly slanted and wrong? And is it any wonder that
so many Americans have difficulty understanding the strides
we're making in the War on Terror? After all, how can we be winning the war when all we see are daily images of car bombings and
body counts?

British journalist Toby Harnden, a reporter for London's
Daily Telegraph, recounted his experience with a hunkered-down
U.S. media in 2004. "The other day, while taking a break by the
Al-Hamra Hotel pool . . . I was accosted by an American magazine journalist of serious accomplishment and impeccable liberal
credentials. She had been disturbed by my argument that Iraqis
were better off than they had been under Saddam and I was
now—there was no choice about this—going to have to justify
my bizarre and dangerous views. I'll spare you most of the details
because you know the script—no WMD, no 'imminent threat'
(though the point was to deal with Saddam before such a threat
could emerge), a diversion from the hunt for bin Laden, enraging
the Arab world. Et cetera. But then she came to the point. Not
only had she 'known' the Iraq War would fail but she considered
it essential that it did so because this would ensure that the 'evil'
George W. Bush would no longer be running her country. Her editors back on the East Coast were giggling, she said, over what a
disaster Iraq had turned out to be. 'Lots of us talk about how
awful it would be if this worked out.' Startled by her candor, I

asked whether thousands more dead Iraqis would be a good thing. She nodded and mumbled something about Bush needing to go. By this logic, I ventured, another September 11 on, say, September 11 would be perfect for pushing up John Kerry's poll numbers. 'Well, that's different—that would be Americans,' she said, haltingly. 'I guess I'm a bit of an isolationist.' That's one way of putting it."[63]

THE WRONG SIDE OF HISTORY

The media's disdainful attitudes and negative reporting incense our troops—and many other Americans, as well. Some soldiers have grown so fed up with the inaccurate reporting that they've tried to bring the truth to the American people directly.

U.S. Army Lieutenant Colonel Tim Ryan, commander of a cavalry unit in Iraq, has written, "Many of the journalists making public assessments about the progress of the war in Iraq are unqualified to do so . . . [and] through their incomplete, uninformed and unbalanced reporting, many members of the media covering the war in Iraq are aiding and abetting the enemy." Referring to a *Rolling Stone* report that described Iraq as the "lost war," Ryan said, "Will someone please tell me who at *Rolling Stone* or just about any other 'news' outlet is qualified to make a determination as to when all is lost and it's time to throw in the towel? . . . How would they really know if things are going well or not?"[64]

In fact, it was dismay at the media's refusal to provide the full story of the War on Terror that prompted my trip to Iraq. Others shared my frustration. I was part of a group of conservative radio talk show hosts who went to Iraq and Kuwait to interview soldiers and broadcast our programs. We called it "The Voices of Soldiers Truth Tour" since we wanted to let the soldiers tell their story directly to America—a story that obviously was not getting through.

Apparently giving the soldiers a voice was too much for the Left to bear. I was always taught as an Air Force pilot that the flak is the heaviest when you're directly over the target. Our group clearly hit our target in calling out Big Media, because even before we touched down in Baghdad, liberal commentators went on the attack.

Leftist comedian and Air America talk show host Al Franken scoffed, "That's how stupid these people are. They think they can walk around and talk to shopkeepers. They don't realize how dangerous it is over there."[65] Actually, Al, I've seen with my own eyes the dangerous conditions that our troops encounter every day. It only increases my respect for the incredible work they are doing under difficult circumstances. And, yes, we walked around and talked with shopkeepers.

Huffington Post antiwar blogger Paul Rieckhoff wrote, "This type of shameless cheerleading and agenda-driven journalism is an insult to those who have sacrificed on the frontlines of this war and experienced its terrible toll." Rieckhoff should have aimed his criticism at the real "agenda-driven journalism"—that of the mainstream media. Our only agenda was to let the troops speak freely, without someone like Matt Lauer insisting that their morale should be low.[66]

Perhaps the most vicious attack came from Peter Beinart, at the time the editor of the liberal magazine *The New Republic*. I respect his intellect. It's his common sense I question. "This [the Voices of Soldiers Truth Tour] is the most pathetic thing I've heard in a long time," Beinart said. "They should be ashamed of themselves. They have no idea what journalism is and to pretend they are journalists is laughable. You do not achieve victory by not facing reality. I think these are the kinds of people that will lead us to lose there."[67]

Beinart missed a simple point: If the so-called real journalists, such as Beinart, had been doing their jobs, our trip would have been unnecessary. And it isn't my associates threatening success in Iraq, it's his.

The media elites would do well to remember the Code of Ethics as promoted by the Society of Professional Journalists. It states that "public enlightenment is the forerunner of justice and the foundation of democracy. The duty of the journalist is to further those ends by seeking truth and providing a fair and comprehensive account of events and issues." The code also lays out a number of responsibilities for every journalist. Among other things, it says journalists should:

- "Make certain that headlines . . . and quotations do not misrepresent. They should not oversimplify or highlight incidents out of context."

- "Examine their own cultural values and avoid imposing those values on others."

- "Distinguish between advocacy and news reporting. Analysis and commentary should be labeled and not misrepresent fact or context."

- "Recognize that gathering and reporting information may cause harm or discomfort. Pursuit of the news is not a license for arrogance."

- "Admit mistakes and correct them promptly."

More vitally, they should take note of federal law under 18 U.S. Code Section 794, subsection (b), which holds:

Whoever, in time of war, with intent that the same shall be communicated to the enemy, collects, records, publishes, or communicates, or attempts to elicit any information with respect to the movement, numbers, description, condition, or disposition of any of the Armed Forces, ships, aircraft, or war materials of the United States, or with respect to the plans or conduct, or supposed plans or conduct of any naval or military operations, or with respect to any works or measures undertaken for or connected with, or intended for the fortification or defense of any place, or any other information relating to the public defense, which might be useful to the enemy, shall be punished by death or by imprisonment for any term of years or for life.

The American people have placed on the media's shoulders an enormous responsibility. We have handed them a burden of trust. They have failed to live up to that responsibility or to fulfill that trust. The establishment media are on the wrong side of history in the War on Terror—just as they were with Vietnam, Reagan's defense buildup, the Grenada invasion, and Nicaragua.

First Sergeant Jeffrey Nuding, U.S. Army, eloquently but forcefully laid out his disappointment with the elite media coverage of the war that he had witnessed while deployed to Iraq. Specifically addressing the U.S. media and liberal elites, Nuding concluded, "You are creating greater risk for me personally [and] you create added danger for my soldiers. You feed into enemy (yes, enemy) propaganda efforts in yielding unlimited access to pre-staged voices with calculated intent. . . . You diminish and demean our service. . . . Never, never claim to support the soldiers, you don't, you never will in any meaningful way until you can see your prejudices for what they are, work to eliminate them, and for once try to view the world with an open and not a closed mind."[68]

The brave men and women of the U.S. military continue to do their duty, to serve honorably, to do everything in their power to protect the American people and win a war they were sent into. But the enemy they can't defeat is the enemy within.

FIVE

STAR WARS

The poet with his words and phrases may be said to lay on the colours of the several arts, himself understanding their nature only enough to imitate them; and other people, who are as ignorant as he is, and judge only from his words, imagine that if he speaks of cobbling, or of military tactics, or of anything else, in meter and harmony and rhythm, he speaks very well—such is the sweet influence which melody and rhythm by nature have.
—Socrates, in Plato's *Republic*

"Welcome to the Suck."

That's the money line from director Sam Mendes's 2005 antiwar, antiwarrior quagmire of a film *Jarhead*. Based on a best-selling book authored by disgruntled ex-Marine Anthony Swofford (played by Jake Gyllenhaal), *Jarhead* pretends to depict Marine Corps training in the months leading up to the 1991 Gulf War. "Welcome to the Suck" more accurately serves as a metaphor for the current state of subversion and intellectual bankruptcy in Hollywood. For Mendes and his colleagues, the American military is "the Suck."

In *Jarhead* the characters are cardboard cutouts of what the

Hollywood elite presume the military to be. It's the Vietnam GI template four decades later, with some homoerotic tendencies thrown in for good measure. Mendes's Marines are a group of idiots, losers, and criminals ("retards and f***ups," to quote the screenplay), and the plot is anchored in the obligatory "the military ruined my life" theme. Young enlisted Marines are portrayed as crazed maniacal killers, dimwitted knuckle-draggers, and warmongers whose sole reasons for existing are sex and alcohol. Marine officers are shown as unprofessional, grossly profane, and conspiratorially distrusting of their superiors. And, of course, back on the home front the wives and girlfriends of the Marines are cheating.

Our protagonist, "Swoff," is a disgruntled soul who joined the Marines, as he tells his drill sergeant, because he "got lost on the way to college" and regrets his decision only days into his service. Swoff reads Camus's *The Stranger* on the toilet, wets his pants at the sound of gunfire, and beseeches one of his squad mates to shoot him so that he can "end the waiting."

In one scene in *Jarhead* a corporal suffers a complete emotional breakdown and physically assaults his commanding officer. Implausible. In another a young trainee panics during a "live-fire" exercise and is accidentally shot and killed by his fellow Marines. Instead of attending to the fallen young man, the drill instructor (played by Jamie Foxx) screams at the corpse, "Why didn't you listen to me when I told you not to stand up?" Impossible. Finally, Swoff and his buddies stage a raging frat-party–like celebration in the middle of the Kuwaiti desert celebrating the end of a war in which they never saw combat. Absurd.

For Mendes, war is obviously hell, and he obligingly pays homage to earlier, similarly dark antimilitary films such as *Apocalypse Now* and *The Deer Hunter.* Tellingly, like virtually all of Hollywood's war and military movies since the 1960s, *Jarhead* does not depict *actual* Marine themes such as honor, courage, and faithfulness—concepts Tinseltown neither understands nor respects. And nowhere in Mendes's film are there portrayals of *real* Marines. There is no room in Hollywood for Marines such as Iraq war hero Sergeant Rafael Peralta.

On the morning of November 15, 2004, Sergeant Peralta and his squad from Company A, 1st Battalion, 3rd Marine Regiment moved house to house during the Battle for Fallujah (Operation Dawn), cleansing the city of al Qaeda and Iraqi insurgents. The first three houses they entered were empty. Then Peralta and his Marines entered a fourth. Kicking in two of the building's entrances, they found nothing. Then Peralta approached the door to an adjoining room and found it unlocked. He pushed it open and prepared to rush in. As he did he was met by three gunmen blazing away with their AK-47s. Peralta, instantly riddled with bullets to his face and torso, fell into the doorway.[1]

Though severely wounded and dying, he managed to wrench himself out of the opening to allow his fellow Marines a clear line of sight. They retaliated with a curtain of gunfire. As the close-quarters battle raged, one of the enemy fighters tossed a grenade at the Marines. Peralta's fellow Marines tried to flee the room but were trapped with no escape. With his last full measure of devotion, Peralta grabbed the grenade and cradled it to his chest. Seconds later it exploded, obliterating the brave Marine's body. Peralta's selfless courage saved his fellow Marines to fight another day.

In honor of his heroism and devotion to duty, Sergeant Rafael Peralta was awarded the Navy Cross for gallantry and courage in combat and is being considered for the Medal of Honor.

Peralta was an immigrant from Mexico who earned his American citizenship while on active duty in the military service of the United States. On his bedroom wall in his parents' home in San Diego, he'd hung copies of the Declaration of Independence, the Bill of Rights, and his graduation certificate from Marine Corps boot camp. In what was to be his final letter to his brother at home, Sergeant Peralta wrote, "Be proud of being an American. Our father came to this country, became a citizen because it was the right place for our family to be."[2]

Sergeant Peralta more properly represents the U.S. Marine Corps than does anything we see in movies. An impartial assessment of the U.S. military is not what we get from Hollywood. Nor do we get an impartial look at America.

No, like their Fifth Column comrades in academic institutions, editorial rooms, and Democratic Party offices, Hollywood's cultural elites care more for their ideology than they do for America.

BLAME AMERICA, NOT THE TERRORISTS

In the years since 9/11, there have been no major films dealing with the realities of the global ideological struggle we find ourselves in or with Western civilization's enemy—Islamofascist terrorism. There have been no movies addressing the evil of al Qaeda, Osama bin Laden, the Taliban, Mullah Omar, or Saddam Hussein, or the many terrorist attacks in the 1980s and 1990s, such as bombings of the embassies in Africa and of the USS *Cole*—nothing. A few major films have focused specifically on the reaction to the 9/11 attacks, such as *United 93* and *World Trade Center*. But none have dealt with the much larger truth of America's global war with jihadists.

In fact, for years Hollywood shied away from the very event that launched the war on terror: 9/11. The first major film to depict that day of infamy, *World Trade Center*, wasn't released until 2006. And what director did Tinseltown line up to treat this important subject? None other than the terminally unhinged and paranoid Oliver Stone, who was responsible for such conspiratorial, America-bashing films as *Salvador, Platoon, Wall Street, Born on the Fourth of July, JFK, Natural Born Killers,* and *Nixon.* Stone was an odd choice to take on a 9/11 film, given that he had referred to the September 11 attacks as a "revolt" and likened images of Palestinians dancing in the streets following the al Qaeda terror to the people in France and Russia celebrating in the wake of their revolutions. The director also charged the Bush administration with kowtowing to U.S. oil companies and letting Osama bin Laden escape from Afghanistan so as not to "piss off the Saudis."[3] And he has said that the "Darth-Vadian Empire of the United States must pay for its many sins in the future. I think America has to bleed. I think the corpses have to pile up. I think American boys have to die again. Let the mothers weep and mourn."[4] *This* is the man to helm a major film about September 11?

The first Hollywood production set in the aftermath of September 11 was *The Great New Wonderful,* which debuted in 2005. Though the film portrays life in New York City soon after the 9/11 attacks, it doesn't mention President Bush, the terrorists, the quick and decisive U.S. military response, the hunt for bin Laden, or the fall of the Taliban. "I just wasn't interested in anything didactic," explained director Danny Leiner.[5] Nor, apparently, was he interested in founding his film in reality.

The movie's lead actress, Maggie Gyllenhaal (*Jarhead* Jake's sister and the daughter of leftist antiwar producer Stephen Gyllenhaal), thought it was "wonderful" to deal with September 11 "in such a subtle, open way that I think it allows it to be more complicated than just, 'Oh, look at these poor New Yorkers and how hard it was for them.' " Typical of the Hollywood elite, she went on to express her enmity for the nation. "I think America has done reprehensible things and is responsible in some way and so I think the delicacy [of the film's approach] . . . allows that to sort of creep in."[6]

Blame America, not the terrorists—that's popular culture's contribution to the global war effort.

When the film *The Sum of All Fears* came out in 2002, the Islamic terror cell depicted in Tom Clancy's original novel was replaced with South African neo-Nazis. In the original draft of Sydney Pollack's *The Interpreter,* the terrorists who attempt the assassination of a head of state hailed from a Middle Eastern country, but after 9/11, writers and producers changed the bad guys into an African guerrilla group. "We didn't want to encumber the film in politics in any way," producer Kevin Misher explained to the *Wall Street Journal.*[7] Or in reality, either.

What makes the film industry's post-9/11 efforts even more troubling is that Hollywood could, if it wanted to, actually lend a hand to the nation in its fight against terrorism. Industry leaders in the 1940s rallied to the U.S. effort in World War II. Back then, Hollywood executives created the War Activities Committee, and President Franklin Roosevelt established the Bureau of Motion Pictures Affairs under the Office of War Information. Brilliant directors such as Frank Capra, William Wyler, and Walt Disney came to the nation's aid and produced films educating America's citizens and fighting men alike to the nobility of the campaigns against fascism and Nazism. Nearly every major studio responded to the war effort. Movies such as *Sergeant York* (1941), *Flying Tigers* (1942), *Guadalcanal Diary* (1943), *Thirty Seconds Over Tokyo* (1944), and *Back to Bataan* (1945) rallied the troops and united a nation during its time of crisis.

Stars stepped up as well. Among those who served with distinction were Jimmy Stewart, Clark Gable (who enlisted at age forty-one!), Gene Autry, Jackie Coogan, Tyrone Power, and Douglas Fairbanks Jr. Stewart, who fearlessly piloted bombers over Europe, earned the Distinguished Flying Cross, four Air Medals, and France's Croix de Guerre. Autry flew C-47 transports in the Burmese Theater. Coogan flew gliders in hazardous special operations for the 1st Air Commando Group. Power was a Marine pilot. Fairbanks was a highly decorated naval officer.

Can you imagine Tom Cruise, Brad Pitt, George Clooney, or

Sean Penn putting their extravagant lifestyles and careers on hold to fight for their country? Can you envision Oliver Stone, Steven Spielberg, or Michael Moore helming films for the White House or the Pentagon designed to encourage patriotism or rally national unity? Of course not.

But it's not as if the current movers and shakers in Tinseltown didn't have their opportunities to help. Shortly after the 9/11 attacks, Bush administration officials flew to Los Angeles hoping to elicit help from the motion picture industry in mobilizing support for the War on Terror. At the Peninsula Hotel in Beverly Hills, White House adviser Karl Rove detailed the nature of the threat in a ninety-minute presentation to approximately fifty of Hollywood's biggest players from all the major studios, including 20th Century Fox, Warner Brothers, Universal Studios, MGM, Columbia Pictures, and DreamWorks. But the industry moguls' eyes were wide shut to their nation's needs. They weren't moved to action by appeals to patriotism or supporting the military.[8] They were resolute, however, in their concerns for Muslim sensitivities and fears of being seen as aligned with the government.

Instead of providing accurate and positive messages of nationalism and pride, Hollywood has released a torrent of films justifying the terrorists' actions and portraying the United States in the worst possible light.

The Oscar-winning film *Syriana,* for example, would have been more appropriately titled *It's the Oil, Stupid* or *It's Our Fault, Sorry.* For the film's creators, the problems in the Middle East are the result not of plundering dictators, anti-Semitism, proliferating nuclear weapons, or plotting jihadists but of corrupt American governmental officials and fat white oil executives.

Set during the administration of President George H. W. Bush, *Syriana* paints the U.S. government as heartless assassins gladly sacrificing the interests of oppressed peoples abroad to guarantee chaos in the Middle East and the safety of its oil interests. George Clooney stars as a burned-out CIA agent, and Matt

Damon plays an oil industry analyst. In one characteristic line, Damon's character tells the prince of a Saudi Arabia–like country, "You want to know what the business world thinks of you? We think one hundred years ago you were living out here in tents in the desert chopping each other's heads off and that's exactly where you are going to be in another hundred. So, yes, on behalf of my firm I accept your money."

One of the heroes of the film, a young Arab prince who is pursuing democracy and Westernization in his country, is killed along with his family by a missile fired by (you guessed it) CIA headquarters. The other hero, a young, handsome disaffected Pakistani, is laid off by an uncaring American oil firm. As a result, he finds refuge in the teachings of radical Islamic fundamentalists. The climax of the film comes when the young jihadist sails his bomb-laden boat into a Persian Gulf oil terminal in a scenario reminiscent of al Qaeda's bombing of the USS *Cole* in 2000. The young terrorist is glorified in his death just as bin Laden's murderers were glorified in theirs following the attack in Yemen.

Try to imagine a feature film produced in the midst of World War II promoting a moral justification for Japan's surprise attack on Pearl Harbor.

NO HEROES

In modern Hollywood, American soldiers are a favorite target. We haven't seen any major motion pictures reflecting on the heroism of our soldiers, sailors, airmen, and Marines and their many successes in tracking down and defeating terrorists. Not one. Perhaps I could suggest a few titles for the struggling Hollywood industry. How about *The Caves of Tora Bora, Shock and Awe, Special Operators in the Hindu Kush, The Road to Baghdad, Establishing Democracy in the Middle East,* or *The Rafael Peralta Story*?

Instead we get movies reflecting the Left's extremely limited, almost childlike perspective, which renders them incapable of differentiating between war and the military. To the Left, the equation is simple: War is bad; the military fights the war; so the military is abhorrent too.

That's why we see movies like Miramax's *Buffalo Soldiers*. Set in the late Cold War years, this is the tale of an American soldier running drug and black-market stolen goods operations from his Army base in West Germany. The film's promotional trailer not-so-cleverly substituted the Army's former recruiting motto of "Be all that you can be" with "Steal all that you can steal." The director, Australian Gregor Jordan, described his movie—which emphasized corruption, drug use, and violence on U.S. Army bases—as factually grounded. Jordan's film shows soldiers marching on an American flag, spewing profanity, abusing drugs, routinely stealing and selling government property, and having illicit sex constantly. Star Joaquin Phoenix said, "I don't know why anyone would be offended. . . . If we don't show things as they really happen, then what's that about?"[9]

Another cinematic outrage is *The Valley of the Wolves: Iraq*, starring has-beens Gary Busey and Billy Zane. The film—produced in Turkey and released in the United States, Britain, Germany, the Netherlands, Denmark, Russia, Egypt, Syria, and Australia—features American soldiers overrunning an Iraqi wedding, indiscriminately killing dozens of innocent people, murdering a little boy in front of his mother, and shooting the groom in the head. The rest of the wedding guests are rounded up and shipped off to the Abu Ghraib prison. Zane's character is an American Army officer who kills innocent civilians while proclaiming to be a "peacekeeper sent by God." In skewed logic only an actor would understand, Zane defended the movie by saying, "This screenplay is not against my country's people. I am doing this movie because I am a patriot."[10] In reality, Zane and Busey are anti-American whores who sold out their country's military for profit in a time of national crisis.

Sinking to the absolute depths of vulgarity is director Joe

Dante's horror film *Homecoming*. Dead American soldiers killed in Iraq crawl out of their flag-draped caskets at Dover Air Force Base intent on overthrowing the politicians (read Bush and the Republicans) for having sent them to war. Dante received a five-minute ovation in Turin, Italy, when the film debuted, according to the *Village Voice*. "Somebody has to start making this kind of movie, this kind of statement," claimed Dante. "But everybody's afraid—it's uncommercial, people are going to be upset. Good, let them be upset."[11]

"DUDE, WHERE'S MY REVOLUTION?"

Hollywood's anti-American and antimilitary message wouldn't be so disturbing if the world didn't take it at face value. But even the most outrageous anti-American propaganda is embraced in elite circles. To see this we need look no further than Michael Moore (who'd be hard to overlook). In his 2004 schlock-umentary *Fahrenheit 9/11*, Moore claims:

- President Bush knew about the 9/11 attacks beforehand and deliberately chose not to act.

- Bush personally allowed members of the bin Laden family to flee the United States in the days immediately following 9/11.

- Attacking Afghanistan was not intended to remove the Taliban or al Qaeda but to establish an oil pipeline for the Texas oil company Unocal.

- Saddam Hussein's Iraq was a bucolic paradise of children flying kites and a burgeoning peaceful society until America's imperial attacks disrupted the tranquillity.

- Saddam never threatened or attacked any Americans.

- The terrorists killing U.S. forces in Iraq are fighting for a noble cause.[12]

You might think mature and sober people would distance themselves from a film with such absurd and reprehensible claims. But Moore became the darling of Hollywood, Big Media, and the Democratic Party in that presidential election year. When *Fahrenheit 9/11* debuted in New York, among those giving Moore a resounding ovation were perennial presidential candidate Al Sharpton, former United Nations ambassador Richard Holbrooke, NBC News anchors Tom Brokaw and Brian Williams, Clinton friend (and Monica Lewinsky facilitator) Vernon Jordan, and actors Richard Gere, Tim Robbins, Mike Myers, Glenn Close, Lauren Bacall, and Lauren Hutton.

When the film premiered in Washington, Moore was saluted by DNC Chairman Terry McAuliffe, Democratic senators Bob Graham, Jon Corzine, Fritz Hollings, and Tom Harkin, and Democratic representatives Charles Rangel, Eleanor Holmes Norton, and William Jefferson, and 9/11 commissioner Richard Ben-Veniste. Most revealingly, at the 2004 Democratic National Convention in Boston, Moore was seated in a place of honor next to former president Jimmy Carter.

While *Fahrenheit* made Moore the toast of the Democratic Party, it didn't endear him to U.S. soldiers. Premiering his movie at the Cannes Film Festival in 2004, he boasted to the press, "When you see the movie you will see things you have never seen before, you will learn things you have never known before. Half the movie is about Iraq—we were able to get film crews embedded with American troops without them knowing that it was Michael Moore. They [the troops] are totally f***ed."[13]

Naturally, copies of the film made the rounds among our soldiers in Afghanistan and Iraq. And it had a "devastating" impact on troop morale, according to Army Specialist Joe Roche, who spent fifteen months in Iraq. "Moore's film is shocking and crushing soldiers, making them feel ashamed," said Roche. "Moore has abused the First Amendment and is hurting us worse than the enemy has. . . . Clearly, this is the type of thing we expect from angry leftists like Moore. What we didn't expect was the full impact this film is having and how it has been embraced and supported by so many Hollywood elites."[14]

Moore has not only seriously damaged the morale of America's sons and daughters in uniform, he has also shamelessly exploited—and distorted—their stories for profit and political gain.

Fahrenheit 9/11 includes video of the funeral of U.S. Air Force Major Gregory Stone, who was killed in Iraq. The Stone family was outraged, since Moore had never contacted them for their consent to use the footage in his movie. "We are furious that Greg was in that casket and cannot defend himself, and my sister, Greg's mother, is just beside herself," Stone's aunt Kandi Gallagher said. "She is furious. She called him a 'maggot that eats off the dead.' " Moore's use of the footage was especially galling because, Gallagher said, Major Stone was a "totally conservative Republican" who would have thought *Fahrenheit* was "putrid."[15]

In another sequence Moore incorporated without asking consent, Army National Guard Sergeant Peter Damon is shown recuperating at Walter Reed Army Medical Center after losing both arms in an explosion that occurred as he was working on a Black Hawk helicopter in Iraq. "I think [Moore] should be ashamed of himself," said Damon. "The whole movie makes soldiers look like a bunch of idiots. . . . It ticked me off. . . . I agree with the president 100 percent. A lot of the guys down at Walter Reed feel the same way."[16] Lieutenant Colonel Chester Buckenmaier, Damon's anesthesiologist, also said he was angered at the Moore film. "I was appalled," Buckenmaier said. "This was Joseph Goebbels–type propaganda. . . . [Moore took] a very positive thing we're doing for soldiers and used it to tell a lie."[17]

It's little wonder that the terror group Hezbollah, with Moore's tacit concurrence, stepped in and promoted *Fahrenheit*. As further evidence of the unholy alliance between the Left and the jihadist terrorists, Moore's Middle East distributor, Front Row, accepted assistance from the terror group in marketing the film in Syria and Lebanon. Having killed and kidnapped Americans for the past twenty-five years, Hezbollah is currently providing support and manpower to al Qaeda in Iraq as it indiscriminately targets Americans and innocent Iraqis and barbarously beheads captives.

In addition to the movie theaters showing Moore's film, television stations across the Arab world (including one owned by Hezbollah) picked up and broadcast portions of *Fahrenheit*. As evidence that it's not just Islamofascists with whom Moore has aligned, Communist dictator Fidel Castro also ran the film on Cuba's state-sponsored television.[18]

Closer to the battlefield, the Iraqi terror cell Rashedeen Army, which is fighting and killing American soldiers, used excerpts from Moore's film in its documentary titled *The Code of Silence*. Talking over scenes from *Fahrenheit 9/11*, the terror group's spokesman concluded, "After all, there are honest and influential guys in America and if Mr. Moore can talk to you like that, so can I."[19]

In truth there is almost no difference between Moore's *Fahrenheit* and the propaganda aired daily on Al Jazeera and other state-controlled media around the Arab world. How many motivated new recruits do you think Moore's film drummed up for the jihadists? How many young American soldiers were demoralized in the field after copies of the DVD circulated among their ranks? How many soldiers saw their friends give their lives in battle only to return home to have to answer to an award-winning film produced by a fellow American alleging that their commander in chief was a criminal and their sacrifices were in vain?

It's natural for Moore to aid and abet America's enemies. Along his journey to leftist idol, Moore has bashed his country at every step. Moore has declared, for example, that Islamofascists murdering women and children are morally equivalent to America's citizen soldiers in the Revolution. "The Iraqis who have risen up against the occupation are not 'insurgents' or 'terrorists' or 'The Enemy,' " grunted Moore. "They are the REVOLUTION, the Minutemen, and their numbers will grow—and they will win. Get it, Mr. Bush?"[20]

In typical hatriot fashion, Moore has saved some of his most virulent America bashing for foreign lands, where he encounters wildly receptive audiences. In an interview with England's *Daily Mirror,* college dropout Moore referred to his fellow countrymen as "possibly the dumbest people on the planet . . . in thrall to conniving, thieving, smug pricks."[21] In a letter to the German people featured in the national *Die Zeit* newspaper, he asked, "Should such an ignorant people [America] lead the world?"[22] On a book tour in Cambridge, England, Moore told yet another audience of foreigners, "You're stuck with being connected to this country of mine, which is known for sadness and misery to places around the globe."[23]

We don't need bin Laden or al Qaeda preaching about the Great Satan America—we have Michael Moore and his traitorous ilk doing it for us.

BRING BACK HUAC

Michael Moore took anti-American propaganda to new heights, but Hollywood has been churning out films attacking America and its military for decades. It began not long after the surge of patriotic support evidenced during World War II. As the Left seized America's major institutions, Hollywood turned against the U.S. government and, ipso facto, the military—largely because of the investigations into Communism in Hollywood.

In November 1947, a group of screenwriters, directors, and producers known as the Hollywood Ten refused to confess to their membership in the Communist Party before the House Committee on Un-American Activities (HUAC) and were jailed by Congress for contempt. The day after the Hollywood Ten were cited for their crimes, executives of the Motion Picture Association of America issued the Waldorf Statement, closing employment opportunities to known or suspected Communist sympathizers. It was Hollywood executives—*not* the U.S. government—who instituted the blacklist. But leftist revisionist history would eventually shift culpability to the American government and Senator Joseph McCarthy.

In April 1952, Elia Kazan, Academy Award–winning director of such legendary films as *On the Waterfront, East of Eden,* and *A Streetcar Named Desire,* testified before HUAC and revealed the identities of a number of his associates who were, in fact, members of the Communist Party. A former Communist himself, Kazan chose to comply with the congressional inquiry after initially refusing, because America was fully engaged in the Cold War with the Soviet Union and he felt that "secrecy serves the Communists and is exactly what they want."[24]

That was the spark. The Hollywood Left divorced themselves from Kazan and the U.S. government. They ridiculed concerns about Communism as paranoid and reactionary. They not only downplayed the Soviet threat, they attacked America as responsible for the increased tensions—just as their progeny today claim that the War on Terror is a fabrication of the Right and that fears of a worldwide jihadist movement are grossly exaggerated. Never mind that hundreds of thousands of innocent Soviets were shot execution-style or exiled to forced labor camps, and that millions more were murdered by Communist regimes in China, North Korea, Vietnam, Cambodia, and Cuba. In the Left's view, it was all America's fault.

Movies began to reflect Hollywood's rebellion against the

supposedly evil and corrupt U.S. government and military. Three films released in 1964 firmly established the industry's alienation from the country and the military: *Seven Days in May, Fail-Safe,* and *Dr. Strangelove or: How I Learned to Stop Worrying and Love the Bomb.*

Seven Days in May is a brazen indictment of America's position in the Cold War and of the Pentagon. In the film, the Joint Chiefs of Staff plan to stage a coup d'état and establish a military junta because the president (who very clearly resembles then-president Lyndon Johnson) intends to sign a treaty with the Soviets calling for bilateral nuclear disarmament. The military is portrayed as a group of right-wing reactionary nuts with complete disregard for civilian authority and the Constitution.

Fail-Safe reflects Hollywood's "anti-anti-Communism" and its fears of an uncontrollable military complex. It was written by blacklisted Communist Walter Bernstein, who, as decrypted Venona Project documents would show decades later, was secretly collaborating with the Soviet Union's KGB.[25] In Bernstein's script, a technological glitch in the Pentagon's strategic nuclear system results in an Air Force bomber dropping a bomb on Moscow. To avoid world war, the U.S. president (played by Jane Fonda's father, Henry—you just knew a Fonda had to be involved somehow) orders an American bomber to drop nuclear weapons on New York as conciliation to the Soviets.

Stanley Kubrick's dark "comedy" *Dr. Strangelove* is overtly antimilitary and anti-American. Its themes echo Hollywood's other blockbuster film themes that year: war is futile, America is to blame, the military is the real enemy, and patriotism inevitably leads to disaster. The characters are bumbling, trigger-happy dolts who get their pleasure from war. The story centers on an insane and paranoid Air Force general, Jack D. Ripper, who unilaterally starts a nuclear war with the Soviet Union because he "can no longer sit back and allow Communist infiltration, Communist indoctrination, Communist subversion, and the international Communist conspiracy to sap and impurify all of our precious bodily fluids."

The U.S. government, working with the Kremlin, develops a plan to shoot down the attacking American B-52s en route to Moscow. Unfortunately for the Kremlin and the world, a single American bomber successfully penetrates the ambush. Whenever the crew of the B-52 is pictured, Kubrick mocks patriotism and the military by playing "When Johnny Comes Marching Home" in the background. The bomber's pilot, Major "King" Kong (Slim Pickens)—a redneck who reads *Playboy* while he flies—rides the bomb down to nuclear Armageddon like a bull rider, waving his cowboy hat and cheering.

These films, trite as they sound today, had a profound impact on the direction Hollywood was to take. When George Clooney, who directed the historically biased and inaccurate McCarthyism film *Good Night, and Good Luck* and starred in *Syriana,* was asked whether any particular movie inspired him to become a film-maker, he replied, "I remember seeing *Fail-Safe* on television and then three nights later seeing *Dr. Strangelove.* It scared the shit out of me."[26]

By the 1970s, the gap between Hollywood and the U.S. military had become a chasm, as the majority of industry executives and artists emerged from the anti–Vietnam War movement. "There's a lot of guilt in those '70s films because very few young filmmakers ever served in the war," contends movie critic and author David Thomson. "It's also why you see so many shattered-Vietnam-vet movies. People in Hollywood thought soldiers should come back without their legs as a symbol of America's decadence and stupidity."[27]

Film critic and national radio talk show host Michael Medved agrees. "Most Americans admire and trust the military, yet Hollywood makes movies which are profoundly antimilitary," says

Medved. He adds, "Hollywood's Vietnam movies were made by people who had a tremendous desire to justify their reasons for avoiding serving in the war."[28]

Hollywood released only one movie about Vietnam during the war years, John Wayne's *The Green Berets* (1968). The postwar years, though, introduced a litany of major film projects portraying the war as decidedly evil (although dominant public opinion and congressional decree had authorized it), America as criminally negligent, and U.S. servicemen as psychologically deranged, drug-abusing, and brutal. The film industry's cookie-cutter approach to "war movies" didn't allow room for depictions of honor, service, patriotism, and accomplishment.

One of the earliest post-Vietnam films, 1977's *Rolling Thunder,* was the first of many "shattered vet" films. It tells the story of an American POW (played by William Devane) who is repatriated after years in North Vietnamese captivity. Devane's character returns to the United States to find his wife in the midst of a torrid affair and a son who doesn't remember him. In an attempt at moral equivalency, the film shows the former POW imagining how he would torture his wife's lover using the same brutal techniques the North Vietnamese practiced on him. Ultimately, the returning veteran proves unable to endure society and launches off on a murderous rampage.

Released in 1978, *Coming Home,* starring Jon Voight, Bruce Dern, and Jane Fonda (surprise!), is brazenly antiwar and antimilitary. Voight plays the stereotypical returning veteran, Luke, who's paralyzed by his injuries and bitter about his involvement in what he perceives as an insignificant war. While in a veterans' hospital he falls in love with a volunteer nurse, Sally (Fonda), whose husband, Bob (Dern), has himself gone off to serve in Vietnam. The film climaxes with the wheelchair-bound Luke chaining himself to the front gate of a Marine base in protest and delivering a biting antiwar soliloquy about what combat has done to him. Meanwhile, Bob returns home to discover his wife's infidelity and ultimately commits suicide by walking into the ocean. In the course of telling this uplifting story, *Coming Home* suggests widespread drug use among soldiers and repeatedly makes mention of war crimes committed by Americans.

Not surprisingly, Hollywood elites applauded the message, rewarding Voight and Fonda with Academy Awards. But *Coming Home* didn't sit well with actual soldiers. Writer-director Patrick Duncan, who served with the 173rd U.S. Army Airborne in Vietnam, said he loathed *Coming Home* and the stereotype of the despondent, shattered Vietnam veteran. "The movies created this new myth of the crazed Vietnam vet when in reality 99 percent of us went back to our lives," Duncan said. "[They] had a big impact on all news coverage. If a guy wore fatigues and carried a gun, every story would say, 'Crazed Viet Vet Shoots Up McDonalds,' even though he turned out to be a nut who'd never served in any war."[29]

Michael Cimino's *The Deer Hunter,* released the same year as *Coming Home,* won the Academy Award for Best Picture. It is yet another film that portrays returning veterans as psychopaths incapable of assimilating back into society after their military service. The three central characters, all friends from a small town in central Pennsylvania, return from Vietnam in various stages of physical and emotional collapse. One is a disabled vet who won't go home because he concludes he "doesn't fit." Another is a psychotic drug addict who eventually kills himself playing Russian Roulette—a game his Vietcong captors forced him to play (although no such technique was ever used in the war). The third character is the troubled loner. The film ends with the characters singing a dirge-like rendition of "God Bless America."

Reading the initial script before production, the U.S. Army quite astutely suggested that the filmmaker "employ a researcher who either knows or is willing to learn something about the Vietnam War."[30] Hollywood passed.

Francis Ford Coppola's *Apocalypse Now,* released in 1979, also portrayed the horrors of war and its devastating effects on war-riors. "My film is not about Vietnam," Coppola said at the time. "My film *is* Vietnam. It's what it was really like."[31]

Coppola's "reality" traces an American officer's mission to track down and assassinate "with extreme prejudice" a Green Beret colonel who has defected to Cambodia. Real-life anti-American peacenik Martin Sheen plays the combat-rattled junior officer whose military experiences have made it impossible for him to re-turn to a normal life. In one line, Sheen's character, Captain Ben-jamin L. Willard, says,

> Every time I think I'm gonna wake up back in the jungle. When I was home after my first tour, it was worse. I'd wake up and there'd be nothing. I hardly said a word to my wife, until I said "yes" to a divorce. When I was here, I wanted to be there; when I was there, all I could think of was getting back into the jungle. I'm here a week now . . . waiting for a mission . . . getting softer; every minute I stay in this room, I get weaker, and every minute Charlie squats in the bush, he gets stronger. Each time I looked around, the walls moved in a little tighter.

Marlon Brando plays Colonel Walter Kurtz, the Army officer who has gone AWOL to a tribal village in Cambodia. During Sheen's mission up the Mekong River in pursuit of the mad Kurtz, the military is shown napalming a beachfront village so that sol-diers can surf, scalping the enemies' dead, smoking dope, water-skiing behind a Swift boat, rioting at a USO show, and massacring innocent civilians on a sampan. In the end, Willard and Kurtz mutually agree that they're both victims of war. Willard kills Kurtz and in the process (according to the gospel of Coppola) as-sumes the colonel's insane interpretation of life.

Producer/director Oliver Stone carried on the antiwar, antimilitary, and anti-American tradition in the 1980s with his films *Platoon* and *Born on the Fourth of July.* Stone is one of the few members of the Hollywood elite who actually served in Vietnam, but his one-sided films depict not reality but the workings of his paranoid liberal mind.

Platoon, for instance, dishonestly relies on scripted liberal myths to portray American soldiers as both bloodthirsty killers and draftees from disadvantaged backgrounds forced to go to war by a morally corrupt government. Officers are characterized as incompetent and inexperienced, and on patrol the soldiers kill innocent civilians, raze villages, and gang-rape children. In one particularly grotesque scene, a U.S. soldier bludgeons a retarded boy with the butt of his rifle and proudly exclaims, "You see that f***ing head come apart?" The main character, played by Charlie Sheen (son of *Apocalypse Now*'s Martin Sheen), also learns that his fellow soldiers abuse drugs, but out of "necessity." (The "good" sergeant in the film is a pothead; the "bad" sergeant is a redneck alcoholic.)

Stone had the gall to dedicate his contemptuous film "to the men who fought and died in the Vietnam War." For the great majority of those who served honorably and their families who do not share Stone's extremist views, that is unforgivable.

In *Born on the Fourth of July,* Stone trumpets his anti-American agenda through the story of paralyzed Vietnam vet Ron Kovic. Tom Cruise stars as Kovic, a young man who enlisted in the Marines specifically to serve in Vietnam but returned from his tour injured, disillusioned, and feeling "betrayed" by his country. Kovic becomes an antiwar activist, joins the Vietnam Veterans Against the War (John Kerry and Jane Fonda's antimilitary organization), and gives a speech at the 1976 Democratic National Convention. Like *Platoon,* this film caricatures the American military as full of bloodthirsty, drug-addled psychotics.

Nowhere to be found in any of these films are the more

familiar stories of the millions of veterans who value their service and sacrifice, chose not to betray their brothers-in-arms, and returned from their service upstanding and contributing members of society.

VIETNAM REDUX

At least in the Vietnam era, Hollywood elites waited until the conflict was over to trot out their nihilistic products. *Coming Home, The Deer Hunter, Apocalypse Now, Platoon,* and *Born on the Fourth of July* were all released years after hostilities ended. In the cases of the latter two films, more than a decade had passed. But that's not the case in today's environment.

While American men and women battle Islamic extremists in Iraq, Afghanistan, the Philippines, and elsewhere, Tinseltown is rushing to push its antiwar and antimilitary agenda on screens worldwide in an unprecedented manner. Hollywood bigwigs make no apologies for this.

For example, Irwin Winkler, director of the 2006 anti–Iraq War movie *Home of the Brave,* said, "Just because [directors in the past] waited longer doesn't mean that I have to wait any longer."[32] Winkler's film, starring Samuel L. Jackson, rapper Curtis "50 Cent" Jackson, and Jessica Biel, follows the simplistic "shattered vets" formula established in such movies as *Coming Home, The Deer Hunter,* and *Born on the Fourth of July.* Like *The Deer Hunter,* the film focuses on three soldiers when they return from combat—and once again the veterans are disconnected and emotionally scarred. In conversations with reporters, Winkler did not hide his agenda. "If we had any political statement to make, it is that everyone is injured by war," he said. He even gloated that he had brushed off the concerns of the Pentagon. The military, Winkler said, was "not very favorably impressed with what we were saying." He chuckled, then added, "They hated it."[33]

Plenty of other Hollywood notables are joining in Winkler's crusade. As of early 2007 at least four other antiwar films were in the works. Academy Award winner Paul Haggis is directing *In the Valley of Elah,* the story of a father looking for his son who has gone missing on his way home from duty in Iraq. Reportedly AWOL, the soldier is discovered as having been murdered by drunken platoon mates in Georgia. Tom Cruise is producing *The Fall of the Warrior King,* the story of a disgraced Army commander, Lieutenant Colonel Nathan Sassaman, who resigns in shame when his soldiers are accused of drowning an Iraqi civilian. Ryan Phillippe is starring in *Stop Loss,* about a soldier who returns home from Iraq and then refuses to return to his unit when the Army recalls him for duty. Mark Gordon and Reason Pictures are producing *The Messenger,* which follows an Army officer who is assigned the very difficult and unpleasant responsibility of notifying families who have lost loved ones in combat. In an overworked scenario, the soldier confronts his moral dilemma when he becomes involved with a fellow soldier's widow.[34]

As with their Vietnam-era predecessors, these films are weapons designed to attack the country and the military during a vulnerable time. For Hollywood, the soldier is no more than a stage prop. That's why there aren't uplifting tales of heroism under fire or victory against overwhelming odds. A normal, healthy, patriotic serviceman isn't at all useful.

EMPTY VESSELS

Of course, Hollywood outrages many Americans not simply because the films themselves so skew reality. Even more maddening are the many Hollywood celebrities who use their fame to preach their ultraliberal, anti-American messages. Robin Bronk, executive director of the Hollywood liberal advocacy group the Creative Coalition, contends, "We live in a society here in the U.S. where

celebrities are put out there as opinion leaders. . . . They are ex-
pected to have their issue."[35] That is certainly true, as stars pontif-
icate on everything from animal rights to the environment to
corporate evils to guns to the War on Terror.

It's well established that Hollywood is a hotbed of liberalism,
but it is nonetheless shocking to examine the never-ending attacks celebrities launch against their country.

Actress Jessica Lange, receiving a Lifetime Achievement
Award at the San Sebastian Film Festival in Madrid, sneered,
"What can I say? I hate Bush; I despise him and his entire admin-
istration. . . . The atmosphere in my country is poisonous, intol-
erable for those of us who are not right-wing." She thanked the
Spanish for inviting her and allowing her to escape the United
States. "It makes me feel ashamed to come from the United
States—it is humiliating."[36]

Natalie Maines of the Dixie Chicks told a reporter for England's *The Telegraph,* "The entire country may disagree with me,
but I don't understand the necessity for patriotism," confessed
Maines. "Why do you have to be a patriot? About what? This land
is our land? Why? You can like where you live and like your life,
but as for loving the whole country . . . I don't see why people
care about patriotism."[37]

Actor Edward Norton told his foreign hosts, "It must be good
to be in Germany and France, because I have completely forgotten what it's like to be proud of your government."[38] I'm not sure
how proud the German and French people are now that their
governments' illicit ties with Saddam's Iraq have been revealed. In
any case, Ed, those people would be goose-stepping or saluting
the hammer and sickle if it weren't for *your* government.

The South African–born actress Charlize Theron, fresh from
shooting a movie about Cuban rappers titled *East of Havana,*
compared her adopted country of the United States to the repressive Communist regime of Fidel Castro. When asked about the

lack of individual freedoms in Cuba, Theron commented, "I would argue that there's a lack of freedom in America." A stunned correspondent gave the actress another opportunity. "Do you think the lack of freedoms in Cuba are parallel to the lack of freedoms in the United States?" asked CNN's Rick Sanchez. "Well, I would," answered the actress, "I would compare those two. Yes, definitely." "It sounds like you don't have a very high opinion of the United States," replied Sanchez (of Cuban descent).[39]

Some celebrities whose stars have faded seek out forums to voice anti-American sentiments. Finding a moment of semiconsciousness between bong hits, hemp activist and former *Cheers* bartender Woody Harrelson penned an op-ed for *The Guardian* in which he said, "I'm an American, tired of American lies. . . . This is a racist and imperialist war. The warmongers who stole the White House (you call them 'hawks' but I would never disparage such a fine bird) have hijacked a nation's grief and turned it into a perpetual war on any nonwhite country they choose to describe as terrorist."[40] Elsewhere he said, "The war against terrorism is terrorism. The whole thing is just bullshit."[41]

Perhaps no one in Tinseltown better represents assumed prerogative and dripping pretension than actor Sean Penn. Before U.S. military operations began in Iraq, Penn, who more closely resembles his *Fast Times at Ridgemont High* brain-dead surfer dude character than a scholarly statesman, went on a much publicized visit to Baghdad as if he'd been dispatched by the White House to conduct vital fact-finding. He said on CNN's *Larry King Live* that as an actor he had "an added responsibility" and that most Americans "don't have the time to attack their own ignorance on issues beyond popular media."[42] For the trip he allied with radical Medea Benjamin, who runs the extreme antiwar, antimilitary nongovernmental organizations Global Exchange, Code Pink, and International Occupation Watch.

In August 2005, Penn became Iran's "useful idiot" when he

visited Tehran to monitor its elections, attend Muslim prayer services, and meet with government officials. One month later, he
showed up in New Orleans in the wake of Hurricane Katrina to
rescue the city's victims—though of course he had his personal
photographer in tow. Unfortunately for Penn, his small boat's
motor wouldn't start and he forgot to put the drain plug in. When
last seen he was bailing out the boat with a plastic cup.

Hollywood celebrities are so uniformly committed to leftist
ideology that many don't even bother to hide it. Calypso singer
Harry Belafonte once claimed, "If you believe in freedom! If you
believe in justice, if you believe in democracy—you have no
choice but to support Fidel Castro!"[43] Actress Julia Roberts declared, "Republican comes in the dictionary just after reptile and
just above repugnant. . . . I looked up Democrat. It's of the people, by the people, for the people."[44]

A favorite rhetorical device is to denounce the "ignorance" of
the American people and our leaders. For example, Jane Fonda
has said, "I don't know if a country where the people are so ignorant of reality and of history, if you can call that a free world."[45]

"Has everyone lost their f***ing minds?" asked singer and actress Cher. "I don't like Bush. I don't trust him. He's stupid. He's
lazy."[46] George W. Bush has degrees from two of the world's foremost academic institutions (a bachelor's degree from Yale and an
MBA from Harvard); Cher dropped out of school in the ninth
grade.

"Bush is a f***ing idiot," said actress Jennifer Aniston, a high
school graduate.[47]

Martin Sheen called Bush "a moron, if you'll pardon the ex-
pression."[48] Sheen flunked his entrance exam for the University of
Dayton and didn't go to college.

Former I Dream of Jeannie and Dallas star Larry Hagman
called Bush "a sad figure—not too well educated, who doesn't get
out of America much. He's leading the country towards fascism."[49] Hagman dropped out of college after a year.

Left-wing celebrities love to prattle about the "ignorance" of the American people, but in the process all they end up doing is betraying their own ignorance.

"FAR REMOVED FROM THE TRUTH"

Emmy Award–winning screenwriter Robert Avrech, one of Hollywood's few out-of-the-closet conservatives, summed it up accurately when he said, "Let's be clear about one thing. Hollywood people are glamorous. But that's about it. They are ill-informed about jihad. They are ill-informed about Islam. They are ill-informed about Israel, the PA, Iraq, and Afghanistan. They are ill-informed about U.S. history, the Constitution, et cetera. The truth is, the movie people I've met are ignorant about most everything—save the weekend grosses of the top ten films."[50]

Ah, but saying that Hollywood liberals are ignorant is not the same as saying that they are inconsequential. Quite the contrary, in fact. In contemporary American society we confer a grossly disproportionate influence on our cultural elites. When Michael Moore, Sean Penn, or George Clooney starts blathering, microphones and cameras appear from everywhere, and their remarks are repeated in a slew of talk shows, lifestyle magazines, and celebrity news programs. Sadly, millions of Americans are listening to the Hollywood Left's hateful, ignorant remarks.

It's not just Americans who listen, either. While Tinseltown liberals repeatedly condemn the U.S. government for imperialism, it's in fact Hollywood that has conquered the world. Movies and the sale of DVDs in Western Europe and the Far East now provide the bulk of Hollywood's income; less than 30 percent of its take comes from sales in the United States.[51] Is it any wonder our Hollywood elite plays to the views of foreign audiences while they increasingly distance themselves from those in the United States?

Movies, television, and popular music don't just entertain;

they communicate messages and attitudes both formally and sub-liminally—and the message is *über*-liberal and decidedly anti-American. We don't need bin Laden, the PLO, the French, or the BBC to falsely indict America—we have American leftists like Clooney, Moore, and Harrelson doing it for them.

More than two thousand years ago Socrates warned that an artist "is a manufacturer of images and is very far removed from the truth."[52] The great Greek thinker warned not to confuse artis-tic talent with education or intelligence. Artists, he said, are mere "imitators," and we must not allow them to influence us in mat-ters of the world.

If only we had listened.

SIX

THE
DHIMMICRATS

Dhimmitude: . . . a behavior dictated by fear (terrorism), pacifism when aggressed, rather than resistance, servility because of
cowardice and vulnerability. The origin of this concept is to be
found in the condition of the Infidel people who submit to the
Islamic rule without fighting in order to avoid the onslaught of
jihad.

—Bat Ye'or, interview with
OldSpeak, June 9, 2005

In the nearly forty years since counterculture leftists snatched
power from Democratic Party moderates, Democrats have
elected two presidents. They are arguably the two worst commanders in chief this nation has known. Their national defense failures are undeniable.

Jimmy Carter betrayed a longtime American ally in the shah
of Iran and facilitated the ascension of the radical fundamentalist
Ayatollah Khomeini. "F*** the Shah," Carter was reported to
have said.[1] That colossal miscalculation created the first Islamic

state-sponsored terror base and led directly to the humiliating Iranian hostage crisis and to a tragically bungled rescue attempt.

Twelve years after Carter left office, Bill Clinton inherited a matured jihadist threat but failed to respond to multiple attacks on America and its citizens, from the first World Trade Center bombing in 1993 through the bombing of the USS *Cole* in 2000. Clinton's first CIA director, R. James Woolsey, aptly summed up Clinton's impotence when he described the former president's "PR-driven" approach to terrorism: "Do something to show you're concerned. Launch a few missiles in the dessert, bop them on the head, arrest a few people. But just keep kicking the ball down the field."[2]

And now we are embroiled in an international War on Terror, a vital struggle to protect our nation from the threat of Islamofascist terrorists intent on bringing down the United States and the Western world. Have Democrats picked up the mantle of John F. Kennedy, who proclaimed in his inspiring inaugural address, "Let every nation know, whether it wishes us well or ill, that we shall pay any price, bear any burden, meet any hardship, support any friend, oppose any foe, in order to assure the survival and the success of liberty"?

Of course not. The contemporary Democratic Party is cut from the cloth of sixties radicalism—in fact, most of today's party leaders were exactly that, New Left radicals.

Today's Democratic politicians flood the airwaves declaring that victory is impossible, calling for immediate withdrawal of troops from Iraq, trying to sabotage the commander in chief at every turn, and denouncing American soldiers as war criminals and cold-blooded murderers.

This is the party that now says, in effect, "Let every nation know that we will pay no price, shrug off all burdens, avoid any hardship, undermine our friends, and oppose no foe. We aren't interested in the survival and success of liberty (unless it's an election year and one of our guys is in office)." In doing so, they provide aid and comfort to America's enemies.

THE VIETNAMIZATION OF THE WAR ON TERROR

All along the Democrats' plan has been simple: Turn the War on Terror into Vietnam.

It was during the Vietnam War, of course, that the radical Left once and for all wrested control of the Democratic Party away from those who took seriously the threats to America's national security. The once proud and patriotic party of FDR, Harry Truman, JFK, and Scoop Jackson gave way to anti-American, anti-military, surrender-happy liberals.

Today, the Democratic Party remains mired in the failed ideology of the anti-Vietnam New Left. Democratic National Committee chairman Howard Dean, proving he understands neither Vietnam nor the War on Terror, succinctly covered all the salient New Left talking points in the span of a short interview with San Antonio's WOAI Radio. "The idea that we're going to win the war in Iraq is an idea which is just plain wrong," said Dean (who avoided Vietnam thanks to a doctor's note and a set of X-rays and then spent the winter skiing in Aspen). "I've seen this before in my life. This is the same situation we had in Vietnam. . . . What we see today is very much like what was going on in Watergate. . . . I think we need a strategic redeployment."[3]

Lets' see: *Vietnam*—check. *Watergate*—check. *War's lost*—check. *Surrender*—check. It's all there. The war changes, but the message stays the same.

Senator Ted Kennedy, who took the lead very early on in attacking the Iraq War, the president, and the troops, has repeatedly invoked the imagery of Vietnam. Speaking about the Iraq War and implying a Gulf of Tonkin–like scenario, he said, "This was made up in Texas, announced in January [2003] to the Republican leadership that war was going to take place and was going to be good politically. This whole thing was a fraud." Another time he said, "Week after week after week, we were told lie after lie after lie."[4] Later he claimed that our troops "are now in a seemingly intractable quagmire."[5] He told the Brookings Institution, "Iraq is George Bush's Vietnam."[6]

As the Senate debated a nonbinding resolution in opposition to the Iraq War, Democratic senator Charles Schumer of New York invoked Vietnam as the strategy for contemporary politicians to pursue. "There will be resolution after resolution, amendment after amendment," promised Schumer, "just like in the days of Vietnam." Sounding eerily similar to something that might have been said about President Richard Nixon in 1973, Schumer concluded, "The pressure will mount, the president will find he has no strategy, he will have to change his strategy and the vast majority of our troops will be taken out of harm's way and come home."[7]

There it is: *It's a quagmire, it's unwinnable, it's based on lies.* The Vietnam clichés all over again—all to undermine the war effort.

The Vietnamization of the War on Terror began almost at the beginning, soon after the September 11 attacks. A few months of political unanimity followed 9/11, but the Left quickly reverted to form. Democratic leaders made it clear that they had no problem tossing aside the decades-old tradition of bipartisan unity during wartime.

Senator Patty Murray stepped forward to defend Osama bin Laden as U.S. troops were fighting and dying in the attempt to capture him. "He's been out in these countries for decades building schools, building infrastructure, building day care facilities, building health care facilities and people are extremely grateful," she protested. "He's made their lives better. We have not done that."[8]

The Democrats' heated anti-U.S. campaign began in earnest in the fall of 2002, after the U.S. military had executed a brilliant campaign in Afghanistan. In September, former vice president Al Gore, showing his bitterness over his loss in the 2000 presidential election, denounced the Bush administration. In a speech at San Francisco's Commonwealth Club, Gore attacked the commander in chief and claimed that U.S. military actions in Iraq "had the potential to seriously damage our ability to win the war against terrorism and to weaken our ability to lead the world in this new century." He downplayed the U.S. military success in Afghanistan, calling the Taliban Afghanistan "a fifth-rate military power." Too bad he and Clinton didn't use their time in the White House to take on that "fifth-rate military power" while it was sheltering al Qaeda; they might have prevented 9/11.[9]

That same month, Democratic congressmen Jim McDermott, David Bonior, and Mike Thompson flew to the Iraqi capital, determined to interfere with U.S. plans to force Saddam Hussein to disarm and comply with UN resolutions. Appearing on ABC's *This Week* from Baghdad on September 29, 2002, McDermott argued that America should accept Saddam at his word but shouldn't take President Bush at his. "I think you have to take the Iraqis on their face value," McDermott said from the grounds of the mass murderer's Baghdad complex. But he would not back down from a previous statement he had made that "the president of the United States will lie to the American people in order to get us into this war." This time he declared that, yes, he thought "the president would mislead the American people."[10]

This Week panelist George Will was rightly shocked by what McDermott had to say. Will remarked on what he called "the most disgraceful performance abroad by an American official in my lifetime, something not exampled since Jane Fonda sat on the antiaircraft gun in Hanoi to be photographed."[11]

Hitler had Lord Haw-Haw (William Joyce) to broadcast Nazi

propaganda into Britain during World War II. North Vietnam had Jane Fonda posing for photographs and making propaganda radio broadcasts aimed at American troops. The Islamofascists have Democrats in the U.S. Congress.

Senate Democrats joined in the attacks. Those attacks became especially heated after the Iraq War began—despite the fact that many outspoken critics had themselves voted to authorize the use of military force in Iraq. (The Senate approved the Authorization for the Use of Military Force in Iraq by a vote of 77–23—with Democrats Harry Reid, Hillary Clinton, Joe Biden, Dianne Feinstein, John Kerry, and John Edwards all voting yea. The House passed it by a vote of 296–133.) Also noteworthy, only two of the authorization's twenty-three clauses detailing rationales for the war mentioned stockpiles of weapons of mass destruction in Iraq. The other clauses demanding military action in Iraq specified numerous violations of the cease-fire agreement, the violation of numerous UN resolutions, the brutal repression of the Iraqi people, and the threat that Saddam posed to the region. All these clauses were conveniently pushed aside by Democrats a few short months later.

At the time, Hillary Clinton testified that "In the four years since the inspectors left, intelligence reports show that Saddam Hussein has worked to rebuild his chemical and biological weapons stock, his missile delivery capability, and his nuclear program. He has also given aid, comfort, and sanctuary to terrorists, including al Qaeda members, though there is apparently no evidence of his involvement in the terrible events of September 11, 2001. It is clear, however, that if left unchecked, Saddam Hussein will continue to increase his capacity to wage biological and chemical warfare, and will keep trying to develop nuclear weapons. Should he succeed in that endeavor, he could alter the political and security landscape of the Middle East, which as we know all too well affects American security."[12]

Senator Jay Rockefeller, Democrat and vice chairman of the Senate Intelligence Committee, agreed. "There is unmistakable evidence that Saddam Hussein is working aggressively to develop nuclear weapons and will likely have nuclear weapons within the next five years," argued Rockefeller. "We also should remember we have always underestimated the progress Saddam has made in development of weapons of mass destruction."[13]

Similarly, John Kerry said, "I will be voting to give the President of the United States the authority to use force—if necessary—to disarm Saddam Hussein because I believe that a deadly arsenal of weapons of mass destruction in his hands is a real and grave threat to our security."[14]

Even Ted Kennedy declared, "We have known for many years that Saddam Hussein is seeking and developing weapons of mass destruction." Nancy Pelosi concurred, "Saddam Hussein certainly has chemical and biological weapons, there is no question about that."[15]

A little over a year later, during Thanksgiving 2003, Senators Hillary Clinton and Jack Reed flew to Afghanistan and Iraq aboard an aircraft the soldiers dubbed *Broomstick One*. The trip was conducted under the pretext of a "fact-finding trip" and morale boost for the troops, but the Democrats turned their mission into a bully pulpit to attack the commander in chief in front of his soldiers on the battlefield.

While overseas, Senator Clinton said, "The outcome of [the war] is not assured," that "there are many questions at home about the administration's policies," and that "the obstacles and problems are much greater than the administration usually admits to." While in Baghdad, she irresponsibly speculated on the motivations for a war she voted for and launched into a personal attack on President Bush, claiming he'd been "obsessed with Saddam Hussein for more than a decade."[16]

It was typically Clintonesque—shameless, selfish, and political.

Our troops thrive on positive messages, encouragement, motivation, and the knowledge that their sacrifices are recognized and
supported at home. Their morale comes from their pride in being
America's defenders of freedom. It's key to what keeps them going
when the going gets tough. That's why the primary obligation of
leadership is to strengthen morale. And you can't slide pap past
them.

But Senators Reed and Clinton offered nothing but doom
and gloom and partisan sniping to young men and women who
were thousands of miles from family on a day of national thanksgiving. Thanks were not what the brave troops got from the Senate Democrats. The terrorists were thrilled, however. The jihadist
Al Jazeera TV network broadcast Clinton's remarks immediately
in Arabic.

Senator John Kerry visited the troops in Iraq in December
2004. Spokesperson April Boyd explained, "He wants to personally thank our troops for their service, focus on the steps that
must be taken to achieve success in Iraq and hear from experts in
the region."[17] In reality, the failed presidential candidate went to
the battlefield only a month after losing the election to President
Bush and trashed the commander in chief for making "horren-
dous judgments" and "unbelievable blunders." In a series of demoralizing comments, Kerry told America's soldiers, "What is sad
about what's happening here now is that so much of it is a process
of catching up from the enormous miscalculations and wrong
judgments made in the beginning." Kerry said that because of the
Bush administration's mistakes, "the job has been made enor-
mously harder."[18]

How much harder was the soldiers' mission after jihadist websites broadcast that ringing endorsement of their progress and
their commander in chief?

Or how much did our enemies love it when Al Gore—who
came within a hair of being elected America's commander in

chief—condemned the U.S. government in a speech to a predominantly Saudi Arabian crowd in Osama bin Laden's hometown of Jeddah? In February 2006 at an event funded in part by bin Laden's family (the Bin Laden Group), the former vice president charged that the U.S. government had committed "terrible abuses" against Arabs after the 9/11 attacks, that Arabs had been "indiscriminately rounded up" and held in "unforgivable" conditions.[19] Jeddah is approximately forty-five miles from Mecca, the holiest site in Islam and the epicenter of the fundamentalist Wahhabi strain, which gave birth to the radical Islamofascism that America wars with today. Fifteen of the nineteen hijackers on 9/11 were Saudi Arabian. Gore's salacious remarks, broadcast all over the region, played right into the hands of al Qaeda.

One of the most stunning retreats into leftist defeatism came from Congressman John Murtha, a former Marine who served in Vietnam. Murtha also voted to authorize the Iraq War in 2002, but he made headlines in 2004 when he declared, "The direction [of the war] has got to be changed or it is unwinnable. . . . We cannot prevail in this war as it is going today."[20]

Those comments were just the beginning for Murtha. The congressman went much further in November 2005, when he called for an immediate withdrawal of U.S. troops from Iraq. "The U.S. cannot accomplish anything further in Iraq militarily," Murtha said. "It is time to bring them home."[21] Many Democrats rallied around Murtha's call for surrender. But when pressed, they didn't have the courage to cast a vote in support of their convictions: a House of Representatives resolution for immediate withdrawal was defeated by a vote of 403–3.[22]

Just a few weeks later, 11 million Iraqis went to the polls to elect a permanent government—a historic step on the Iraqis' path to democracy. But sure, the U.S. military hadn't accomplished anything in Iraq.

Once in the national spotlight, though, Murtha wouldn't cede his place. Two weeks after calling for withdrawal, he said, "The Army is broken, worn-out, and living hand to mouth."[23] An Air Force buddy of mine in Iraq caught this last bit of news as he left the weekly steak-and-lobster dinner at the dining hall en route to his room with wireless Internet, air conditioning, and television.

The concept of cutting and running is not a new one for Murtha. After the United States suffered the loss of soldiers in a land-mine detonation in Mogadishu, Somalia, in 1993, he urged then-president Clinton to pull our troops out. Clinton accepted Murtha's advice and initiated the withdrawal that bin Laden would later cite as evidence of America's lack of resolve and war-fighting ability. "Our welcome has been worn out," said Murtha at the time. The president has been "listening to our suggestions. And I think you'll see him move those troops out very quickly," he told NBC's *Today* show in September of 1993.[24]

No, the politician that Democrats have appointed as their chairman for the House Armed Services Committee and the one they most often point to as their expert on military affairs is anything but. On NBC's *Meet the Press* on June 11, 2006, Murtha bragged about his encouraging Clinton to cut and run in Somalia and laid out his plan for Iraq to Tim Russert and the nation. Advocating for a "redeployment" of American soldiers currently stationed in Iraq (in other words, "retreat"), Murtha suggested moving our 140,000 troops to Okinawa. "We can go to Okinawa," said Murtha. "We can deploy there almost instantly," he said. "When I say Okinawa . . . I'm saying troops in Okinawa. When I say a timely response, you know, our fighters (aircraft) can fly from Okinawa very quickly."[25]

The facts, however, point to just how clueless the congressman is when it comes to military affairs. Okinawa is more than 4,000 nautical miles from Baghdad, and any U.S. aircraft that would be based on the Japanese island would have to overfly China and Iran on their way to Baghdad, not a likely scenario. A redeployment of 140,000 troops would take several months to plan and execute. For a single U.S. Air Force fighter aircraft to make the journey, the pilot would have to refuel in flight more than ten times to make the round-trip. But that's not important when you're trying to lose a war.

On another occasion, in April of 2006, Murtha conducted a town hall meeting along with Congressman Jim Moran, a Democrat from Virginia, with the participation and support of the radical antiwar organizations Code Pink and moveon.org. One of the audience members was former Army Sergeant Mark Seavey, recently returned from duty in Afghanistan. During the question and answer portion of the event, Seavey stood and said, "I know you keep saying how you have talked to the troops and the troops are demoralized, and I really resent that characterization. The morale of the troops I talk to is phenomenal, which is why my troops are volunteering to go back despite the hardships. . . ." Murtha said nothing and Moran brushed off the soldier's comment stating, "That wasn't in the form of a question, it was a statement," and moved on.

On May 17, 2006, former Marine Murtha went well beyond the pale when he told reporters that Marines had killed innocent civilians "in cold blood" in the town of Haditha, Iraq, and suggested that ranking officers had covered up the murders. In spite of the fact that the Pentagon was conducting an investigation of the accusation and charges had not yet been conferred on the Marines, Murtha convicted them in the courtroom of mass media.

Speaking at a press conference, where one would assume the congressman had prepared his remarks, Murtha claimed, "Our troops overreacted because of the pressure on them. And they killed innocent civilians in cold blood."[26] A week later, speaking with ABC's George Stephanopoulos on *This Week,* Murtha added, "I will not excuse murder and this is what has happened. . . . There

has to have been a cover-up of this thing. No question about it."[27]
Innocent until proven guilty, unless you're in the military.

Murtha's comments and grandstanding have outraged many
in the military. In a letter to the congressman, Army Lieutenant
colonel Christopher Stark voiced the displeasure of many in the
armed forces when he wrote:

> It is indeed fitting that you are a member of the same politi-
> cal party as another traitor and seditionist, former Lieu-
> tenant John Kerry USN. . . . We are at war, Representative
> Murtha, and your actions and conduct give aid and comfort
> to our enemies. . . . You have dishonored all of those who
> have fought and died up to the day you stood on the floor of
> the House of Representatives and demanded that we with-
> draw immediately. Yes, Representative Murtha, you have
> given aid and comfort to our enemies in a time of war. You
> have given them hope, which they have fast been losing, due
> to all of the victories and sacrifice by our sons and daughters
> on the field of battle in Iraq and Afghanistan. You have been
> honored by our enemies on the front page of Al Jazeera. . . .
> Be advised, my son is a Marine Officer. He has commanded
> men in battle through two (2) tours and he is due to return
> to Iraq on a third tour. If he should be harmed in any way as
> a result of your actions on the floor of the House this week, I
> will do everything in my power to see to it that you are dri-
> ven from office and that you are charged and tried for trea-
> son and sedition.[28]

PROGRESS? WHAT PROGRESS?

If you're continually asserting that everything is going wrong in
Iraq, what do you do when real progress is made in the war?

Usually Democrat politicians simply deny that any real gains

are being made. Take the case of Senator Joseph Biden, who offered a clinic in how to ignore the facts to advance your storyline.
Biden, then looking ahead to a presidential run in 2008, delivered
a speech to the Brookings Institution in June 2005 that catered to
the antiwar Left. Recently returned from Iraq, he offered a dire assessment of the situation there. The reconstruction project in Iraq
had thus far been "a disaster," he claimed. "The disconnect between the administration's rhetoric and the reality on the ground
has opened not just a credibility gap, but a credibility chasm."[29]

Well, I visited Iraq in July 2005, just a matter of days after
Biden's trip. This is what I confirmed without the luxury of a
team of congressional staffers:

- Iraq's gross domestic product in 2004 was up 14 percent
  over prewar levels.

- Per capita income doubled between 2003 and 2005 and was
  30 percent higher than it had been before the war.

- Iraq's unemployment had dropped to 28 percent from
  prewar levels of 33 percent; Biden's claim of 40 percent was
  greatly exaggerated.

- U.S. efforts added 1,400 megawatts of electrical power
  across Iraq, expanding the grid to reach 4.2 million citizens.

- Oil production had nearly reached prewar levels of
  2 million barrels a day, despite sabotage to the delivery
  systems.

- An independent media of 170 newspapers, 72 radio
  stations, and 29 television stations had risen after the
  collapse of Saddam's regime.

- Between 2003 and 2005, renovations were completed on
  3,211 schools, 20 hospitals were renovated, and

construction was finished on 76 water treatment plants, 30 sewer plants, and 33 fire stations.[30]

Not letting the facts deter him, Biden went on NBC's *Meet the Press* in August and asserted that the Iraq Army had only 3,000 troops capable of fighting without U.S. support. Retired U.S. Army Generals Barry McCaffrey and Wayne Downing revealed that Biden was woefully misguided. They confirmed that at least thirty-six battalions, or about 22,000 Iraqi troops, were self-sufficient and capable of operating without oversight.[31] During my trip to Iraq I interviewed Iraqi General Abdul Qadr Jassim, who informed me that in fact U.S. forces had successfully trained *155,000* Iraq Army members.[32]

Shortly after the revolutionary and highly successful elections in Iraq in January 2005, Senator John Kerry warned that "No one in the United States should try to overhype this election. . . . The real test is not the election. . . ."[33]

But who cares about the truth when you're trying to lose a war?

Of course, sometimes Democratic politicians simply can't ignore good news coming out of Iraq. But even then they resist acknowledging it as a victory for their nation; instead they scramble to explain it away.

We got a clear example of this phenomenon in June 2006, when U.S. forces killed al Qaeda terrorist Abu Musab al-Zarqawi. Taking out Zarqawi—the leader of the insurgency, and the most wanted man in Iraq—was a major victory for the United States in Iraq.

Some Democrats were quick to deny the significance of the hit, however. Congressman Dennis Kucinich claimed that Zarqawi was just a small part of "a growing anti-American insurgency" and then reasserted his opposition to the war. "We're there for all the wrong reasons," said the former presidential candidate (who has called for a federal Department of Peace). Congressman Pete Stark of California said the killing was "just to cover Bush's [rear]." He added, "Iraq is still a mess—get out."[34] Representative Jim McDermott (Baghdad Jim) said, "This insurgency is such a confused mess that one person, dead or alive at this point, is hardly significant today."[35]

Many other Democrats acknowledged that taking out Zarqawi was an important step, but they made sure to stress that it didn't change anything. Like Pete Stark, many of them seized the opportunity to call for withdrawal. John Murtha said, "We should be able to substantially reduce our presence in Iraq and redeploy our military outside of Iraq." Similarly, Senator John Kerry said the Zarqawi killing was "another sign that it's time for Iraqis to stand up for Iraq . . . and run their own country."[36]

Nancy Pelosi, then the House minority leader and now the speaker of the House, offered the obligatory commendation of the troops and then claimed that they should come home. Why? Because military personnel records had been hacked into at the Veterans Administration. "As many as 2.2 million military personnel were among the 26.5 million records mishandled and lost by the Department of Veterans Affairs," she said, which is "simply the latest example of incompetence in the Bush administration."[37]

There's almost no good news that the Dems can't spin against the war effort.

TORTURED POLITICS

The Vietnamization of the War on Terror wouldn't be complete if the Left didn't portray our fighting forces as torturers, baby killers, and murderers.

John Kerry made such claims a familiar part of the Left's rhetorical arsenal back in April 1971, when, as a Navy lieutenant, he testified before the Senate Foreign Relations Committee. In a speech that would define him and his generation of Democrats, Kerry demonized his fellow soldiers. He testified that American troops in Vietnam "had personally raped, cut off ears, cut off heads, taped wires from portable telephones to human genitals and turned up the power, cut off limbs, blown up bodies, randomly shot at civilians, razed villages in fashion reminiscent of Genghis Khan, shot cattle and dogs for fun, poisoned food stocks, and generally ravaged the countryside of South Vietnam."[38] Kerry hadn't actually witnessed the events to which he testified, mind you. It was hearsay gathered at the Winter Soldier conference in Detroit a few months earlier. Much of the information came from impostors pretending to be war veterans. Still, it was Kerry's national coming-out party—and it would provide antiwar leftists with tropes that they would repeat for decades thereafter.

In December 2005, Kerry dusted off his 1971 testimony and adapted it for the Iraq War. Sounding creepily as he did thirty-four years earlier, Kerry told CBS *Face the Nation* host Bob Schieffer, "There is no reason, Bob, why American soldiers need to be going in the homes of Iraqis in the middle of the night, terrorizing kids and children, you know, women, breaking sort of the customs of—of the historical customs—religious customs—whether you like it or not."[39]

Forget about the insurgents in Iraq setting off bombs and killing innocent civilians. In Kerry's view American soldiers are the real terrorists.

Kerry's comments only added to the Left's treacherous assault on America and her troops, one of the most egregious and damaging aspects of which has been the hysterical exaggerations and distortions of "torture." Seeking to strip away the legitimate moral authority of victories in Iraq and Afghanistan, the Left has portrayed the Abu Ghraib prison and the detention facilities at Guantánamo Bay as medieval torture chambers.

When left-wing writer Seymour Hersh "broke" the Abu Ghraib story, the U.S. Army's criminal investigation of the reprobates was already three months old. In fact, Hersh's story wasn't even a scoop. The U.S. military had announced the probe into the abuses in January 2004, and CNN had reported the incident that month as it related to the Army's investigation.[40] But Hersh's celebrity power carried the story to new heights. The *New York Times* then ran Abu Ghraib on its front page for thirty-two days in a row.[41]

It was just like Vietnam. Abu Ghraib became this war's My Lai massacre. Not surprising when one recalls that Hersh was also the reporter who documented My Lai.

Democratic politicians seized on the chance to attack America. Al Gore screamed, "How dare the incompetent and willful members of this Bush/Cheney administration humiliate our nation and our people in the eyes of the world and in the conscience of our own people? How dare they subject us to such dishonor and disgrace? How dare they drag the good name of the United States of America through the mud of Saddam Hussein's torture prison?"[42]

Senator Ted Kennedy haughtily remarked, "On March 19, 2004, President Bush asked, 'Who would prefer that Saddam's torture chambers still be open?' Shamefully, we now learn that Saddam's torture chambers reopened under new management— U.S. management."[43]

The behavior of the National Guardsmen at Abu Ghraib was indeed disgraceful, even reprehensible. It was a tremendous failure of leadership on the part of then–Brigadier General Janis Karpinski (now demoted to colonel). In the end, though, humiliation, intimidation, uncomfortable environments, and aggressive interrogation hardly rise to the level of torture. How callously thoughtless for one of the most senior members of the U.S. Senate to morally equate the humiliation and bullying of ten or twelve terrorists committed by a few miscreants with Saddam's systemic murder, torture, and rape of more than 300,000 innocent men, women, and children. And to say this at a time when American soldiers were in the field of combat was absolutely appalling.

Panties on the head of a terrorist or no head at all on an American hostage, Senator?

After Democratic congressman Pete Stark of California voted to condemn U.S. abuse of Iraqi prisoners, Army National Guardsman Sergeant Daniel Dow urged the congressman to stop the politicization of the war and support the troops. Stark showed his support for the troops by leaving a scathing, insulting, antimilitary screed on the sergeant's voice mail:

> Dan, this is Congressman Pete Stark, and I just got your fax. And you don't know what you're talking about. So if you care about enlisted people, you wouldn't have voted for that thing either. But probably someone put you up to this, and I'm not sure who it was, but I doubt if you could spell half the words in your letter, and somebody wrote it for you. So I don't pay much attention to it. But I'll call you back later, and let you tell me more about why you think you're such a great Goddamned hero. And why you think that this general, and the Defense Department who forced these poor enlisted guys to do what they did, shouldn't be held to account. That's the issue. So if you want to stick it to a bunch of enlisted guys, have your way. But if you want to get to the bottom of the people who *forced* this *awful* program in Iraq, then you should understand more about it than you obviously do. Thanks.

Sergeant Dow, who *is* an enlisted guy (ergo the rank of "sergeant"), followed up Stark's unhinged antimilitary attack by giving a tape of the voice mail to my good friends at KSFO-560 in San Francisco, who aired the message for several days.*

---

*Oh, and next time you hear a Democrat utter the liberal mantra that they "support our troops," remember also that Democrats have tried their hardest to block the soldiers'

Democrat politicians did even more to advance the hopes of America's enemies when they denounced the Guantánamo Bay detention camp. On the basis of an e-mail (an uncorroborated e-mail) alleging loud music, extreme temperatures, and the rough handling of a Koran, Democratic senator Dick Durbin of Illinois—the second-ranking member of the Senate's Democrat leadership—took to the Senate floor and compared U.S. servicemen to Nazis, the keepers of the Soviet gulags, and the Khmer Rouge. Sounding hauntingly similar to John Kerry in 1971, Durbin charged,

> On one occasion, the air conditioning had been turned down so far and the temperature was so cold in the room, that the barefooted detainee was shaking with cold. . . . On another occasion, the air conditioner had been turned off, making the temperature in the unventilated room well over 100 degrees. The detainee was almost unconscious on the floor. . . . On another occasion, not only was the temperature unbearably hot, but extremely loud rap music was being played in the room and had been since the day before, with the detainee chained hand and foot in the fetal position on the tile floor.
>
> If I read this to you and did not tell you that it was . . . describing what Americans have done to prisoners in their control, you would most certainly believe this must have been done by the Nazis, Soviets in their gulags, or some mad

---

fundamental right to vote. In the 2000 postelection controversy, while Democratic presidential candidate Al Gore, Jesse Jackson, and company were blubbering about "disenfranchised voters" in Palm Beach, Florida, the Democrats and their hordes of lawyers were systematically negating the votes of men and women serving their country abroad. The Democrats went to great lengths to prevent military absentee ballots from being counted, challenging the authenticity of signatures, noting the lack of postmarks (even though not all military mail is processed through U.S. postal services), and contesting incomplete or, in some cases, handwritten entries.

regime—Pol Pot or others—that had no concern for human beings. Sadly, this is not the case. This was the action of Americans in the treatment of their prisoners.[44]

The willful attempt to relate the U.S. military to the killers of tens of millions of innocents is deeply insulting not only to our men and women in uniform but also to the millions of family members of those who were killed. What kind of moral calculus does it take to connect mass starvations, gas chambers, mounds of skulls, and shots to the heads in Siberia with hot and cold temperatures and loud music?

"Temperatures over 100 degrees"? Do you know how hot it gets in Iraq, Senator? In the summer 120 degrees is balmy . . . and that's before you strap on your Kevlar and torso vests on top of your long-sleeved battle dress uniforms (BDUs), wool socks, and leather boots and head out on patrol.

"Cold temperatures"? It was air conditioning in Cuba!

"Loud infidel music while chained to a cell"? Sounds like just another Friday night at the Clintons'.

Within minutes Durbin's comments were broadcast across the Arab world and posted on the Internet. An American soldier voiced his outrage. "What the hell is that all about?" he asked. "Doesn't he understand how this crap hurts us? Doesn't that S.O.B. have a clue about morale? God, Osama couldn't pay enough to get that kind of free propaganda. Zarqawi is cackling with glee! We have to stop this diarrhea of the mouth—someone is going to get killed! And it might be me or one of my buddies!"[45]

I spoke to a number of soldiers in Iraq about Durbin's comments. Over and over I heard similar expressions of shock and outrage. Air Force Major Eric Egland told me, "Senator Durbin's remarks about Gitmo were an insult. The false reporting by the media and irresponsible remarks by Durbin and crew had a tremendous negative effect on us. It inflamed the Iraqis at a time when we were really making strides in their confidence and willingness to help. We were relying on their help in rooting out the bad guys . . . [and] comments like these made our job much more difficult. . . . He set us back immeasurably."[46]

An Army specialist in Baghdad put it more bluntly. When I asked the specialist about Durbin's comments, he said of the senator, "I don't know who he is—but I hate him."[47]

Similar reactions came from U.S. forces assigned to Guantánamo. A female Army private working at Gitmo remarked, "It hurts my feelings to hear that junk. We try to do as good a job as possible down here. The detainees are dangerous. They try to kill us every time we get close to them and would certainly kill Americans if released."[48] Another said, "We hear all that, of course. But we try not to let it get us down."[49]

Sadly, but not surprisingly, Democratic leaders did not rush to condemn Durbin's treasonous behavior. In fact, some echoed his claims.

House Democratic leader Nancy Pelosi declared, "The treatment of detainees is a taint on our country's reputation, especially in the Muslim world, and there are many questions that must be answered."[50]

Former president Jimmy Carter committed the spineless act of criticizing his country overseas, telling an international conference of the Baptist World Alliance in Birmingham, England, "I think what's going on in Guantánamo Bay and other places is a disgrace to the U.S.A. . . . I'm embarrassed about it, and I think it's wrong."[51] Al Jazeera wasted no time in airing his subversive comments.

Former president Bill Clinton called for shutting down the detention facility at Gitmo. "It's time that there are no more stories coming out of there about people being abused. . . . If we get a reputation for abusing people, it puts our own soldiers much more at risk."[52]

Senator Hillary Clinton, in a fundraising letter to supporters, wrote, "Who knew Vice President Cheney would start lobbying for the right to torture?"[53]

THE LEFT'S TORTURE MYTH

So Democrats run around screaming about "torture" committed by Americans at Guantánamo. But this is just another leftist myth, as a look at the facts reveals.

One of the antiwar Democrats' favorite talking points about Guantánamo was that the United States had been guilty of "torture" because the government had concluded that captured al Qaeda fighters were not covered by the Geneva Conventions. (The Left even began referring to the Justice Department memorandum on this matter as the "torture memo.")

Jimmy Carter led the charge in his 2005 book *Our Endangered Values,* saying that the Bush administration had "decided to violate" the Geneva Conventions in the War on Terror because it consider the enemy to be "subhuman."[54]

But the fact is that it's not the United States who violated the Geneva Conventions; *it's the terrorists.* The Geneva Conventions embody the idea that even in as brutal an activity as war, civilized nations could obey humanitarian rules: no attacking civilians and no retaliation against enemy soldiers once they fall into your hands. Destruction is to be limited as much as possible to professional soldiers on the battlefield. That rule requires, unconditionally, that soldiers distinguish themselves from civilians by wearing uniforms and carrying arms openly. Any soldier captured on a battlefield *wearing a uniform* is a *prisoner of war* and is entitled to all the rights of the Geneva Conventions.

A jihadist captured in Afghanistan, Iraq, or Pakistan, in contrast, is an *unlawful combatant* and is entitled to no protections under the Geneva Conventions. Why? Because he cheated.

He violated the principle of sanctuary. Not only did he hide behind civilians, he targeted them. He eliminated any distinction between himself as a legitimate target and the innocent people around him—between the battlefield and the world of civilians.

Keep in mind, the 380 people detained at Guantánamo aren't innocent foot soldiers or innocent victims. They represent some of the most high-value detainees out of the more than 70,000 al Qaeda and Taliban jihadists captured on battlefields and vetted since 9/11. Most of these terrorists are well educated, with advanced degrees in law, engineering, and medicine. Some are experts in demolition and some have been trained in former Soviet camps. They are murdering terrorists who, if allowed to fight another day, will come after Americans once again. They regularly attack the Gitmo guards by throwing "cocktails" of feces, urine, and semen and by shouting death threats, such as "One day I will enjoy sucking American blood."[55] They use their blankets as garrotes and attempt to construct weapons out of anything they can get their hands on.

In short, the Guantánamo detainees are the baddest of the bad. Among those held at Gitmo are the so-called twentieth 9/11 hijacker, Mohamed al-Kahtani, and Osama bin Laden's personal aide and driver, Salim Ahmed Hamdan.

All that aside, there is this elemental fact: What has gone on at Guantánamo simply does not constitute torture, no matter what Hillary and Co. insist. The truth is that Gitmo is the most culturally sensitive detention center in the history of warfare—to a fault, in my opinion. Terrorists who would otherwise be killing or plotting to kill are guaranteed prayer rugs, skullcaps, and Korans, five broadcasts of Muslim prayer each day, painted arrows pointing to Mecca in each cell, access to a jihadist library, and superb medical care. Each detainee receives three hot halal meals a day in accordance with Muslim regulations on food. The U.S. government spends more than $2.5 million a year to feed the detainees at Gitmo, which averages to $12.68 a day per prisoner. Meanwhile, the Pentagon spends $8.85 per day to feed each of the soldiers deployed to Iraq; convicts in U.S. federal penitentiaries average $2.78 per day.[56]

The Defense Department very carefully scrutinized interrogation practices in Gitmo and reviewed specific techniques that Army officials requested permission to employ on these unlawful combatants. As Heather Mac Donald pointed out in *City Journal,* "To read the techniques requested is to understand how restrained the military has been in its approach to terror detainees—and how utterly false the torture narrative has been." Mac Donald documented some of the practices the interrogators at Guantánamo felt they could *not* use unless they had express clearance from the secretary of defense. Those included:

- yelling at detainees—and even when they had permission, they could never yell in someone's ear

- deceiving detainees, such as by telling them that the interrogator was a Saudi agent

- serving the detainees cold meals (except in the most extreme circumstances)[57]

After some six months of careful Pentagon deliberation, in April 2003 Secretary of Defense Donald Rumsfeld approved a list of twenty-four techniques that could be used on terrorists at Guantánamo. These are the techniques that the media present as the source of "torture," both at Guantánamo and at Abu Ghraib. How terrible were they? Well, here are some of the "torturous" practices the memo approved:

- poking detainees in the chest in a "mild, noninjurious" fashion, or engaging in "light pushing"—activities that could be conducted only after review by the commander of the U.S. Southern Central Command in Miami

- stroking the ego of detainees

- insulting detainees, but "not beyond the limits that would apply to a POW"

- repeating the same question

- playing good cop/bad cop—or "Mutt and Jeff," as the Defense Department labeled the technique

- isolating detainees from other prisoners "while complying with basic standards of treatment"[58]

In reality, nothing occurs to the world's most extreme and dangerous terrorists that most U.S. military warriors haven't endured in training. In my first few years as an Air Force pilot, I was required to attend Survival, Evasion, Resistance, and Escape training (SERE), which prepares Air Force pilots and crew members who might someday be shot down and captured by America's enemies. We learned how to survive off the land, to evade to a rescue site, and ultimately how to resist and survive in a prisoner-of-war situation. Individually we were subjected to the anticipated practices and techniques of America's enemies. It was a miserable experience but invaluable training.

The specific techniques the U.S. military uses in training its own people are classified, but without violating that I can tell you that the techniques share strong similarities with those used by the military at Guantánamo Bay and the CIA. Grabbing the prisoner for attention, slapping him to create fear, forcing him to stand for long periods of time and in cold cells, making him disrobe, splashing him with cold water, blaring loud music or distorted noise, and "water boarding" are all common methods of "coercive interrogation." Water boarding is the most extreme of these; the prisoner is placed on an inclined board, his feet above his head, his face is wrapped, and water is poured over him, which induces a drowning sensation. Heather Mac Donald reported that the CIA used this technique on Khalid Sheikh Mohammed, the mastermind of the September 11 attacks.

In their rush to condemn the United States, liberals miss a critical point about such interrogation techniques: Sometimes they represent the only way to get vital information out of the terrorists. In the case of Kahtani, the twentieth hijacker, he began talking only after an intense eighteen-hour interrogation (all of which, by the way, was carefully monitored by "a medic, a psychiatrist, and lawyers, to make sure that no harm was done," as Mac Donald reported).[59] He ended up providing key details about bin Laden and other terrorist leaders.

As the Kahtani case illustrates, top-level terrorists detained at Gitmo have information that might stop the next attack. We want that information; indeed, we *need* that information. The Left's moral relativism prevents them from appreciating this crucial need in the War on Terror.

To be sure, that need does not justify any and all techniques to induce testimony. But it should be clear to anyone who bothers to investigate the record that in fact our military and the Defense Department have taken great pains to determine precisely which techniques are warranted. And the truth is that most of what the Left calls "torture" actually amounts to anything from cheap high school pranks to standard coercive interrogation.

That's a truth you won't learn from the hysterical Left. It sounds much better to them to equate the U.S. military with Nazis and the Khmer Rouge.

THERE'S AN ELEPHANT IN THE ROOM

At a fundraising event in April 2003, Senator Hillary Clinton shrieked, "I'm sick and tired of people who say that if you debate and disagree with this administration somehow you're not patriotic. We are Americans. We have the right to participate and debate any administration."[60]

There is no doubt that Americans can criticize their country and be patriotic. Debate is necessary and dissent is good. Freedom of speech and protest are all foundations of the American political process and protected by the U.S. Constitution's First Amendment. And there should be no more lively or rigorous debate than the one that precedes the nation's decision to send its military to war. But the Left consistently and conveniently overlooks two critical points regarding speech and dissension. First, not all speech is protected by the First Amendment. Subsequent constitutional amendments place limits on certain acts of dissent and protest should they harm the country. That's called treason. Second, the right to free speech in America brings along with it an obligation of responsibility.

Dissent is good, betrayal is bad. Liberals who speak out against the War on Terror because they oppose America and seek their country's defeat have crossed the line from dissent to betrayal, because their anti-American comments are broadcast around the world, encouraging and motivating the enemy. There is no patriotism in encouraging America's defeat and there is no honor in demoralizing the American soldier.

Sadly, many liberal politicians have crossed the line. Comparing the U.S. military to Communist regimes that murdered millions is rhetoric beyond the pale. It is reckless and irresponsible. It goes beyond partisan criticism of a president and extends to horribly slandering the soldiers sent to defend our nation.

Ask yourself: Is it responsible dissent to compare the Iraq War to the Holocaust? That's exactly what Democratic congressman Charles Rangel did in 2005, when he said the Iraq War was "just as bad as the 6 million Jews being killed."[61]

John Kerry, sitting just feet from former Iranian president Mohammad Khatami in Davos, Switzerland, said, "I've never seen our country as isolated, as much as a sort of international pariah for a number of reasons as it is today."[62]

These elected representatives should know better. They should know that their rhetoric is a weapon for the enemy. They should know that Al Jazeera will pick up their words and immediately broadcast them to all corners of the Arab world.

But the Democrats rant anyway. They are aiding and abetting the enemy. They are prolonging the conflict and causing the needless sacrifice of American servicemen and women. They have American blood on their hands.

Memo to the Democrats: If you find yourself frequently quoted by Al Jazeera or featured on jihadist websites, you can assume you've crossed the line from dissent to betrayal.

President Abraham Lincoln found a solution under similar circumstances during the Civil War. Congressman Clement L. Vallandigham of Ohio opposed the war and the emancipation of slaves. "The men in power are attempting to establish a despotism in this country, more cruel and oppressive than ever existed before," he yelled. "I can see nothing before us but universal political and social revolution, anarchy, and bloodshed."[63]

Lincoln suspended habeas corpus and had Vallandigham arrested for sympathy to the enemy and deported. "Must I shoot a simple-minded soldier-boy who deserts, while I must not touch a hair of a wily agitator who induces him to desert?" Lincoln concluded. "I think that in such a case to silence the agitator and save the boy is not only constitutional, but withal a great mercy."[64]

Oh, were we to have that conviction today.

SEVEN

THE WAHHABI LOBBY

On February 15, 2003, the largest antiwar demonstration in the history of the world occurred. Twenty-five million people took to the streets in more than three hundred cities around the globe, from America's largest cities to London, Berlin, Madrid, Amsterdam, Rome, Dhaka, Jakarta, Amman, Bombay, Islamabad, Hong Kong, and Bangkok.[1] This demonstration, the most well-orchestrated and choreographed exhibition of anti-Americanism ever, was all to protest a military action (in Iraq) that hadn't even begun.

While this event was the biggest, it was by no means the only notable "peace rally" held during the War on Terror. On September 29, 2001, less than a month after the 9/11 attacks, protests were held in Washington, D.C., and San Francisco to condemn the U.S. invasion of Afghanistan. On April 20, 2002, more than 100,000 demonstrators marched in Washington in support of Palestine. On January 18, 2003, more than 500,000 people marched on Washington, and another 200,000 took to the streets in San Francisco in an *earlier* protest against the possible invasion of Iraq.

These protests didn't arise from the ether. Such demonstrations require complex logistics, media interface, meticulous planning, and substantial funding. They weren't put together by average citizens, despite what one might think based on the mainstream media's focus on suburban moms and dads and other ordinary Americans at the protests.

No, left-wing radicals don't just "come together for peace." Anti-American activities such as these are funded and directed by a carefully organized network of leftist organizations. The groups that constitute this radical movement—the nongovernmental organizations, their donors, and their left-wing protectors in the legal community—form another integral element of America's Fifth Column.

In the many antiwar protests that have been held since 9/11, we've seen the same people and the same props we saw during the Left's Vietnam salad days—the tie-dyed shirts and bandannas, the signs protesting the "Pentagon war machine" and "American imperialism." Except these days the signs are mass-produced, thanks to the well-coordinated and well-financed network of radical antiwar organizations, and the message has evolved from "Make Love, Not War" to "We Support Our Troops When They Shoot Their Officers," "No Blood for Oil," "Bush Lied, Thousands Died," "9-11 = Inside Job / U.S. Fascists Guilty!" and "No War but the Class War!"

The parallels to the anti-Vietnam movement run deeper. Like the "peace" movement of the 1960s, today's radical opposition is about opportunity. In years past, antiwar movements were founded on love of country, religious precepts, and caution regarding the use of military power. But during Vietnam, the Left found that cloaking themselves in their supposed concern for human rights provided a convenient opportunity to attack the United States and secure political leverage.

Today something similar is going on. The antiwar movement has little to do with opposing U.S. involvement in the Middle East and everything to do with the Left's continuing war on America. If antiwar radicals had authentic empathy for the Iraqi people, they would caution against removing U.S. troops from the region, since bloody civil war would inevitably follow. After all, they've been down this road before. Remember, with the Left's insistence on U.S. withdrawal from Southeast Asia in the early 1970s, 2.5 million were slaughtered by Communist regimes in Vietnam and Cambodia. Recall, too, the destruction caused by the Communist and socialist regimes leftist radicals defended during the Cold War; according to *The Black Book of Communism,* 25 million people were murdered in Stalin's Soviet Union and 65 million in Mao Tse-tung's China.[2]

Just as those millions of lives were inconsequential to the Left, so too are the lives of Iraqis meaningless today. The emptiness of the "peace" movement's stated concern for human rights shouldn't surprise us. Today's leftist radicals are led by unreconstructed Stalinists and Maoists who, in the words of former fellow traveler David Horowitz, "supported America's totalitarian enemies during the Cold War." Previously, he wrote, these "neo-Communists" supported "the Vietcong, the Sandinista Marxists, and the Communist guerillas in El Salvador. Before that they marched in behalf of Stalin and Mao." Now, he commented, "They still support ('critically' of course) Castro and the nuclear lunatic in North Korea, Kim Jong-Il."[3]

The reality is that supposed "peace" organizations are among the most radical and destructive elements in our society. Yet, in another frightening commentary on the contemporary Left, these radical groups have immense influence—influence that extends far beyond the many antiwar protests they have organized. Indeed, supposedly reputable Democratic politicians and other prominent liberals routinely line up with them to support their anti-American agenda.

One reason the politicians get away with doing so is that the radical organizations with which they align themselves typically don't endure much scrutiny of their true objectives, their leadership, or their financial backers.

It is well past time to confront the truth about this crucial element of the Fifth Column.

OSAMA'S USEFUL IDIOTS

A close look at the most prominent "peace" organizations reveals that David Horowitz was spot-on when he described the radical nature of the movement.

The principal organization behind almost every major antiwar demonstration since 9/11 has been an umbrella group known as International ANSWER (Act Now to Stop War and End Racism). Officially founded shortly after 9/11, ANSWER is the largest of the antiwar NGOs and is in reality a front group for several radical Left causes. In spite of Big Media's characterization of the antiwar protests as a mainstream American movement, ANSWER and its associated organizations are anything but representative of patriotic citizens simply opposed to war. For ANSWER, the United States is imperialist, racist, militarist, sexist, and homophobic and responsible for the majority of the world's human rights violations.

ANSWER uses the antiwar movement as its primary vehicle for condemning capitalism and attacking American society and foreign policy. The group launched into action just days after the tragedies of 9/11, holding the first of its many mass anti-U.S. demonstrations in Washington, D.C., on September 29, 2001. And it didn't let up. The organization's hate-America machine was so primed for action that ANSWER organized more antiwar protests in four months—from the United Nations' deadline for Iraq in November 2002 to the first day of the American invasion—than occurred during the first six years of U.S. involvement in Vietnam.[4]

Giving the lie to claims that ANSWER is an organization founded on pacifist ideals, the group relies heavily on its close connections to the Marxist-Leninist group the Workers World Party, which contends that capitalism (and therefore the United States) is the source of all the world's problems and revolution is the only answer. The ANSWER staff and many of its rally speakers are drawn from the membership of the party, which renowned liberal thinker Christopher Hitchens refers to as an "especially venomous little Communist sect."[5] The Workers World Party was founded in 1959 when five members of the Socialist Workers Party split off, accusing their old party of becoming too "rightist." Over the past three decades, the World Workers Party supported the Soviet invasion of Afghanistan, China's Tiananmen Square massacre, and the repressive regimes of Slobodan Milošević in Yugoslavia, Kim Jong Il in North Korea, and Fidel Castro in Cuba; meanwhile it opposed the conciliatory Russian presidencies of Mikhail Gorbachev and Boris Yeltsin.[6]

The head of ANSWER's steering committee and its most notable front man is Ramsey Clark. Clark, once President Lyndon Johnson's attorney general, is a radical leftist anti-imperialist with an impressive résumé of hatred for his own country:

- During the Vietnam War, Clark traveled to Hanoi to demonstrate his support for the North Vietnamese. He returned to the United States to testify to Congress that American prisoners were being treated well by their captors—this at a time when American POWs were being tortured and killed.

- In 1979, Clark traveled to France to meet with the Ayatollah Khomeini. Shortly thereafter, a mob of approximately 500 Iranian students under Khomeini's direct control seized the American Embassy in Tehran, capturing sixty-six hostages and beginning one of the most humiliating foreign policy disasters in American history. In spite of Iran's deliberate act of war in attacking the U.S. Embassy, Clark later visited Tehran as a stooge for Khomeini and publicly denounced America's "crimes."

- In 1986 Clark demonstrated his affinity for terrorists when he served as legal counsel to the leaders of the Palestine Liberation

Organization (PLO) after PLO terrorists hijacked the Italian cruise liner *Achille Lauro* and shot and killed the elderly, wheel-chair-bound Leon Klinghoffer.

- Also in 1986, Clark flew to Libya to announce his support for tyrannical ruler Muammar Qaddafi after President Ronald Reagan launched a bombing campaign in response to a Libyan terrorist attack in Berlin that killed three people and injured more than 200.

- After Islamofascists bombed New York's World Trade Center for the first time in 1993, Clark stepped forward to defend the terrorists. To this day he continues to represent the "Blind Sheikh" Omar Abdel Rahman, who worked closely with al Qaeda to carry out the attack and was convicted for plotting to destroy other New York facilities, such as the United Nations building and the Holland and Lincoln tunnels, and possibly the George Washington Bridge.

- After al Qaeda successfully bombed the U.S. Embassies in Kenya and Tanzania in 1998, Clark represented Mohammad Daoud al-Owhali, a disciple of Osama bin Laden and a principal in the two near-simultaneous attacks.

- Proving there's not an American enemy he doesn't gravitate to, Clark stepped forward to defend Yugoslav president Slobodan Milošević against charges of genocide, and Saddam Hussein after U.S. forces captured him on the run in Iraq.[7]

When he's not defending tyrants and terrorists, Clark also heads the International Action Center, whose credo is "Information, Activism, and Resistance to U.S. Militarism, War and Corporate Greed."[8] The Center and ANSWER have much more in common than just Clark. In fact, they could be considered as one and the same entity, as the two organizations share the same office address in New York City and the same phone numbers.[9]

Another figure who splits his duties between ANSWER and the International Action Center is Brian Becker. Becker is a member of ANSWER's steering committee and a codirector of the International Action Center (not to mention a member of the secretariat of the Workers World Party). Less than two months after the 9/11 attacks, Becker called America's military intervention in Afghanistan "one of the greatest crimes and acts of terrorism." "Let us not forget," Becker said, "that September 11 was not the beginning of violence, but just one point in a long continuum of violence that is fundamentally a consequence of U.S. policies around the world."[10]

Besides ANSWER, one of the most significant antiwar and antimilitary organizations is Not in Our Name, which is also a Communist front group. The organization was created in March 2002 by C. Clark Kissinger, a longtime Maoist activist who was the national secretary of the Students for a Democratic Society at one time during the 1960s. Kissinger is also a member of the Revolutionary Communist Party, whose platform states that "of all the tyrants and oppressors in the world, there is none that has caused more untold misery and committed more screaming injustices against the people of the world than the rulers of the U.S. . . . The rulers of the U.S. have plundered and slaughtered their way to the top position within the worldwide system of capitalist-imperialism—a system of global exploitation, of political and military domination, and of murderous rivalry among the imperialist powers themselves."[11] Kissinger echoes such claims when he says, "The problem in this country [is] the oppressive system of capitalism that exploits people all over the world, that destroys our planet, that oppresses minority people, that sends people to the death chambers in droves. That is a problem that has to be done away with." The solution? "Revolution is the solution."[12]

Kissinger's Not in Our Name began its anti-U.S. "peace" campaign with the release of its "Statement of Conscience," which morally equated the 9/11 terrorist attacks with previous

U.S. military actions in Iraq, Panama, and Vietnam. "We too mourned the thousands of innocent dead [on 9/11] and shook our heads at the terrible scenes of carnage—even as we recalled similar scenes in Baghdad, Panama City, and, a generation ago, Vietnam," read a portion of the statement.[13]

Many of those who endorsed the "Statement of Conscience" were avowed Communists or members of radical pro-Communist organizations like the Revolutionary Communist Party, the International League of Peoples' Struggle, the Black Radical Congress, and the National Lawyers Guild. But none of this radicalism has deterred high-profile liberals from hopping onboard with Not in Our Name. Among the tens of thousands to publicly align with Not in Our Name are Jesse Jackson, Al Sharpton, Congressman Jim McDermott, Congresswoman Cynthia McKinney, Martin Luther King III, and Gloria Steinem, as well as Hollywood figures Kevin Bacon, Ed Asner, John Cusack, Oliver Stone, Marisa Tomei, Danny Glover, Susan Sarandon, Jessica Lange, and Martin Sheen.[14]

Kissinger also created one of the newer anti-American organizations when he started the World Can't Wait project in June 2005. In November of that year, the group held its coming-out party in San Francisco, and various signs and placards emphasized ideas such as that the Bush administration planned 9/11 and that a Maoist revolution was overdue.[15] On December 12, 2005, World Can't Wait ran an advertisement in the *New York Times* claiming, "YOUR GOVERNMENT, on the basis of outrageous lies, is waging a murderous and utterly illegitimate war in Iraq. . . . YOUR GOVERNMENT is openly torturing people, and justifying it. . . . YOUR GOVERNMENT is moving each day closer to a theocracy, where a narrow and hateful brand of Christian fundamentalism will rule. . . . YOUR GOVERNMENT enforces a culture of greed, bigotry, intolerance and ignorance. People look at all this and think of Hitler—and they are right to do so."[16]

Oh—and this shocking, I know—World Can't Wait is also a front for the Revolutionary Communist Party. Nevertheless, the group has earned the endorsement of not only ANSWER and Not in Our Name but also Jesse Jackson, Al Sharpton, Harry Belafonte, Jane Fonda, Sean Penn, Martin Sheen, Susan Sarandon, Ed Asner, Ed Begley Jr., Casey Kasem, Gore Vidal, Kurt Vonnegut, Howard Zinn, Ward Churchill, Bill Ayers, and Janis Karpinski, the disgraced and retired Army colonel who was the commander of the Abu Ghraib miscreants.[17]

The largest coalition of antiwar organizations is United for Peace and Justice, which claims to represent more than 1,300 local and national groups "to oppose our government's policy of permanent warfare and empire-building."[18] This group was officially created on October 25, 2002, in the Washington, D.C., offices of the also deceptively titled and anti-Christian leftist organization People for the American Way. United for Peace and Justice was intended to put a more mainstream face on the antiwar movement, but in reality this supposedly moderate group's agenda is the same as the others'. Its "Unity Statement" denounces "the 'preemptive' wars of aggression waged by the Bush administration 'in its alleged' drive to expand U.S. control over other nations and strip us of our rights at home under the cover of fighting terrorism and spreading democracy."[19]

The head of United for Peace and Justice is Leslie Cagan, a committed Communist and an anti-U.S. agitator with a forty-year history of shilling for totalitarian regimes. During that time she has been a prolific organizer of anti-American demonstrations, turning out millions of protesters. She is also a devoted supporter of Fidel Castro and she proudly aligns her politics with those of the Communist dictator.

Closely linked to Cagan's United for Peace and Justice is Code Pink, which claims more than 250 chapters worldwide. Launched in December 2002, this organization describes itself as a "grassroots peace and social justice movement" of women activists, but in fact its members are anything but pacifists. More honestly, they are cut from the same cloth of such Communist revolutionaries as Clark, Kissinger, and Cagan.

Code Pink was founded by radicals Medea Benjamin, Jodie Evans, Diane Wilson, and a Wiccan activist who refers to herself only as "Starhawk." Benjamin most personifies the militant core of the organization. Born Susie Benjamin, she changed her name to Medea during her freshman year at Tufts University after the Greek character known for murdering her father, brother, and children to exact revenge on her husband.

Benjamin organized the anticapitalist and antiwar organization Global Exchange in 1988, which promotes itself thusly: "Whether it is US companies such as Nike abusing the women who make its shoes, the US government fueling an illegal, unjustified, murderous war in Iraq, or the World Trade Organization (WTO) undercutting consumer and environmental protections, Global Exchange offers itself as a partner for peace and social justice."[20] In 1999, she played a key role in organizing the World Trade Organization protest riots in Seattle, which caused property damages totaling millions of dollars.[21]

Since 9/11, Benjamin and her allies at Code Pink have shifted their sights toward the U.S. military, the Bush administration, and America's War on Terror. Benjamin laid out much of Code Pink's strategy in an article she penned titled "Toward a Global Movement," published in *The Nation* in April 2003. In it, she urged fellow radicals to "send grassroots teams to the world's hot spots—North Korea and South Korea, Iran, Syria—to link up with appropriate local and regional groups."[22] Let's be clear here—this is an American citizen who, as the head of an international antiwar organization, is attempting to rally activists to collude with anti-U.S. groups.

And she's done just that. In December 2004, Benjamin and

her associates traveled to Amman, Jordan, to donate more than $600,000 in cash and medical supplies to the "other side"— terrorists and their supporters locked in bloody house-to-house fighting with U.S. Marines in Fallujah, Iraq. In a press conference celebrating her organization's subversion, Benjamin chortled, "I don't know of any other case in history in which the parents of fallen soldiers collected medicine . . . for the 'other side.' It is a reflection of a growing movement in the United States . . . opposed to the unjust nature of this war. . . . Our hearts go out to the people of Fallujah."[23]

The only major media outlet to cover her sedition was Agence France-Presse. The U.S. media completely ignored the story. Here, perhaps, is the reason: According to the online publication *Peace and Resistance,* in an unbelievable act of complicity in wartime, Benjamin's entourage received logistical support from an elected politician. Congressman Henry Waxman, Democrat from California, wrote a letter to the U.S. ambassador in Jordan that may have helped expedite the aid from America's leftists to our enemies.[24]

Benjamin's mission to undermine the U.S. military and directly aid the enemies of America didn't start with providing support and comfort for embattled terrorists in Fallujah. In the early months of the Iraq War she began sabotaging U.S. and Iraqi security and reconstruction efforts by opening an organization called the Iraq Occupation Watch in Baghdad. Allying with fellow radical soul mate and professional activist Leslie Cagan, Benjamin set out, according to the watchdog website discoverthenetworks.org, to "(a) undermine the Bush administration's reconstruction efforts in Iraq through propaganda and dissimulation in the American media; (b) demoralize U.S. troops by relaying tales of wavering public support; (c) encourage widespread desertion by 'conscientious objectors.' "[25]

To put the efforts of Benjamin and Cagan into context, actress

Jane Fonda also defied U.S. law when she visited Communist North Vietnam in 1972 and encouraged U.S. troops to desert. Fonda recorded several radio broadcasts for Hanoi and posed for photos showing her smiling as she pretended to shoot down America's military aircraft. But not even the traitorous Hanoi Jane physically approached American soldiers at war, on enemy soil, and attempted to facilitate their desertion.

In yet another act of subversion, Code Pink and United for Peace and Justice in June 2005 sent representatives to a mock "war crimes" trial in Istanbul, Turkey, and signed a joint declaration backing the Iraqi insurgency. The "World Tribunal on Iraq" concluded, "The popular national resistance to the occupation is legitimate and justified. It deserves the support of people everywhere who care for justice and freedom."[26]

Code Pink showed its contempt for the U.S. military when it spent most of 2005 staging weekly protests just outside the perimeter of the Walter Reed Army Medical Center in Washington, D.C. Walter Reed is the primary convalescent home for wounded soldiers returning from battle. Positioning themselves directly in front of the military hospital's main entrance, the "Pinkos" held signs proclaiming that the injured troops were "Maimed for a Lie." Recovering soldiers and their families were forced to walk through a gauntlet lined with mock caskets and placards reading, among other things, "Enlist here to die for Halliburton."[27]

This kind of cruel protest has a devastating effect on our proud soldiers and their families. One of the soldiers treated at Walter Reed was Kevin Pannell, a member of the Army's First Calvary Division who lost both of his legs in a grenade ambush near Baghdad in 2004. He was outraged. Pannell recalled, "We went by there one day and I drove by and [the antiwar protesters] had a bunch of flag-draped coffins laid out on the sidewalk. That, I thought, was probably the most distasteful thing I had ever seen. Ever. You know that 95 percent of the guys in the hospital bed lost guys whenever they got hurt and survivor's guilt is the worst thing you can deal with." Referring to the Code Pink activists, Pannell said, "We don't like them and we don't like the fact that they can hang their signs and stuff on the fence at Walter Reed."[28]

Another soldier, Sergeant Mark Leach, responded to Code Pink in an e-mail from Afghanistan:

> What angers and hurts me as a soldier is that they parade their anti-war views in the face of my brothers and sisters who are recovering from the same battlefield that I fought on and am still fighting on as I type this e-mail. Is there no honor or dignity left in the anti-war movement? Do they have no shame? Do they have no integrity? Do they have no heart? Do they have no soul? I can answer that with a simple no! How can they say they support the troops but protest where they try to recover from war? You interviewed one gentleman, and I use that term loosely, who stated 'If I was injured I would want someone to speak for me like this.' Well let me tell him something, we do not want you to speak for us and we do not need you to speak for us![29]

The military blogger Froggy Ruminations asked, "What must it be like to look in the mirror after spending a long day outside Walter Reed Army Hospital in Washington, D.C., mocking and tormenting wounded soldiers? This is déjà vu all over again when the parents of these contemptible slime were calling the parents of fallen soldiers in Vietnam and telling them how glad they were that their 'baby killer' son had died."[30]

CINDY SHEEHAN: THE "PEACE MOM"

Nobody to date has personified the anti-American peace movement since the attacks of 9/11 more than Cindy Sheehan. She, of course, is the mother of U.S. Army Specialist Casey Sheehan, who was killed in action in Baghdad's Sadr City in April 2004. Specialist Sheehan was a Humvee mechanic who heroically volunteered to go to the aid of his fellow soldiers under attack. He was killed along with seven other American warriors in a fierce firefight.

The grieving Mrs. Sheehan met with President Bush within two months of her son's death. After meeting with Bush, she told her hometown paper, "I now know he's sincere about wanting freedom for the Iraqis. I know he's sorry and feels some pain for our loss. And I know he's a man of faith."[31] Soon she changed her tune, however.

Embracing a radical ideology while adroitly turning the tragic and patriotic sacrifice of her son into her own selfish fame, Sheehan became the face of the Left's anti-American movement. The media lavished attention on Sheehan as soon as she began sounding off against President Bush and the War on Terror.

But little noticed in her elaborate campaign was her close coordination and collaboration with the vast network of radical "peace organizations."

She created the antiwar organization Gold Star Families for Peace in 2004, lifting the name of her antimilitary and anti-American organization from the highly patriotic and virtuous American Gold Star Mothers organization. The latter organization was founded in 1918 by President Woodrow Wilson for grieving mothers of soldiers killed during World War I; its charter states that the organization's mission is to "keep alive and develop the spirit that promoted [military] service; inculcate a sense of individual obligation to the community, State, and Nation; maintain true allegiance to the United States of America; and inspire respect for the Stars and Stripes in the youth of America."[32] Hmm, hardly the motivation for Sheehan and her ilk.

When the "Peace Mom" went to Crawford, Texas, in August 2005 to stake out President Bush's ranch, she received support and funding from United for Peace and Justice, Code Pink, and moveon.org, to name a few far-left groups. This was not a grieving mother trying to get a personal meeting with President Bush, as Sheehan claimed (glossing over the fact that she had *already* met personally with the president). No, this was a left-wing political campaign.

Sheehan and fellow leftists arrived in Crawford in a red-white-and-blue bus with "Impeachment Tour" emblazoned on the side, suggesting her true motives. In a calculated attempt to promote herself further, she began blogging on leftist sites such as michaelmoore.com, dailykos, and huffingtonpost.[33]

Overlooking these connections, Big Media outlets were all too happy to position Mrs. Sheehan as a spokesperson for all the families who had lost loved ones in Iraq. *New York Times* columnist Maureen Dowd even insisted, in a transparently illogical line that was repeated incessantly, that the "moral authority" of mothers like Sheehan was "absolute."[34] Perhaps Dowd and her liberal colleagues should have looked more closely at who was supporting Sheehan, and also at what the "Peace Mother" was revealing about her true intentions.

In one revealing exchange, Sheehan showed that she had little concern for anyone but herself. The only opinion that counted was hers, she made clear. Referring to other grieving families who didn't agree with her, Sheehan said, "I am starting to lose a little compassion for them. I know they have been brainwashed."[35]

At another point, appearing on CNBC's *Big Idea with Donny Deutsch,* she ruthlessly attacked a courageous and pregnant female veteran who was just days from delivering a child conceived with her late husband—a Navy corpsman killed in Iraq. "Well, sweetie, you know what?" Sheehan condescendingly scoffed. "Your baby is going to be fatherless for a lie, two lies: weapons of mass destruction and terrorism." The grieving widow shot back, "My child will never be fatherless because his father is an angel."[36]

Elsewhere Sheehan declared, "The person who killed my son, I have no animosity for that person at all."[37] No, when you hate America it doesn't matter who really pulled the trigger; it's always George Bush's fault.

The more support Sheehan received from the Fifth Column "peace" organizations, the more unhinged she became. In a speech to an assembled group of folks claiming to be Veterans for Peace, she declared, "You get that evil maniac [the president] out here, 'cause a Gold Star Mother, somebody whose blood is on his hands, has some questions for you." She added, "And you [the president] tell me what the noble cause is that my son died for. And if [you] even start to say freedom and democracy, I'm gonna say 'bullshit.' You tell me the truth. You tell me that my son died for oil. You tell me that my son died to make your friends rich. You tell me my son died to spread the cancer of Pax Americana, imperialism in the Middle East."[38]

Nothing illustrates how powerful the antiwar movement is or how deeply the Left has co-opted the Democratic Party more than the fact that Sheehan, despite her radical statements, has been embraced by Democratic politicians. In the midst of her staged Crawford stunt, more than forty congressional Democrats signed a letter asking President Bush to meet with Sheehan.

While she was grandstanding for cameras and journalists in a ditch, Democratic congresswoman Jan Schakowsky phoned to convey her support, gushing, "I'm just so proud of you. . . . My heart is with you." Joe Trippi, Democratic National Committee chairman Howard Dean's 2004 presidential campaign strategist, joined Code Pink cofounder and activist fundraiser Jodie Evans to webcast the charade from Crawford. Democratic presidential candidate Al Sharpton visited Sheehan to announce his support, and Congressman John Conyers, Michigan Democrat, invited her to "testify" in a mock impeachment trial on Capitol Hill.[39]

In her same summer of fame, Sheehan met with the following

Democratic Party leaders, who, by association, legitimized her extreme politics: Senators Hillary Clinton, Ted Kennedy, Harry Reid, Robert Byrd, Russ Feingold, and Barbara Boxer, and Representatives Nancy Pelosi, Charles Rangel, Maxine Waters, Henry Waxman, Pete Stark, Cynthia McKinney, Barbara Lee, Sheila Jackson Lee, Lynn Woolsey, Shelley Berkeley, John Barrow, and Frank Pallone. These meetings and public displays of alliance with at least twenty members of Congress occurred *after* Sheehan had referred to the terrorists fighting Americans and democracy in the Middle East as "freedom fighters," the U.S. government as a "morally repugnant system," and the commander in chief as a "lying bastard."[40]

In an interview I conducted with Air Force Major Eric Egland in Iraq, I asked about the antiwar movement at home. Egland became incensed, particularly with the way the media gave a platform to Sheehan. "Cindy Sheehan was lionized by the press," Egland said. "She claims moral authority? She's one person! I see a lot of moral authority in the families who've sacrificed here. Objectivity is not part of their [the media's] equation."

Sergeant Walter J. Rausch, a member of the 101st Airborne Division deployed to Iraq, agreed. "I watched Cindy Sheehan sit on the president's lawn and say that America isn't worth dying for. Later she corrected herself and said Iraq isn't worth dying for," said Rausch. "She badmouthed all that her son had fought and died for. I bet he is rolling over in his grave."

Rausch, speaking with the moral authority that is achieved on battle fields, concluded, "I have watched brave souls give their all and lose their lives and limbs for this cause. . . . For these brave souls who gave the ultimate sacrifice, including your son, Cindy Sheehan, I will shout till I can no longer. These men and women are heroes. Their spirit lives on in their military and they will never be forgotten. They did not die in vain but rather for a cause that is larger than all of us."[41]

One soldier felt the need to reach out directly to Sheehan to counter her claims. Specialist First Class C. J. Grisham, serving in Iraq, posted an online "Open Letter to Cindy Sheehan," in which he wrote:

President Bush did not kill your son, Casey. A radical Islamic terrorist from another country and/or disillusioned Iraqis killed him. President Bush had the backing of Congress when he authorized military action in Iraq. In October AND November of 2002 Congress authorized the use of force against Iraq. . . . There are 535 members of Congress that you should also petition if you truly want this question answered. . . .

What did [your] son die for? Casey died for a number of things, not the least of which is peace, democracy, humanity, love, loyalty, and patriotism. He died giving more than 25,000,000 people a better life. While Iraq today is not an ideal environment right now, history will prove that your son is personally responsible for Iraq's future prosperity. In addition to those 25,000,000+ Iraqis, your son died for the more than 1,000,000 other soldiers serving in Iraq, and the few specific soldiers that were privileged to have known and worked with Casey. . . .

I really do hope that you can be comforted in the knowledge that Casey died for something beyond the scope that many of us can comprehend. I hope that you can begin to celebrate his sacrifice as something honorable. I pray that each American will live their life worthy of his sacrifice. In Casey's death, we all have life. In his death, other nations will be able to partake of the same fruits of liberty for the first time that we've enjoyed for the past 229 years.[42]

Of course, Cindy Sheehan went right on getting headlines; Specialist Grisham's response escaped the notice of Big Media.

COUNTER-RECRUITING: TARGETING THE SOLDIER

While Sheehan and celebrity protesters attract most of the attention in the antiwar movement, other elements of the antimilitary campaign exert a great deal of influence as well. These groups support the work of ANSWER, United for Peace and Justice, and the rest, and they pursue the same ultimate goal: defeat of imperialist America. A military defeat for the United States in Iraq and Afghanistan and a return to isolationism would allow the Left to reclaim its lost political leverage and pursue its destructive agenda.

Not content with relying on symbolic "antiwar" protests alone, the hate-America Left has developed a new "direct action" campaign designed specifically to destroy the lifeblood of the armed forces—the soldier, sailor, airman, and Marine. If the Left can hollow out the military, they will make U.S. military defeat more likely in Iraq and Afghanistan and in future battles as well.

During the Vietnam War, leftists artfully used fear of the draft as the tool to "bring down the American war machine." How, though, do you generate the massive public support required to destroy the military and lose the War on Terror with an all-volunteer Army? You create unsubstantiated fear that America will return to the draft (as Democratic politicians and left-wingers attempted in the run-up to the 2004 presidential election). Or you try to block the military from attracting enough quality recruits.

Complementing the Left's assault on America through its immense network of "peace organizations" is its "counter-recruitment" campaign, which seeks to destroy the nation's ability to augment its fighting forces. At the forefront of this campaign, not coincidentally, are the same Communist-affiliated organizations that dominate the "peace movement"—most notably Cagan's United for Peace and Justice and Benjamin's Code Pink. These groups carefully divide their efforts, with Code Pink attacking military recruiting operations in major cities along the West Coast and in the Midwest, and United for Peace and Justice focusing primarily on the East Coast, especially the New York City area. Augmenting their well-organized counter-recruitment campaign are groups like the Ruckus Society, Leave My Child Alone, Central Committee for Conscientious Objectors (CCCO), National Network Opposing the Militarization of Youth, Veterans for Peace, and the Campus Antiwar Network.

The counter-recruitment campaign uses a range of tactics to stop young men and women from joining the military: "training camps" for aspiring activists; a massive disinformation campaign disseminated through DVDs, handbooks, and publications; aggressive efforts to disrupt recruiters on campuses and in their offices.

The disinformation campaign is rooted in the stereotypical lies we see over and over from the Left and discussed in Chapter 2: The military preys on the poor, the uneducated, and minorities who have no other options in life. The counter-recruitment effort of the Left includes one more precept: Recruiters lie.

For example, Code Pink's official website declares, "The military is desperate for young people to fight in Iraq and they are doing everything they can to pull in young people: promising them a college education, big cash bonuses, and trying to guarantee that new enlistees won't get sent to the Middle East. Recruiters roam the halls of high schools luring students into conversation with free goods, rock-climbing walls, war simulation video games, and, worst of all, fancy Hummers. Join CODEPINK and the national counter-recruitment movement in standing up to these warmongers and liars. Stop the next war now by stopping the next generation from becoming cannon fodder in this illegal and immoral war!"[43]

In association with Leave My Child Alone, Code Pink also tries to coerce school boards, faculties, and parents into ignoring or challenging Section 9528 of the Bush administration's 2002 No

Child Left Behind Act.[44] This law grants the U.S. military the same access to high school student directory information that is readily available to prospective employers, colleges, and universities. Those schools choosing not to comply with the law risk losing their federal funding. This provision is similar in principle to the Solomon Amendment passed by Congress in 1995, which requires colleges and universities to allow military recruiters on campus or risk forfeiting federal funding.

The Ruckus Society takes an even more aggressive approach to this issue. This violent anarchist organization grew out of the 1990s ecoterrorist group Earth First!, and it helped organize the 1999 World Trade Organization riots in Seattle. Ruckus executive director John Sellers defended his group's actions, saying, "I think you can be destructive, you can use vandalism strategically."[45] The Ruckus Society has emerged to conduct "training camps" that are zealously anti-American, antimilitary, and anticapitalist. These training camps introduce and indoctrinate aspiring anarchists and radicals with tools ranging from street protests to shutting down military recruiting offices to forcing military recruiters out of taxpayer-funded educational institutions. Activists are, for instance, taught to block entrances to job fairs, stop school presentations, and interrupt recruiting efforts by staging "die-ins." On its official website, Ruckus promotes its Not Your Soldier Project, which provides "youth the tools they need to stop the military invasion of their schools and their communities."[46] (Ruckus teaches such techniques to other "activists" as well, hosting boot camps in "street blockades," "police confrontation strategies," and "using the media to your advantage.")[47]

Another group critical to the antimilitary crusade is the Central Committee for Conscientious Objectors (CCCO), headed by former Black Panther Wendy Carson. Its sponsors include America-haters Ed Asner, Joan Baez, Noam Chomsky, former Democratic congressman Ron Dellums, NAACP executive director Julian Bond, and moonbat musician Jello Biafra.[48]

The CCCO, through its Military Out of Our Schools program, floods inner-city junior high and high schools with antiwar, antimilitary posters and conducts "peace" seminars for students and parents. Although, as we've seen, it's a myth that minorities are overrepresented in military service, the organization nevertheless builds its campaign around the idea that rich white people are exploiting poor minorities in the military.

One of CCCO's counter-recruiting posters, for example, portrays an African-American boy with a devilish white military recruiter pulling on his ear and human skulls peering over his shoulder. On the child's right side we see the words "War" and "Death" and images of a tank, a mushroom cloud, and the earth in flames; to the boy's left and the words "Peace" and "Life" and a pastoral setting with a family, sunshine, wildlife, and flowers.[49]

Subtle.

Among CCCO's claims is that "Joining the Military is Hazardous to your . . . education . . . future . . . to people of color . . . to women . . . to your civil rights . . . to your mental health . . . and to the environment."[50]

CCCO also publishes a magazine titled *AWOL: Youth for Peace and Revolution* (representing the military crime of being "absent without leave," which is a punishable offense but one that the Left champions). This publication promotes, among other anti-U.S. messages, the writings and music of convicted cop killer Mumia Abu Jamal.[51]

Aiding the antimilitary efforts are the National Network Opposing the Militarization of Youth and Veterans for Peace, a group of disgruntled veterans (and those claiming to be veterans). Both groups counter-recruit at the high school level, with Veterans for Peace sending its members to dissuade students from military service through antimilitary "testimonials." Like other organizations in the antiwar and counter-recruiting efforts, Veterans for Peace has a history of supporting America's enemies and opposing its military. Founded in 1985, the organization actively supported Nicaragua's Marxist Sandinistas, aligned itself with Fidel Castro, denounced America's actions in Iraq, and with the assistance of ANSWER, held a "Korean War Tribunal" convicting the United States of war crimes during the Korean War.[52]

Another pro-Communist, anti-American group is the War Resisters League, created in 1923 by pacifists opposed to World War I. This organization has opposed every U.S. military involvement since the Great War. Today, the War Resisters League sabotages the U.S. military via its Revolution Out of Truth and Struggle (ROOTS) program. The ROOTS program primarily focuses on high school Junior Reserve Officer Training Corps (JROTC) military classes. Amazingly replete with misspelled words, poor grammar, and heavy-handed racism, ROOTS's official statement declares that "the goal of JROTC is to brainwash us into believing the rich white man's version of history, of other races and their solutions n [*sic*] to get us to fight in their military." After all, the radical organization asks, "How often do u [*sic*] see an advertisement on how the military could lead u [*sic*] to have a disease, lose your life, be psyhcologically [*sic*] screwed, be homeless, face severe sexual violations, racism, gay bashing, not get your benefits, work 12–18 hours day, not be able to quit, etc.?"[53]

And sometimes radical groups simply try to block recruiters from going into schools. The Campus Antiwar Network is the tip of the spear for the counter-military campaigns on America's college campuses. It is run directly by college students and has organized a comprehensive counter-recruitment campaign that focuses on in-your-face tactics, including threatening and verbally harassing recruiters and physically forcing them off campuses. As noted in Chapter 3, these protesters have been very effective both in keeping military recruiters out of campus job fairs and in disrupting their presence once they are there.[54]

THE DEEP POCKETS

Also flying below the radar are the groups who provide the resources to support the work of the antimilitary, anti-America campaign. These are the deep pockets of the "peace movement"—the leftist foundations that fund the vast network of antimilitary organizations. While few Americans are aware of these organizations or the tremendous damage they wreak upon America, our military, and our ability to fight the War on Terror, these groups work tirelessly to undermine the efforts of the U.S. armed forces.

The rather innocuous-sounding Peace and Security Funders Group pulls together much of this funding. This association of more than fifty private and public foundations provides a significant portion of its $27 billion cache to leftist organizations pursuing anti-American causes. Established in 1999, the Peace and Security Funders Group argues that American society is too militaristic and seeks to confront the "root causes" of war. Among the significant funders are the Ford Foundation, the Tides Foundation, and left-wing billionaire George Soros's Open Society Institute. The fortunate beneficiaries include the antiwar groups ANSWER, Not in Our Name, United for Peace and Justice, Code Pink, Global Exchange, the Ruckus Society, the War Resisters League, and the leftist legal entities that defend them—the Center for Constitutional Rights, the National Lawyers Guild, and the ACLU.

The largest private contributor for leftist causes is the Ford Foundation. Most Americans, if even aware of the Ford Foundation, probably assume it's an entity of the Ford Motor Company. Once upon a time that was true. The foundation was originally built upon the estates of Henry and Edsel Ford. But in 1977 Henry Ford II, the grandson of Henry, resigned from the Ford Foundation's board of trustees, thoroughly disgusted with the organization's gravitation toward leftist causes and away from American values. As he left the foundation, Ford remarked, "I tried for thirty years to change it from within to no avail."[55]

Today the Ford Foundation is wholly independent from the car manufacturer and serves as the world's largest source of monetary support for anti-American agendas. In fact, the Ford Foundation alone contributes approximately *fifteen times* as much to liberal causes as the three largest conservative foundations *combined* give to conservative causes. It is one of the largest and most dangerous sources of unchecked power, with assets of approximately $12.2 billion as of 2006.[56] On average, it pays out approximately 2,500 grants worth a total of $500 million annually, nearly all of it earmarked for leftist and radical causes.[57] This anti-American, anticapitalist, and antimilitary leviathan makes Soros and his Open Society Institute look insignificant.

The president of the Ford Foundation is Susan Berresford, who, like most members of the leftist elite, is a child of the sixties. In the aftermath of 9/11, Berresford joined the throng of other hatriots urging Americans to "explore the issues behind the headlines and broaden [their] understanding about the countries from which the attacks came."[58] In the wake of an unprovoked and overwhelming attack on her homeland, Berresford wasn't driven by anger or indignation at the attackers but by her inherent need to blame the United States.

One of the many leftist beneficiaries of the Ford Foundation is the Tides Foundation and the associated Tides Center, which receive substantial grants. In turn, these groups give millions of dollars in grants each year to hundreds of decidedly left-wing political organizations and causes. For 2004, the Tides Foundation showed assets of $144 million and the Tides Center $37 million. One of the more visible donors is Teresa Heinz Kerry, wife of Senator John Kerry, who has given more than $8 million to Tides.[59]

To support the antiwar movement, Tides established the Iraq

Peace Fund, which underwrites United for Peace and Justice, the Ruckus Society, Peaceful Tomorrows, the Council for American-Islamic Relations (CAIR), and moveon.org. Tides also funded "A Better Way Project," which opposed the war in Iraq and coordinated the efforts of United for Peace and Justice, the Hollywood antiwar campaign Win Without War, and the Ruckus Society. Since 1999, the Tides Foundation has donated more than $150,000 to the Ruckus Society.

Together, the Ford Foundation and Tides also fund the "legal Left," which day by day hacks away at the Constitution and the U.S. military's ability to wage war. For example, immediately following the 9/11 attacks, the Ford Foundation gave $150,000 to the Center for Constitutional Rights, which was founded in 1966 by radicals who were either members of the Communist Party or politically allied with the New Left. The foundation designated the grant to be used for "racial justice litigation, advocacy, and educational outreach activities related to the detention and racial profiling of Arab Americans and Muslims following the World Trade Center attack."[60]

It was a fitting contribution. One of the center's founders, the wild-haired radical William Kunstler, had defended terrorist El Sayyid Nosair, a leader in the 1993 plot to bomb the World Trade Center. The center's clients over the years have included the Armed Forces of National Liberation (FALN) of Puerto Rico, which were responsible for approximately fifty bombings in the United States from 1974 to 1983; Japanese Red Army member Yu Kikumura, who was convicted of attempting to bomb a U.S. Army recruiting station; Red Army Baader-Meinhof terrorists who carried out bombings on U.S. military facilities in Germany during the 1980s; and Black Panther H. Rap Brown, who murdered a Georgia law-enforcement officer.[61]

At its 2004 annual convention, the Center for Constitutional Rights honored convicted terrorist enabler and attorney Lynne

Stewart for abetting the terrorist activities of her client Sheik Omar Abdel Rahman. Instead of characterizing Stewart's work as what it was—subversion—the center condemned those who had prosecuted her, calling it "an attack on attorneys who defend controversial figures, and an attempt to deprive these clients of the zealous representation that may be required."[62]

Since the War on Terror began, the Center for Constitutional Rights has filed multiple "nuisance" lawsuits against various antiterrorism measures the United States has attempted to implement, including our military's detention of captured Taliban and al Qaeda fighters at Guantánamo Bay. The center has also campaigned against the surveillance and the detention of terrorist suspects, seizing on everything from wiretaps to voluntary interviews of Middle Eastern men as evidence of authoritarian overreach.

Perhaps not surprisingly, the Center for Constitutional Rights is a member of United for Peace and Justice.

The Ford and Tides foundations also fund the National Lawyers Guild, which was founded in 1936 by the Communist Party USA and today boasts chapters in every major U.S. city.[63] In 2002, the Ford Foundation gave $100,000 to the Guild's National Immigration Project "as core support for activities to ensure the human rights of non-citizens detained in the United States in the aftermath of the attacks of September 11, 2001."[64] True to its origins, the National Lawyers Guild is still saturated with Communists and other far-left ideologues. According to member Chip Berlet, Guild meetings are overrun with "cadres from Leninist, Trotskyist, Stalinist, and Maoist groups, along with Marxists, anarchists, libertarians, and progressive independents—interacting with a preponderance of reluctant Democrats."[65] The Guild also supports ANSWER, endorsing its March 2004 "Call to End Colonial Occupation from Iraq to Palestine & Everywhere."[66]

No organization has benefited more from Ford Foundation largesse than the ACLU. One of this group's founders candidly stated in 1935, "I am for socialism, disarmament, and ultimately, for abolishing the state itself as an instrument of violence and compulsion. I seek social ownership of property, the abolition of the propertied class, and sole control of those who produce wealth. Communism is the goal."[67]

Little has changed. The ACLU, supposedly a "guardian of liberty," consistently undercuts the Constitution and America's right to defend its national security.

Despite those efforts—or, more likely, because of them—in 1999 the Ford Foundation donated $7 million to the ACLU, the largest single gift the legal organization had ever received.[68] So what kind of efforts have we seen from the ACLU since receiving such extraordinary funding?

Since September 11, 2001, the ACLU has fought tooth and nail against the Patriot Act, military detentions of terrorists, coercive interrogation, heightened security of airline passengers from countries that sponsor terrorism, and just about anything else the U.S. government has attempted to do to prevent the next 9/11 from happening.[69]

When FBI and Homeland Security agents were searching for illegal Iraqi immigrants in the weeks prior to the invasion of Iraq, the ACLU set up telephone hotlines advising illegals how to avoid deportation.

When the INS and the Justice Department instituted a program requiring males visiting the United States from Arab and Muslim nations to register with the Bureau of Citizenship and Immigration Services, the ACLU organized protests against what it called a "discriminatory" policy.

When commercial airlines implemented the Computer-Assisted Passenger Profiling System (CAPPS) to check its passengers against known terrorist profiles, the ACLU aggressively lobbied against the safety measure.

When the National Football League instituted a policy of increased security, the ACLU objected and convinced a judge in

Florida to bar professional football teams from searching fans entering their stadiums for weapons.

When the National Security Agency's terrorist surveillance program was revealed, the ACLU filed suit.

When several states attempted to pass legislation preventing antiwar groups from protesting at military funerals, the ACLU filed suit against such legislation—showing that even deceased soldiers and their families aren't beyond their anti-American reach.

When counter-recruiters wanted to challenge the provision of the No Child Left Behind Act that requires school boards to provide military recruiters with student information, the ACLU stepped up to file litigation in New Mexico.

When questions were raised about the detainment and interrogation of captured terrorists at Guantánamo Bay, the ACLU agreed to represent these terrorists as their clients. The organization's attorneys have intervened at every opportunity to obstruct the interrogation sessions, despite the fact that these high-level terrorists have information that could prevent the next attack.

The ACLU pops up everywhere to fight against the U.S. military and harm America's national security. It couldn't do nearly so much without the extraordinary funding from left-wing groups like the Ford Foundation.

Since left-wing groups have millions and millions of dollars and powerful legal teams at their disposal, it is little wonder that they have developed such a well-coordinated effort to undermine the War on Terror—an effort most Americans are completely unaware of.

THE FIFTH COLUMN'S EFFORTS PAY OFF

Though the so-called peace movement's numerous antimilitary campaigns do not draw much notice, they very effectively undermine America's ability to win wars. By portraying America as a militaristic, imperialist, and racist nation responsible for the terror attacks it receives, and by characterizing our military actions as illegal, illegitimate, and immoral, these left-wing groups contribute to the cause of the Islamofascists.

Their efforts do even more damage because they receive the support of other elements of the Fifth Column, including politicians and the mainstream media. Just look again at how Democratic political leaders and major media figures gave a major platform to Cindy Sheehan. Her hateful rants against the president and her country became international news, demoralizing American troops while also emboldening our enemy. The Left knew all this and yet continued to celebrate Sheehan anyway. Why? Because she had "absolute moral authority."

Linda Ryan lost her son too. Marine Corporal Marc T. Ryan was killed in an explosion in Ramadi at the hands of Sheehan's "freedom fighters." Linda Ryan has absolute moral authority as well. Referring to Sheehan, Mrs. Ryan said, "George Bush didn't kill her son, it's the evildoers who have no value of life who killed her son. Her son made a decision to join the Armed Forces and defend our country, knowing that, at any time, war could come about. George Bush was my son's commander in chief. My son, Marc, totally believed in what he was doing. [Sheehan]'s going about this not realizing how many people she's hurting. When she refers to anyone killed in Iraq, she's referring to my son. She doesn't have anything to say about what happened to my son."[70]

Robert Hoffman has moral authority too. His son, Marine Sergeant Justin Hoffman, was one of fourteen Marines killed on August 3, 2005, in one of the bloodiest terrorist roadside bombings to occur in Iraq. " 'Freedom is not free' is a phrase we hear every day, but few of us understand what it means," Hoffman said at his son's funeral. "Justin and the Lima Company understood. They gave up their lives for it."[71]

William McNaughton also has moral authority. His son, James D. McNaughton, had two professions: serving the citizens of New York City as a police officer and serving freedom and democracy as a U.S. military policeman in Iraq. Staff Sergeant McNaughton died by sniper fire in Baghdad on August 2, 2005. His father remarked, "Most people don't know what the word 'samurai' means. It means to serve. He's been serving his whole life."[72]

Of the thousands of parents who have buried children killed in America's War on Terror, why do we never hear from the Linda Ryans, Robert Hoffmans, and William McNaughtons? Why is Cindy Sheehan the one and only family member the Left and Big Media trot out as the marker for the feelings and opinions of military families?

It's the Wahhabi Lobby and their joint endeavors with the hate-America Left . . . that's why.

EIGHT

THE MEASURE OF A NATION

The name of American, which belongs to you, in your national capacity, must always exalt the just pride of Patriotism, more than any appellation derived from local discriminations. . . . Citizens by birth or choice of a common country, that country has a right to concentrate your affections.

> —President George Washington,
> Farewell Address,
> September 17, 1796

I've often wondered why great civilizations fail. I've walked through the ruins in ancient Rome, Athens, Cairo, and Venice reflecting on what once was. And I've always left wondering, "What in the hell happened?"

Now I understand. I'm watching it happen to my country. With our nation engaged in a struggle to defend its civilization, I've seen my military brothers and sisters fighting valiantly and achieving countless successes. Yet I'm also watching as fellow Americans, leading Democratic Party politicians, and the Left's "hate-America" ideologues not only work tirelessly to subvert the military's valiant efforts but in many cases actually want their nation to *lose the war.*

This awful but indispensable ideological struggle has done much more than reveal the valor and courage of our military and the unfathomable evil of our Islamofascist enemies. What has shocked and dismayed me more than the enemy's capacity for unspeakable horrors is the realization that millions of nominally "fellow Americans" willingly and eagerly joined our enemies' cause. This conflict, which clearly sets good versus evil, has unmasked the enemy within—the American Left.

As I pondered in Rome, Athens, Cairo, and Venice, I now ask:

What country sends its men and women to war through national decree knowing some will give their all in sacrifice—yet withers in resolve at the first signs of difficulty and abandons the will to fight?

What country grossly distorts the malfeasance of a few of its people in uniform at a detainee prison while remaining completely blinded to hundreds of thousands of better men and women and their supreme acts of courage and bravery under fire?

What country levels allegations of "torture" at its military without a shred of context while granting more human rights to terrorists than it does to its own warriors?

What country seeks to extend legal representation to those who would rejoice at dragging a cold blade across the throats of its own citizens?

What country grants a national stage and "absolute moral authority" to anti-American radicals while simultaneously denying the voice and moral authority of thousands of similarly grieving families?

What country underwrites an educational system that cultivates hatred for the nation so deep that scholars openly cheer for the country's defeat and the deaths of its soldiers?

What country's moral compass is so skewed that it worships popular culture, bestowing untold wealth, fame, and popularity on its actors and musicians even as their contemptible words and subversive actions embolden enemies around the world?

What country's duly elected politicians, often from both sides of the aisle, shamelessly exploit a conflict they voted to authorize and, by pursuing non-binding resolutions and timetables for withdrawal, barter the sacrifice of American soldiers for political capital?

I'm thoroughly disgusted to say *my* country.

Great civilizations don't collapse because foreign enemies breach the fortress walls—great civilizations die because they rot from within.

The American Left is seeking this outcome. The Left believes America's military is a jackbooted heel to the throat of the world no matter how evil our foe. We rape underdeveloped nations and cause poverty, famine, and tyranny. We—not self-defeatist cultures, murderous ideologies, tyrannical rulers, or stupid ideas— are to blame.

As the radical fringes drag along their more moderately liberal but increasingly impotent fellow travelers, they bring the war home. As they do, they unite in a de facto alliance with America's Islamofascist enemies, their common causes fashioned from the belief that they share the same enemy—the United States and its military.

America as a nation has had to go to war for much of the past hundred years. We have been at war with radical Islamic extremists for decades: Iranian-sponsored attacks on our embassy and Marines in Beirut, Lebanon; the bombing of Pan Am Flight 103 over Lockerbie, Scotland; the World Trade Center bombing in 1993; and the embassy bombings in Kenya and Tanzania are just a few of the many instances of Islamofascist terrorists targeting America. In the years *before* 9/11, Islamic terrorists attacked the

United States more than forty times, murdering more than 450 U.S. citizens (see the chronology in the appendix). In spite of the obvious realities, the Left has chosen to side with our enemies.

In response to years of terror attack upon terror attack, reaching an unspeakable day of destruction on September 11, 2001, America has successfully launched and prosecuted robust military campaigns in Afghanistan and Iraq. We've done so with professionalism and dispatch built upon the sweat, blood, and tears of the greatest military history has ever known. No doubt, there are more battles to come.

From 9/11 on, the Bush Doctrine has been as clear and decisive as the Carter and Clinton years were obtuse and feckless. Composed of ideological retreads from George McGovern's 1972 "Come Home, America" campaign and from the abysmal malaise of the Carter years, the Clinton administration in the wake of Cold War and Gulf War victories turned the world's greatest defense force into a "meals on wheels" service and a petri dish for social engineering. Eight years of Clintonian faux diplomacy, appeasement, and feigned resolve encouraged and emboldened our enemies while making America appear weak and vulnerable.

With the grossly mistaken belief that the end of the Cold War was the end of armed conflict, liberals viewed the crumbling of the Soviet Empire as "the end of history," as an influential book by Francis Fukuyama put it. For the Left it was easier that way.

With history supposedly over—*No more war!*—Bill Clinton swept into power and immediately began pursing social experimentation in the armed forces at the express cost of military capability and morale. And now we have his wife aiming to be commander in chief starting in January 2009.

The Clinton years are best characterized by Mogadishu and the *Black Hawk Down* atrocity; inconsequential excursions into Haiti, Rwanda, and Bosnia; and the failure to respond with military force to eight separate terrorist attacks on America (almost all from al Qaeda).

The Islamofascists were taking notes. In May 1998, Osama bin Laden, referring to Clinton's decision to cut and run in Somalia, told ABC's John Miller:

> After our victory in Afghanistan [over the Soviets] and the defeat of the oppressors who had killed millions of Muslims, the legend about the invincibility of the superpowers vanished. Our boys no longer viewed America as a superpower. So, when they left Afghanistan, they went to Somalia and prepared themselves carefully for a long war. They had thought that the Americans were like the Russians, so they trained and prepared. They were stunned when they discovered how low was the morale of the American soldier. America had entered with 30,000 soldiers in addition to thousands of soldiers from different countries in the world. . . . As I said, our boys were shocked by the low morale of the American soldier and they realized that the American soldier was just a paper tiger.[1]

But the failures aren't limited to just Carter and Clinton. The Left has opposed American military operations for decades. Consider that in the past seventy years, the Left has opposed intervening against Adolf Hitler until Germany attacked the Soviet Union (the political surrogate for American Communists and the Left); opposed U.S. efforts during the Cold War to save Turkey, Greece, South Korea, South Vietnam, Cambodia, Afghanistan, and Grenada from Communist takeover; opposed Ronald Reagan and the military buildup and aggressive posture toward the Soviet Union that won the Cold War; opposed the liberation of Panama from an anti-American drug-trafficking dictator threatening the region; opposed the liberation of Kuwait from Saddam Hussein's Iraq; opposed a military response to 9/11; and opposed the war in Iraq to enforce seventeen United Nations resolutions and to liberate that country from Saddam's murderous regime.

When it entered the White House, the Bush administration clearly understood that the U.S. military's raison d'être was toe-to-toe, tank-to-tank, jet-to-jet dominance based on overwhelming numbers and lethal force. The surest way to defeat the new millennium's first threat *to* freedom was *with* freedom.

AMERICA'S FUTURE

I've seen my country's future. But it wasn't where most Americans would think to look.

I didn't see it strolling across the campus at Stanford University or walking along Hollywood Boulevard amid the glam and glitz of a movie premiere. I looked but couldn't find it while working in the Clinton White House. Nor did I ever experience it listening to politicians blather on the floor of Congress. I certainly didn't see it in our Big Media or in their false idols Cindy Sheehan and Michael Moore.

I saw America's future on the evening of July 14, 2005, while standing just inside the gates of Camp Victory in Baghdad, Iraq. It was approaching 7 P.M. and temperatures still hovered well over 120 degrees. With sand hanging thick in the air, it was a suffocating environment—more oppressive than any I ever experienced in my twenty years as an Air Force pilot.

From nearby, I observed a group of U.S. soldiers preparing to head "outside the wire" (off the camp) to patrol for terrorists. Only an hour earlier I had watched these young men eating dinner at the dining hall, laughing and joking and stealing occasional glances at the large TV blaring news from home. Now, as they manned their Humvees, I detected a wholly new bearing and demeanor. Replacing the pink-faced boys raised on video games and MTV I'd seen in the chow hall were seasoned American warriors sharing encouragement and sober conviction.

With assured calm and trust earned through months together,

they strapped on their battle armor of ceramic helmets and flak vests lined with ceramic plates. Almost in unison, there were sounds of ripping Velcro as the body armor was adjusted and gloves were tightened. In the heat and the blowing sand, their long-sleeve battle dress uniforms (BDUs), wool socks, and boots were already stifling. The armor added another thirty-three pounds.

The gunners climbed into the turrets atop each vehicle. The young Army captain commanding the patrol shared a few thoughts with his driver in solemn confidence before initiating a radio check between the vehicles. "Game faces" on, they rolled out the gates and into the streets of Baghdad, on the hunt for freedom's enemies.

Terrorists were all around—earlier that day a suicide car bomber had plowed into a crowd of children receiving candy from U.S. soldiers, killing twenty-four of them. Yet the soldiers betrayed no sign of trepidation or false bravado. Studying them, I found nothing but quiet, professional resolve in each of them.

These soldiers, I suddenly realized, were members of an exclusive club whose dues are paid in sweat, toil, death, and sorrow.

I had been involved in military operations most of my adult life, in conflicts ranging from Grenada to Somalia to Bosnia to the Persian Gulf, but it wasn't until that moment that I truly understood: I was watching America's best.

The best we have to offer isn't found in our clerisy—the privileged professors, reporters, politicians, or actors—I concluded. It is in America's military—grunts, squids, flyboys, and jarheads.

Out of an American population of some 300 million people, less than one-tenth of 1 percent are involved in this war. Why do they do it? Why do these young men and women leave the relative comfort of the civilian world to serve their nation? How can they go "outside the wire" day after day for several months knowing that this time might be their last?

They go even though they've seen their friends killed or

maimed. They go *because* they've seen their friends killed or maimed. Many refuse to leave the combat zone and many demand to return. They do it because they believe in something—the *idea* of America. They believe that America must do all it can to fight evil, hatred, and oppression. They do all of that and they still smile, they joke, and they have enormous capacity for compassion for the Iraqi and Afghan people.

Major Eric Egland, a veteran of Afghanistan and Iraq, told me, "The highlight of my job [in Iraq] is getting to work with America's sons who leave the gate every day, at least six days per week, every week for at least one year. Each day, they try to accomplish their missions while scanning every inch of roadway wondering if today might be the day that they get hit by a roadside bomb, just like their friend did a few days ago. Whether that friend has returned to duty and is riding next to them, or is in the hospital, or is waiting for them in heaven, each troop gets up, puts his kit together, studies the mission, and goes back out of the gate. Every single day."[2]

Marine Corps Captain Rory Quinn testified, "In four months spent last year near Iraq's border with Syria, I was exposed to the full gamut of emotions and experiences typical of any modern combat tour. I saw corrupt, wicked men captured or killed by 19-year-old Americans who possessed maturity in applying different levels of force that left me in awe. Eleven years ago when I was their age, I wouldn't have held a candle to our 19-year-olds of today. On patrol last year, I saw one old friend and 17 new ones killed by sniper's bullets, exploding artillery shells or hidden land mines. I grieved in the desert and saw 900 comrades do the same. Then I saw our marines lock their grief and rage behind a mental door and go back out the gate to patrol again."[3]

The American soldier is a paradoxical combination of military might and uncommon compassion. Our soldiers are capable of striking our enemies with a devastating fury and a lethality defying description, but they are equally capable of extraordinary decency—they soothe, heal, and build.

Tellingly, they have no difficulty with right and wrong. President Bush is right, Osama bin Laden is wrong. While the Left grasps for nuance, our men and women in uniform don't tolerate moral relativism. The returning vets of World War II internalized the distinctiveness of being an American in their trials and sacrifices and became, as Tom Brokaw put it, America's "greatest generation." Something similar is happening with today's generation of warriors.

America's men and women in uniform—calm, brave, and confident—have recaptured the American spirit lost since the 1960s. American values that have been discarded by recent, more liberal generations flourish among our service members. Classics scholar Victor Davis Hanson picked up on this in the early months of the Iraq War. What drove these men and women to take on the overwhelming challenges they face, Hanson wondered. He concluded that there was "transcendence at work." The military, he realized, "has somehow distilled from the rest of us Americans an elite cohort with the most direct ties to the old breed of the sort who fought at Okinawa, rolled with Patton, and reconstituted Japan."[4]

Directly contrary to what our presumed elites believe to be true, our soldiers stand apart from us because of their extraordinary commitment to selflessness and service. They will come home to a culture that will continue to idealize its elites, but these Americans embrace the value of something much larger. They have found a meaning in their lives that others can never know.

War is an ugly and brutal thing, no doubt. Lord Byron concluded, "War's a brain-spattering, windpipe splitting art." But it's "not the ugliest of things," as John Stuart Mill reminded us. Imagine our world without America's willingness to bear arms when necessary. Where would the world be if the United States had chosen not to intervene militarily in World War I, World War II, the Korean War, the Vietnam War, the Cold War, and the first Gulf War?

In the days following 9/11, Bryan Appleyard wrote a column for the *Sunday Times* of London addressing anti-Americanism and asked his readers to "ponder exactly what the Americans did in that most awful of all centuries, the 20th. They saved Europe from barbarism in two world wars. After the Second World War they rebuilt the continent from the ashes. They confronted and peacefully defeated Soviet Communism, and thereby enforced the slow dismantling—we hope—of Chinese communism, the most murderous system ever devised by man. America, primarily, ejected Iraq from Kuwait and helped us to eject Argentina from the Falklands. America stopped the slaughter in the Balkans while the Europeans dithered."[5]

Indeed, America has used its unmatched military power to liberate the oppressed rather than to claim dominion over others. A rational look at history, as well as the contemporary world, finds much to be grateful for in America's dominance. Through six decades as the world's preeminent military power, America has not expanded its territory by an inch. We only ask for the land necessary to bury our dead.

The U.S. military marches not for conquest but for liberty— even when the liberty we are defending is not our own.

Just consider some of our armed forces' extraordinary accomplishments in the War on Terror. Can you comprehend the impact they are having on our world? Is there any other U.S. institution that can claim to have such a profound influence? In the face of a monstrous enemy, thousands of car bombs and ambushes, relentless naysaying at home, seditious efforts from fellow countrymen specifically designed to circumvent their success, and logistical challenges no other army in the history of the world could have overcome, our men and women in uniform have changed history:

- They have hunted down and killed tens of thousands of al Qaeda terrorists and captured thousands more, preventing further death and destruction; more than two-thirds of the existing al Qaeda leaders have been eliminated or taken into custody.

- They have freed 50 million subjugated people in Afghanistan and Iraq by deposing the barbaric Taliban government and the bloody dictatorship of Saddam Hussein.

- They have captured Saddam, forcing him finally to face justice for his decades of crimes against humanity—and it's doubtful he met his seventy-two virgins.

- They have halted the nuclear black market of A. Q. Khan, which worked covertly with the rogue regimes in North Korea, Iran, and Libya; they also forced Libyan dictator Muammar Qaddafi to come clean on nuclear weapons development—at a time when the vaunted International Atomic Energy Agency was completely unaware he even had a nuclear program.

- They have given stateless populations of Kurds and Shia self-determination.

- Their success in bringing democracy to Iraq inspired Syria to end its twenty-eight-year occupation of Lebanon, Egypt to move toward democratic elections for the first time ever, and Saudi Arabia to hold its first democratic elections at the local level.

- They have treated wounded enemy terrorists; built schools, hospitals, fire stations, electrical grids, and water systems; and immunized millions of children in a blighted region.

Their achievements are astounding. And these accomplishments have come in less than six years since the first American GI boot stepped onto Afghan soil.

Yes, what has America ever done for the world?

This generation of American warriors is redefining itself and our nation. With its unique spirit, honor, and courage, today's U.S. military will dictate the future of our nation just as they've dictated the future for Afghanistan, Iraq, and the Middle East.

Their experiences in Afghanistan and Iraq will underscore their lives forever. Their beliefs have been forever altered and their priorities redefined. Their experiences will affect the career paths they choose, the people they marry, and the ways they raise their children.

They have stared the evil of Islamofascism in the face and have personally seen that pacifism and appeasement are miserably failed concepts. They have seen the depths of evil.

Marine Lieutenant Brian Donlon recalled his experiences in Fallujah in a letter to his friends and supporters back home. "(U.S. Marines) shot dogs and cats caught feasting on the dead, found the mutilated corpse of aid worker Margaret Hassan, discovered a torture chamber with full suits of human skin and refrigerated body parts right out of 'Silence of the Lambs,' opened a cellar with chained men who had starved to death and broke down doors to find rooms full of corpses, hands tied behind their backs, bullet holes in the back of their heads. . . . The enemy they encountered was fanatical and often fought as if pumped up on drugs. His ethnicity was varied and his tactics ranged from insurgents attempting to cross the Euphrates River on inflated beach balls to houses detonated on top of Marines as they entered the first floor."[6]

In another letter written home by a Marine officer and posted on the military weblog 2Slick's Forum, he describes his experiences cleaning out a city full of terrorists. "Along the way, [we] found HUGE caches of weapons, suicide vests, and many foreign fighters. (We) also found unbelievable amounts of drugs, mostly heroin, speed, and cocaine. It turns out, the enemy drugged themselves up to give them the 'courage' and stupidity to stay and

fight. . . . We were very disturbed to find one house with 5 foreigners with bullets in their head, killed execution style. Marines
also came upon a house where an Iraqi soldier in the Iraqi National Guard had been shackled to the wall for 11 days and was
left there to die. . . . [Two] mosques were not being used for
prayer . . . but rather for roadside bomb making. They were literally IED assembly line factories, with hundreds of IEDs complete
or being built. Soldiers [also] . . . came across the dead bodies of
fighters from Chechnya, Syria, Libya, Saudi Arabia, Jordan,
Afghanistan, and so on. . . . No, this was not just a city of pissed
off Iraqis, mad at the Coalition for forcing Saddam out of power.
It was a city full of people from all over the Middle East whose
sole mission in life was to kill Americans."[7]

As the U.S. Army's 3rd Armored Calvary Regiment prepared
to return home from its deployment to Tall 'Afar, Iraq, the local
mayor, Najim Abdullah Abid Al-Jibouri, sent the troops a letter of
thanks. It read,

To the Courageous Men and Women of the 3d Armored
Cavalry Regiment, who have changed the city of Tall 'Afar
from a ghost town, in which terrorists spread death and destruction, to a secure city flourishing with life.

To the lion-hearts who liberated our city from the grasp of
terrorists who were beheading men, women and children in
the streets for many months.

To those who spread smiles on the faces of our children,
and gave us restored hope, through their personal sacrifice
and brave fighting, and gave new life to the city after hope-
lessness darkened our days, and stole our confidence in our
ability to reestablish our city.

Our city was the main base of operations for Abu Mousab
Al Zarqawi. The city was completely held hostage in the
hands of his henchmen. Our schools, governmental services,
businesses and offices were closed. Our streets were silent,

and no one dared to walk them. Our people were barricaded in their homes out of fear; death awaited them around every corner. Terrorists occupied and controlled the only hospital in the city. Their savagery reached such a level that they stuffed the corpses of children with explosives and tossed them into the streets in order to kill grieving parents attempting to retrieve the bodies of their young. This was the situation of our city until God prepared and delivered unto them the courageous soldiers of the 3d Armored Cavalry Regiment, who liberated this city, ridding it of Zarqawi's followers after harsh fighting, killing many terrorists, and forcing the remaining butchers to flee the city like rats to the surrounding areas, where the bravery of other 3d ACR soldiers in Sinjar, Rabiah, Zumar and Avgani finally destroyed them.

I have met many soldiers of the 3d Armored Cavalry Regiment; they are not only courageous men and women, but avenging angels sent by The God Himself to fight the evil of terrorism.

The leaders of this Regiment, COL McMaster, COL Armstrong, LTC Hickey, LTC Gibson, and LTC Reilly, embody courage, strength, vision and wisdom. Officers and soldiers alike bristle with the confidence and character of knights in a bygone era. The mission they have accomplished, by means of a unique military operation, stands among the finest military feats to date in Operation Iraqi Freedom, and truly deserves to be studied in military science. This military operation was clean, with little collateral damage, despite the ferocity of the enemy. With the skill and precision of surgeons they dealt with the terrorist cancers in the city without causing unnecessary damage.

God bless this brave Regiment; God bless the families who dedicated these brave men and women. From the bottom of our hearts we thank the families. They have given us something we will never forget. To the families of those who have given their holy blood for our land, we all bow to you in reverence and to the souls of your loved ones. Their sacrifice was not in vain. They are not dead, but alive, and their souls hovering around us every second of every minute. They will never be forgotten for giving their precious lives. They have sacrificed that which is most valuable. We see them in the smile of every child, and in every flower growing in this land. Let America, their families, and the world be proud of their sacrifice for humanity and life.

Finally, no matter how much I write or speak about this brave Regiment, I haven't the words to describe the courage of its officers and soldiers. I pray to God to grant happiness and health to these legendary heroes and their brave families.

Najim Abdullah Abid Al-Jibouri
Mayor of Tall 'Afar, Ninewa, Iraq[8]

Yet the American Left considers the "insurgents" to be "freedom fighters" and America's military to be barbarians.

They should read this letter from Special Forces Captain Jeffrey P. Toczylowski to his family:

If you are getting this e-mail, it means I have passed away. . . . Please don't be sad for me. It was an honor to serve my country, and I wouldn't change a thing. It was just my time.

Don't ever think that you are defending me by slamming the global war on terrorism or the U.S. goals in that war. As far as I am concerned, we can send guys like me to go after them, or we can wait for them to come back to us again. I died doing something I believed in and have no regrets except that I couldn't do more.[9]

I have seen America's future and it is bright.

IT'S A WAR AND YOU'RE THE TARGET

"You may not be interested in war, but war is interested in you."
—Leon Trotsky, 1917

Let's be brutally clear. This war is not about Iraq or Afghanistan; those are simply battles in a greater war. Radical Islam has set out to establish a Grand Caliphate, embarking on a religious war in order to implement extremist Salafism and Islamic law across the world. The enemy stretches from North America to Indonesia and involves at least eighty al Qaeda–affiliated movements. This is a war whose plan was written in blood 1,400 years ago.

Al Qaeda's number two, Ayman al-Zawahiri, laid it all out in the letter he wrote to the terrorists' key man in Iraq, Abu Masab al-Zarqawi, in the summer of 2005: The first stage in their plan is to expel America from Iraq; after that they will establish the caliphate in Iraq, expand the caliphate to Iraq's neighbors, destroy Israel, and expand the caliphate across the region.[10]

The truth is that today wars cannot be won solely on the battlefields, and they can most definitely be lost off of them. This is why the Left represents the single greatest obstacle to U.S. success in the War on Terror. At their nation's time of need in this global ideological battle, the American Left has climbed into bed with our enemies.

While we battle our fundamentalist Islamic enemy abroad, the Left insidiously works from within. They demoralize our brave men and women in uniform and drain our nation of its resolve to fight by convincing politicians and the general public that this is a war we cannot endure fighting any longer. Such erosion of America's resolve is precisely what the Islamofascists want, for they understand that the United States cannot be beaten militarily. Their only hope is that Americans become so demoralized that they run from the fight. The terrorists represent a grave danger, without doubt, but it is only through their unholy alliance with the American Left that they threaten the survival of America.

The American people are the only ones who can decide whether to carry on to victory or give up in failure and defeat. This is our war. And our military. We are the soldiers. We are the weapons. We are the targets of the enemy strategy. Our hearts, our spirit are the front line. This is our war, more than it is the Marines' or the Army's, or the Islamofascists'.

When I asked Army Sergeant Joe Skelly what he thought about the constant undermining of the media and politicians back home, he succinctly answered, "The American people are the center of gravity in this war. They need to understand that."[11]

Are we really going to let them do it again? Are we going to let tremendous military successes and burgeoning democracies in Iraq and Afghanistan give way to another demoralizing national embarrassment? Are we going to return to the failed policies of another Carter or Clinton? Are we really that weak? Our troops deserve so much more. Our response will forever define us and shape the century to come.

Sergeant Eddie Jeffers provided the overwhelming sentiment of the men and women in uniform I spoke with in the hundreds of interviews I conducted for this book. In a letter he wrote to his father, retired Army Master Sergeant Dave Jeffers, he noted that "People like Cindy Sheehan are ignorant. Not just to this war, but to the results of their idiotic ramblings, or at least I hope they are," concluded Jeffers. "They don't realize its effects on this war. . . . The enemy slinks in the shadows and fights a coward's war against us. It is effective though, as many men and women have died since the start of this war. And the memory of their service to America is tainted by the inconsiderate remarks on our nation's news outlets. And every day, the enemy changes . . . only now, the enemy is becoming something new. The enemy is transitioning from the Muslim extremists to Americans. The enemy is becoming the very people whom we defend with our lives. And they do not realize it. But in denouncing our actions, denouncing our leaders, denouncing the war we live and fight, they are isolating the military from society . . . and they are becoming our enemy."[12]

To win this long ideological war with Islamofascism we need our media to present a balanced picture, our schools to address their bigotry toward their nation, our elected leaders to stand together, our popular culture to root for the home team—none of which is occurring at this point.

In his address to the nation soon after the attacks of September 11, 2001, President George W. Bush laid out in unmistakable terms the nature of the war that lay ahead. The War on Terror would be a "long struggle," he made clear. He reminded Americans that "our resolve must not pass," for America now had a mission it had no choice but to see through to the end.

"We have suffered great loss," Bush said. "And in our grief and anger we have found our mission and our moment. Freedom and fear are at war. The advance of human freedom—the great achievement of our time, and the great hope of every time—now depends on us."

President Bush was absolutely right about the stakes involved in the global War on Terror. Unfortunately, he did not anticipate the strength of the enemy within.

"We will," Bush said, "rally the world to this cause by our efforts, by our courage. We will not tire, we will not falter, and we will not fail."[13]

Less than five years later, we are already tiring, already faltering—all owing to the relentless efforts of the American Left. And if they have their way, we will ultimately fail.

It's up to us to keep that from happening.

APPENDIX

———

WHY WE FIGHT

FEBRUARY 1, 1979—THE FIRST RADICAL ISLAMIC TERROR STATE IS BORN: With encouragement from President Jimmy Carter, Iranian shah Reza Pahlavi, a longtime American ally, is forced from power. Radical cleric Ayatollah Khomeini assumes the Iranian leadership. "We will export our revolution to the four corners of the world," Khomeini declares only ten days later. "Islam makes it incumbent on all adult males, provided they are not disabled or incapacitated, to prepare themselves for the conquest of countries so that the writ of Islam is obeyed in every country in the world. But those who study Islamic Holy War will understand why Islam wants to conquer the whole world." Carter's decision to support Khomeini's ascension leads directly to the first radical Islamic state-sponsored terrorism and will launch a series of cataclysmic events in the Middle East.

FEBRUARY 14, 1979—ISLAMIC EXTREMISTS KIDNAP AND KILL THE U.S. AMBASSADOR TO AFGHANISTAN: Ambassador Adolph Dubs is taken hostage by Islamic extremists attempting to secure the release of several "religious figures." He is killed in a rain of gunfire between Afghan police and his captors.

JULY 16, 1979—SADDAM HUSSEIN BEGINS HIS MURDEROUS REIGN IN IRAQ:
In a ruthless coup within his Baath Party, Saddam Hussein seizes power from his frail older relative President Ahmed Hassan al-Bakr. His first act of leadership is to identify all "spies" and "conspirators" among his party and have them assassinated—the first of some 2 million people his regime will murder or torture.

NOVEMBER 4, 1979—KHOMEINI DECLARES WAR ON THE UNITED STATES:
Under Ayatollah Khomeini's direct control, a mob of approximately 500 Iranian students calling themselves the "Imam's Disciples" overrun and seize the American Embassy in Tehran. Sixty-six American diplomats are taken hostage in this act of war, and one of the most humiliating foreign policy disasters in American history unfolds over 444 days. Carter's bumbling foreign policy and betrayal of the Shah has launched a series of cataclysmic events in the Middle East and Islam's war with America has begun.

Immediately Iran positions itself on the front lines in the conflict between the Palestinians and the Israelis, establishing the terror group Hezbollah ("The Party of God") in Lebanon. It also begins attacks on the United States. "We are at war with America as our Prophet was at war against the corrupt regimes of his time," Khomeini declares. "Because we believe that Islam is the one and only true faith, it is incumbent on us to fight until the entire humanity either converts or submits to Islamic authority."

NOVEMBER 20, 1979—ISLAMIC FUNDAMENTALISTS SEIZE THE GRAND MOSQUE IN MECCA, SAUDI ARABIA: Just days following the storming of the American Embassy in Tehran, hundreds of well-armed Islamic fundamentalists seize the Grand Mosque, the holiest site in Islam. Juhayman al-Utaybi, the leader of the insurgents, is a direct descendant of the Wahhabi warriors who helped the Al Saud family assume power in the 1920s.

Al-Utaybi's radicals call for a return to pure Islam and denounce modernization, accusing the Saudi royal family of corruption and loss of legitimacy because of dealings with the West. Saudi and French forces eventually retake the mosque in a battle in which 250 are killed and 600 wounded.

Iran's new ruler, Ayatollah Khomeini, blames the United States for the takeover, inflaming the Muslim world. The U.S. embassies in Pakistan and Libya are attacked and torched, and four are killed.

The House of Saud is forced to increase its religious standing in the kingdom by implementing a more fundamental Islamic agenda. Saudi Arabia begins pumping millions of dollars into religious education, creating new theological schools designed to produce large numbers of Wahhabi clerics.

DECEMBER 25, 1979—THE SOVIET UNION INVADES AFGHANISTAN: Once the United States loses its strategic foothold in Iran, the Soviets invade neighboring Afghanistan.

The war will last until 1989, when the Soviet Union finally is forced to retreat. More important, the conflict will establish the epicenter for young Muslim jihadists from across the world. Between 1980 and 1989, approximately 35,000 Muslim radicals from forty Islamic countries will come together in Afghanistan to fight the Soviet Union. Tens of thousands more will come to study in Pakistani madrassas. Eventually, more than 100,000 foreign Muslim radicals will be directly influenced by the Afghan jihad, including Saudi national Osama bin Laden.

DECEMBER 26, 1979—OSAMA BIN LADEN GOES TO AFGHANISTAN TO FIGHT THE SOVIETS: Only days after the Soviet Union invades Afghanistan, bin Laden sets up a base in Peshawar, Pakistan, and begins raising funds to provide the mujahedeen with logistical and humanitarian aid. He forms the Maktab al-Khadamāt (the "Office of Services") with his mentor Abdullah Azzam.

From 1986 on, bin Laden fights in numerous battles as a guerrilla commander, including a fierce battle at Jalalabad that ultimately leads the Soviets to withdraw. It is in Peshawar that bin Laden first meets Egyptian doctor Ayman al-Zawahiri.

OCTOBER 6, 1981—ISLAMIC EXTREMISTS ASSASSINATE EGYPTIAN PRESIDENT ANWAR SADAT: Three years after making peace with Israel, President Sadat is assassinated by Muslim extremists as he presides over Egypt's annual military parade. Cleric Sheikh Omar Abdel Rahman, the "Blind Sheikh," who will later be convicted for his involvement in the 1993 World Trade Center bombing, issued the fatwa sanctioning Sadat's assassination.

JANUARY 18, 1982—LEBANESE TERRORISTS MURDER U.S. ARMY LIEUTENANT COLONEL CHARLES RAY: Ray, a military attaché to the American Embassy in France, is shot and killed outside of his Paris apartment by the Lebanese Armed Revolutionary Faction.

AUGUST 11, 1982—PALESTINIAN TERRORISTS BOMB PAN AM FLIGHT 830 TO HONOLULU, HAWAII: A Pan Am jet traveling from Tokyo, Japan, to Honolulu, Hawaii, explodes at 36,000 feet as the plane prepares to descend. A Japanese student is killed and 15 people are injured. The bomber is Mohammed Rashid, a member of the radical Palestinian organization known as the 15 May Organization. Rashid will eventually be captured and tried for his role in the 1986 bombing of TWA Flight 840 near Athens, Greece.

APRIL 18, 1983—HEZBOLLAH BOMBS THE U.S. EMBASSY IN BEIRUT, LEBANON: Sixty-three people, including the CIA's Middle East director and 16 other Americans, are murdered, while 120 are injured, when an explosives-laden vehicle laden is detonated in the U.S. Embassy compound. U.S. intelligence intercepted a pre-attack cable from the Iranian foreign ministry to the Iranian Embassy in Syria approving payment for a terrorist attack in Beirut. The attack is carried out by Iranian-backed Hezbollah guerrillas operating in Lebanon using "Islamic Jihad" as a cover name.

This marks the first of several Hezbollah attacks on the United States.

OCTOBER 23, 1983—HEZBOLLAH BOMBS THE U.S. MARINES HEADQUARTERS IN BEIRUT: Hezbollah terrorists send a large truck loaded with 2,500 pounds of TNT through the main gate of the U.S. Marine headquarters, killing 241 Americans. The Marines are part of a multinational force sent at the request of the Lebanese government to assist in separating warring factions.

Two minutes later, another truck packed with explosives slams into a French paratrooper base two miles away, killing 58 soldiers and the driver.

Thirteen individuals are connected to the attack, including Mohammed Hussein Fadlallah, the leader of the Hezbollah group, and Hussein Musawi (Mussavi), a leader of the Islamic Amal group, also linked to Iran. Syrian officers and the then-Iranian ambassador to Lebanon, Ali Akbar Mohtashami, are also implicated in the bombings.

DECEMBER 12, 1983—IRANIAN-SPONSORED TERRORISTS BOMB THE U.S. EMBASSY ANNEX IN KUWAIT: An explosives-laden truck crashes into the compound of the U.S. Embassy Annex in Kuwait, killing 6 and wounding 80. The Embassy Annex is one of six installations attacked in Kuwait that day, including the French Embassy, the control tower at the airport, the country's main oil refinery, and a residential area for employees of the American corporation Raytheon.

Seventeen terrorists who are members of the Iranian-sponsored Al Dawa ("The Call") Party are arrested and convicted for the attacks. One of those convicted is Mustafa Youssef

Badreddin, the cousin and brother-in-law of Hezbollah senior officer Imad Mughniyah. Saddam Hussein's forces will release all seventeen terrorists after Iraq invades Kuwait in 1990.

1982–1992—HEZBOLLAH KIDNAPS AND MURDERS NUMEROUS U.S. OFFICIALS IN LEBANON: The kidnapping of American University of Beirut president David Dodge in July 1982 commences a series of kidnappings and murders of Americans conducted by Hezbollah. In all, 30 Westerners are kidnapped over ten years, including Americans Dodge; William Buckley, the CIA Beirut station chief; Terry Anderson, a journalist; Peter Kilburn, an American University of Beirut librarian; Benjamin Weir, a Presbyterian minister; Edward Tracy, a businessman; Jesse Turner; Thomas Sutherland; and Alann Steen.

One of the most gruesome atrocities is the abduction, torture, and killing of U.S. Marine Lieutenant Colonel Richard Higgins, a United Nations official observing the peace in Lebanon. Higgins is kidnapped in February 1988 and is interrogated and tortured before his murder. In a videotape distributed by the terrorists, Higgins's body is shown hanging from a rope. Hezbollah dumps his body onto the street in Beirut in 1991.

JANUARY 18, 1984—HEZBOLLAH MURDERS AMERICAN UNIVERSITY OF BEIRUT PRESIDENT MALCOLM KERR: Two Hezbollah gunmen shoot and kill Kerr while he walks to his office.

SEPTEMBER 20, 1984—HEZBOLLAH BOMBS THE U.S. EMBASSY ANNEX IN AUKAR, LEBANON: The Iranian-sponsored terror group strikes once again, sending an explosive-laden van into the compound at the U.S. Embassy, which has been relocated from Beirut. The resulting explosion 30 feet from the embassy annex kills 9 and injures 58.

APRIL 12, 1985—TERRORISTS BOMB A RESTAURANT NEAR TORREJON AIR BASE IN MADRID, SPAIN: A bomb is detonated in a restaurant popular with American servicemen near the U.S. Air Force Base outside of Madrid, Spain, killing 18 and wounding 82 (including 18 Americans). It is the worst act of terrorism in Spain since the end of the Spanish Civil War in 1939. Spanish authorities determine that Hezbollah is responsible. No arrests are ever made, however. According to Spanish officials, it is the only major terrorist attack in the country's modern history that has not been solved.

JUNE 14, 1985—TERRORISTS HIJACK TWA FLIGHT 847: TWA Flight 847, bound for Rome with 39 Americans aboard, is hijacked over the Mediterranean Sea by members of Hezbollah and forced to land in Beirut, Lebanon. The hijackers, demanding the release of hundreds of Shiite Muslim prisoners held by Israel, single out U.S. Navy diver Robert Stethem, beat him, shoot him in the head, and throw his body onto the tarmac. The four hijackers are eventually set free after being offered transportation to Damascus and the release of the 435 Lebanese and Palestinian Shiite prisoners in Israel.

In 1987 German officials will arrest hijacker Mohammed Hamadei at the Frankfurt airport with a suitcase containing liquid explosives. German authorities convict Hamadei and sentence him to life imprisonment for the murder of Stethem. The remaining three terrorists are never captured and their whereabouts remain unknown.

Hamadei will be released by Germany in 2005.

AUGUST 8, 1985—LEFT-WING TERROR GROUP BOMBS RHEIN-MAIN AIR BASE IN FRANKFURT, GERMANY: A car bomb detonates at the main U.S. Air Force base in Germany, killing 2 and wounding 20. The next day a U.S. serviceman's body is found; he apparently was killed for his identification card. The terrorists responsible for the bombing come from the Red Army Faction, or Baader-Meinhof Group, a radical left-wing German terror organization that trained at a Palestinian terror camp in 1970.

OCTOBER 7, 1985—PALESTINIAN TERRORISTS HIJACK THE *ACHILLE LAURO*: Four Palestinian hijackers commandeer the Italian cruise liner *Achille Lauro* off the Egyptian coast and hold more than 700 tourists hostage. Demanding the release of Palestinian prisoners held in Israel and elsewhere, the terrorists shoot and kill elderly wheelchair-bound New Yorker Leon Klinghoffer and push his body overboard.

The Palestine Liberation Front's Abu Abbas facilitates the terrorists' surrender and release. The four hijackers and Abbas fly out of Egypt for safe haven but are intercepted by four U.S. Navy F-14 Tomcat jets and forced to land at Sigonella Naval Air Base in Sicily, where U.S. special operations forces await them.

Italian authorities arrest the four hijackers but refuse to hold Abbas, who is allowed to fly to Belgrade, Yugoslavia, under diplomatic cover. Abbas will be arrested by U.S. forces in Baghdad in April 2003.

NOVEMBER 23, 1985—TERRORISTS HIJACK EGYPT AIR FLIGHT 648: The Abu Nidal Organization hijacks Egypt Air Flight 648 en route from Athens to Cairo, forcing it to land on the island of Malta. The terrorists shoot 3 Americans and 2 Israelis in the head and dump their bodies onto the tarmac. Egyptian commandos storm the plane, and 60 more are killed in the ensuing battle.

Abu Nidal, perhaps the most ruthless terrorist in the world and "the father of the struggle," will receive safe haven in Saddam Hussein's Iraq in 1999. But in late 2002 Saddam's security forces will assassinate him, because they knew the United States was coming and they were covering up their terror ties.

DECEMBER 27, 1985—THE ABU NIDAL ORGANIZATION ATTACKS AIRLINE COUNTERS IN ROME AND VIENNA: Terrorists from the Abu Nidal Organization storm airports in Rome and Vienna, tossing hand grenades and firing automatic weapons at TWA and El Al airline ticket counters. They kill 20 and wound 110. Airport security forces kill 4 of the 7 terrorists.

In January 1986, Italy issues an international warrant for the arrest of Abu Nidal for mass murder. He will be tried in absentia and sentenced to life imprisonment in 1988.

APRIL 2, 1986—THE ARAB REVOLUTIONARY CELL BOMBS TWA FLIGHT 840: A terror group calling itself the Arab Revolutionary Cell, with ties to Abu Nidal and Yassir Arafat, detonates a bomb on board TWA 840 as it descends into Athens for landing. Four Americans, including an infant, are sucked out of the fuselage to their deaths. Five others are injured.

APRIL 5, 1986—ABU NIDAL, WITH THE HELP OF THE LIBYAN REGIME, BOMBS A WEST BERLIN DISCO: A bomb placed in the restroom of a discotheque frequented by U.S. military personnel explodes, killing 3 and injuring more than 200, including 44 Americans. Libya and Abu Nidal are responsible for the attack, and in response President Ronald Reagan launches Operation El Dorado Canyon, sending U.S. Air Force and Navy fighters and bombers to attack Tripoli and Benghazi, Libya. Forced to fly around French airspace, Air Force F-111s accidentally bomb the French Embassy in Tripoli.

SEPTEMBER 5, 1986—ABU NIDAL HIJACKS PAN AM FLIGHT 73 IN KARACHI, PAKISTAN: Four terrorists from the Abu Nidal Organization storm Pan Am Flight 73. Jordanian terrorist Zayd Hassan Safarini shoots American passenger Rajesh Kumar in the head execution-style and pushes Kumar's body onto the tarmac. After dark, Safarini and the other hijackers order all of the passengers to the center of the aircraft, then say a martyrdom prayer and unleash a barrage of hand grenades and automatic weapons. Twenty passengers are killed and more than 100 are injured in the attack.

1988—BIN LADEN ESTABLISHES AL QAEDA ("THE BASE"): Bin Laden starts al Qaeda, seeing the need to shift the fighting away from the Soviets and toward an international jihad that will reunite the Muslim world under a single leader and reestablish "the Caliphate." According to the CIA, al Qaeda will eventually establish terror cells in fifty countries.

APRIL 14, 1988—TERRORISTS BOMB THE USO CLUB IN NAPLES, ITALY: A car bomb explodes outside of the United Service Organization club in Naples, killing 5 (including one U.S. naval sailor) and injuring 15 (including four U.S. sailors). The terror group Japanese Red Army, working at the direction of the Popular Front for the Liberation of Palestine, is responsible for the attack.

DECEMBER 21, 1988—PALESTINIAN TERRORISTS AND THE LIBYAN REGIME BOMB PAN AM FLIGHT 103: En route from London to New York, Pan Am Flight 103 explodes over Lockerbie, Scotland, killing 270 innocent people, including 189 Americans. The bomb was packed into a Toshiba radio-cassette recorder in the luggage compartment. The Popular Front for the Liberation of Palestine and the Libyan government are responsible for the attack. Libyans Abdelbaset Ali Mohmed Al Megrahi and Al Amin Khalifa Fhimah will be indicted for murder. Libyan president Muammar Qaddafi will turn over the terrorists in 1999 and formally accept responsibility for the attack in 2003.

1989—OSAMA BIN LADEN RETURNS TO SAUDI ARABIA: After the Soviets pull out of Afghanistan, bin Laden returns to Saudi Arabia as a hero. He opposes the Saudi monarchy while working for his family's construction firm, the Bin Laden Group.

JANUARY 18–19, 1991—IRAQI AGENTS ATTEMPT BOMBINGS OF AMERICANS IN INDONESIA, THE PHILIPPINES, AND THAILAND: In Indonesia, an Iraqi posing as a contractor plants a bomb at U.S. ambassador John Monjo's residence. The bomb is discovered by a gardener before it detonates and is immediately defused.

In the Philippines, two Iraqi agents target Manila's Thomas Jefferson Cultural Center, but as they prepare the bomb it explodes, killing one of the terrorists. Iraqi diplomat Muwafak al-Ani is deported after Philippine investigators discover that an embassy car dropped the bombers off at the target and find al-Ani's card in one of the terrorist's pocket. Later, the Iraqi Embassy's second secretary, Husham Z Hussein, will also be expelled after it is determined that he was in close contact with members of the al Qaeda–associated terror organization, the Abu Sayyaf Group.

In Thailand, two Iraqi diplomats are deported after they are found smuggling explosives into the country. According to former UN weapons inspector Richard Butler, their targets were the U.S., Israeli, and Australian embassies in Bangkok.

APRIL, 1991—BIN LADEN FLEES SAUDI ARABIA FOR SUDAN: Bin Laden flees Saudi Arabia after his opposition to Saudi Arabia's alliance with the United States lands him in detention. After briefly staying in Afghanistan, he relocates to Khartoum, Sudan, where in 1992 he reestablishes al Qaeda headquarters. Hundreds of suspected terrorists and former mujahedeen also relocate to Sudan for safe haven, and bin Laden establishes a number of camps for training in firearms and explosives. In 1994, Saudi Arabia will revoke bin Laden's citizenship and his family will disown him.

DECEMBER 29, 1992—AL QAEDA'S FIRST ATTACK: A bomb is detonated in a hotel in Aden, Yemen, where U.S. troops stayed on their way to the humanitarian mission in Somalia. The soldiers depart the hotel prior to the attack, but two Austrian tourists are killed. Two Yemeni Muslim militants who trained in Afghanistan are injured in the blast and arrested. They will eventually be released, only to collaborate in the bombing of the USS *Cole* in 2000.

JANUARY 25, 1993—A LONE GUNMAN ATTACKS CIA HEADQUARTERS IN LANGLEY, VIRGINIA: Pakastani Mir Aimal Kasi jumps from a car outside Central Intelligence Agency headquarters in Langley and fires an AK-47 assault machine gun, killing two CIA employees and wounding three others. Kasi trained with Afghani jihadists during the war with the Soviet Union.

After the attacks at Langley, Kasi quickly boards a flight to Pakistan. After years of investigation, in 1997 the FBI will apprehend Kasi on the border between Afghanistan and Pakistan and return him to the United States to stand trial. He will be convicted of murder and killed by lethal injection on November 14, 2002.

In retaliation for Kasi's guilty verdict, four American oil company employees and their driver will be gunned down in the Pakistani port city of Karachi.

FEBRUARY 26, 1993—THE FIRST WORLD TRADE CENTER BOMBING: Thirty-eight days into President Bill Clinton's presidency, an explosive-laden Ryder van is detonated in a hotel parking garage beneath New York's World Trade Center, killing 7 people (including an unborn child) and wounding 1,040. The blast creates a 100-by-100-foot crater.

Al Qaeda associate Ramzi Yousef, also a veteran of bin Laden's camps in Peshawar, Pakistan, planned the attack. The morning after the blast, Yousef escapes to Pakistan, disappointed he hasn't had more success. He vows to return and finish the job. "Our calculations were not very accurate this time. However we promise you that next time it will be very precise and the Trade Center will be one of our targets." Eventually, Yousef will move on to the Philippines at the direction of bin Laden and begin early preparation for Operation Bojinka—the precursor to the 9/11 attacks.

In the first of his many failures to confront terrorism, President Clinton cautions Americans not to overreact to the World Trade Center bombing, and in an interview for MTV he attributes the attack to someone "who did something really stupid." At first Clinton even downplays the possibility that terror was involved, preferring to believe that the explosion was the result of an electric generator—even though several radical Islamic groups claimed responsibility.

Fortunately, bomber Mohammed Salameh's stupidity tips off law enforcement. His incessant demands for a refund of $400 for the van give the FBI the lead it needs. Salameh becomes the first of eight terror suspects arrested. Some are actually caught in the act of mixing explosive materials for attacks on the United Nations, the George Washington Bridge, and two tunnels into the city.

In July 1993, Sheik Omar Abdel Rahman, the blind cleric who was behind the assassination of Egyptian president Anwar Sadat, is indicted along with fourteen other suspects.

In March 1994, four of the terrorists—Nidal Ayyad, Mohammed Salameh, Ahmad Ajaj, and Mahmud Abouhalima—are convicted and each is sentenced to 240 years in prison without parole.

In October 1995, Sheik Rahman and nine of his followers are convicted of plotting the bombings and planning other acts of terror in New York. In January 1996, Rahman is sentenced to life without parole plus 65 years and the others are given terms from 25 years to life.

APRIL 14, 1993—IRAQI INTELLIGENCE AGENTS ATTEMPT THE ASSASSINATION OF PRESIDENT GEORGE H. W. BUSH: The Iraqi Intelligence Service attempts to assassinate former president Bush as he visits Kuwait to celebrate the coalition victory and the removal of Saddam Hussein two years earlier. Kuwaiti security forces uncover the plot to load 175 pounds of explosives into a Toyota Land Cruiser and detonate them in proximity to President Bush; the security forces immediately round up seventeen suspects associated with the plot.

OCTOBER 3–4, 1993—"BLACK HAWK DOWN": The Battle for Mogadishu occurs, thanks to the miscalculation of President Bill Clinton. President George H. W. Bush originally deployed 28,000 U.S. troops to Mogadishu, Somalia, as part of a humanitarian mission to feed drought-stricken Somalis. But when President Clinton inherited the mission, he immediately reduced troop levels to only 4,500. In a demonstration of ignorance and tragic miscalculation, he also dramatically expanded the scope of the mission, moving from humanitarian aid to nation-building and targeting Somali warlord Mohammad Farah Aidid.

In the days leading up to the Battle for Mogadishu, U.S. Army General William Garrison, commander of the U.S. troops, formally requests much-needed armored vehicles, tanks, and AC-130 Spectre gunships. The Clinton administration, through Secretary of Defense Les Aspin, denies the request.

On October 3, members of the U.S. Task Force Ranger are ambushed as they raid the Olympic Hotel in Mogadishu, where a meeting of warlord Aidid's lieutenants is under way. The Somali fighters, who have been trained by al Qaeda and bin Laden, shoot down two Black Hawk helicopters and drag the American dead in the streets through wildly cheering mobs. Eighteen elite U.S. soldiers are killed and 84 wounded.

Democratic congressman John Murtha urges Clinton to begin an immediate and complete pullout of U.S. troops from the region. Clinton takes the advice and orders the withdrawal only four days after the battle.

Osama bin Laden learns a valuable lesson that day. He will

later say that America's withdrawal was what convinced him that America could be attacked with impunity: "Our boys no longer viewed America as a superpower. So, when they left Afghanistan [after defeating the Soviet Union], they went to Somalia and prepared themselves carefully for a long war. They had thought that the Americans were like the Russians, so they trained and prepared. They were stunned when they discovered how low was the morale of the American soldier. . . . They realized that the American soldier was just a paper tiger. After a few blows, it forgot all about those titles and rushed out of Somalia in shame and disgrace, dragging the bodies of its soldiers."

DECEMBER 8, 1994—OPERATION BOJINKA BEGINS IN THE PHILIPPINES: Al Qaeda member Ramzi Yousef joins his uncle Khalid Sheikh Mohammed, Wali Khan Amin Shah, and Abdul Hakim Ali Hashim Murad in Manila to begin Operation Bojinka, the precursor to the 9/11 attacks.

The planned operation has three phases: (1) the assassination of Pope John Paul II, (2) the bombings of multiple commercial airliners as they head to the United States, and (3) piloting and crashing commercial airliners into U.S. targets: CIA headquarters, the Pentagon, the World Trade Center, the Sears Tower in Chicago, the Transamerica Tower in San Francisco, and a nuclear power plant. The money for the operation comes to the terrorists in Manila from Osama bin Laden through his brother-in-law Mohammed Jamal Khalifa.

The assassination of the pope is designed to be a diversion for the second phase. To prepare for the last phase, Murad has trained as a pilot in North Carolina, and several other al Qaeda operatives now attend flight schools in the United Sates.

On the night of January 6, 1995, a fire begins inside the terrorists' apartment as Yousef and Murad inadvertently cross bomb-making chemicals. Responding to the complaints of residents, the

Philippine police stumble onto a treasure trove of terrorist evidence. Just two weeks prior to its implementation, Operation Bojinka is busted.

Murad confesses and is extradited to the United States, where he is sentenced to life imprisonment. Shah is arrested in Malaysia and extradited to the United States, where he also is sentenced to life imprisonment. Khalifa, bin Laden's brother-in-law and al Qaeda's moneyman, is arrested in Mountain View, California, as he prepares to fly to Manila; he is arrested for his involvement in the 1993 World Trade Center bombing.

In March 1995, Philippine authorities forward the information about the foiled Bojinka plot to the U.S. government, including specific details that Khalifa was the funding source for the terrorist operation. The FBI argues to detain Khalifa for questioning, but the Clinton administration sides with the State Department and deports Khalifa to Jordan, where he is acquitted on murder charges unrelated to the attack in the United States and is allowed to flee to Saudi Arabia.

In April 1995, the Clinton administration receives specific evidence of terror plans to hijack airliners and use them as flying weapons in New York and Washington, D.C. Nothing is done. Only a year later the president will personally turn down an offer from the Sudanese government for Osama bin Laden's arrest and extradition to the United States.

FEBRUARY 7, 1995—RAMZI YOUSEF IS CAPTURED IN PAKISTAN: Operation Bojinka planner Yousef is apprehended while staying at a hotel in Islamabad, Pakistan, by members of the U.S. Diplomatic Security Service. After extradition to the United States, he will be convicted and sentenced to life imprisonment plus 240 years for his involvement in the 1993 World Trade Center bombing.

Khalid Shaikh Mohammed will successfully escape Manila and rejoin al Qaeda in Afghanistan, becoming the architect for future operations. He will propose turning Yousef's Operation Bojinka into a new attack on a grander scale. Mohammed's plot will be executed on September 11, 2001. Yousef will watch his plan unfold on cable TV from his cell in Colorado's "Supermax" penitentiary.

MARCH 8, 1995—AL QAEDA–AFFILIATED TERRORISTS MURDER U.S. DIPLOMATS IN PAKISTAN: Three armed gunmen in a stolen taxi step from their vehicle and begin firing on a U.S. Embassy van in Karachi, Pakistan. U.S. diplomats Jacqueline Keys Van Landingham and Gary C. Durell are killed and Mark McCloy is wounded.

The attack comes as retaliation for the capture of Ramzi Yousef a month earlier and is carried out by the al Qaeda–affiliated Abu Sayyaf Group.

NOVEMBER 13, 1995—BIN LADEN–CONNECTED TERRORISTS BOMB THE U.S. MILITARY TRAINING COMPLEX IN RIYADH, SAUDI ARABIA: A powerful car bomb rips through an American military training complex in Riyadh, killing 7 people, including 5 Americans, and wounding 60 others.

Officials quickly arrest four Saudi nationals and will behead them in June 1996 in an effort to stem potential unrest and preserve relations with the United States. The terrorists involved are all veterans of the mujahedeen in Afghanistan and boast of their relationship to Osama bin Laden.

1996—THE TALIBAN CONQUERS JALALABAD AND KABUL AND TAKES CONTROL OF AFGHANISTAN.

MAY 1996—SUDAN EXPELS BIN LADEN; HE RETURNS TO AFGHANISTAN: Sudan expels bin Laden because of international pressure from the United States and Saudi Arabia and for his involvement in a failed assassination attempt on Egyptian president Hosni Mubarak in June 1995. President Bill Clinton turns down the offer from the Sudanese government to bring bin Laden to the United States, which allows the terror chief to return to Afghanistan and reestablish al Qaeda and jihadist training camps.

JUNE 25, 1996—HEZBOLLAH BOMBS THE KHOBAR TOWERS AT DHAHRAN AIR BASE, SAUDI ARABIA: At about 10 P.M. a fuel truck loaded with 20,000 pounds of explosives detonates just outside the fence of the U.S. military complex in Dhahran, Saudi Arabia, killing 19 Americans and wounding more than 500. The blast creates a crater 85 feet by 35 feet.

On June 21, 2001, a federal grand jury in Alexandria, Virginia, will indict 13 members of the pro-Iran Saudi Hezbollah for the attack. The entire operation was planned, funded, and coordinated by Iran's security services on orders from the highest levels of the Iranian government. In 2004, the 9/11 Commission will note the possibility that Osama bin Laden was involved as well.

JULY 17, 1996—TWA FLIGHT 800 EXPLODES ON DEPARTURE FROM NEW YORK.

AUGUST 23, 1996—OSAMA BIN LADEN ISSUES THE FIRST OF TWO DECLARATIONS OF WAR: Bin Laden issues his first fatwa, published in *Al Quds Al Arabi,* a London-based newspaper. The fatwa is titled "Declaration of War against the Americans Occupying the Land of the Two Holy Places."

FEBRUARY 23, 1997—A PALESTINIAN GUNMAN OPENS FIRE ON TOURISTS ATOP NEW YORK CITY'S EMPIRE STATE BUILDING: Ali Hassan Abu Kamal, a Palestinian teacher, kills a young Dutch tourist and wounds 6 other people before turning the gun on himself. A handwritten note on his body claims that the attack was in retaliation against the "enemies of Palestine."

NOVEMBER 12, 1997—ISLAMIC TERRORISTS MURDER FOUR AMERICAN OIL COMPANY EMPLOYEES IN KARACHI, PAKISTAN: Thirty-six hours after Mir Aimal Kasi is pronounced guilty of the murder of two CIA employees at the front gate of CIA headquarters in 1993, two gunmen assassinate four Americans and their driver in Karachi. The Islamic Revolutionary Council and the Aimal Khufia Action Committee are responsible.

FEBRUARY 23, 1998—BIN LADEN AND AYMAN AL-ZAWAHIRI REUNITE AND DECLARE WAR ON THE UNITED STATES: Bin Laden and Zawahiri of the Egyptian Islamic Jihad reunite in Afghanistan. Zawahiri has just recently returned to Afghanistan from Baghdad, where he met with Saddam Hussein and other Iraqi leaders on February 3, 1998. According to *U.S. News & World Report,* Saddam provided $300,000 in funding for al Qaeda and Zawahiri. Three weeks later, bin Laden and Zawahiri declare war on the United States, saying, "We—with God's help—call on every Muslim who believes in God and wishes to be rewarded to comply with God's order to kill the Americans and plunder their money wherever and whenever they find it. We also call on Muslim ulema, leaders, youths, and soldiers to launch the raid on Satan's U.S. troops and the devil's supporters allying with them, and to displace those who are behind them so that they may learn a lesson. The ruling to kill the Americans and their allies—civilians and military—is an individual duty for every Muslim who can do it in any country in which it is possible to do it."

AUGUST 7, 1998—AL QAEDA BOMBS THE U.S. EMBASSIES IN NAIROBI, KENYA, AND DAR ES SALAAM, TANZANIA: A small pickup truck packed with explosives is driven to the delivery entrance of the U.S. Embassy in Nairobi and detonated. The blast destroys the left and rear of the embassy and the adjacent business building. At the same time, a vehicle containing a large explosives cache approaches the main gate of the U.S. Embassy in Dar es Salaam and explodes. The east wing of the concrete block building is destroyed and debris rains on streets and houses for a mile in every direction.

The two near-simultaneous attacks kill 224 and wound more than 5,000.

Within days Pakistan announces the arrest of Palestinian Mohammed Saddiq Odeh, who admits his role in the blasts and that he was recruited and financed by Osama bin Laden. Odeh describes al Qaeda as a terror network of 5,000 with intent to attack American interests abroad. He also details a litany of attacks on the United States, including the ambush in Somalia. He confirms al Qaeda's involvement in the attacks against the American military in Riyadh and Dhahran in 1995 and 1996.

Federal officials publicly charge bin Laden's al Qaeda with the Kenya bombing in a complaint made public on August 28. In November, a federal grand jury returns an indictment against bin Laden and his top military commander, Muhammed Atef, also believed to be hiding in Afghanistan. In December 1998, an unnamed bin Laden aide—identified only as "Confidential Source-1"—confesses that he participated in a plot to attack American military facilities around the world, implicating the Saudi millionaire and his disciples in the embassy explosions in Africa, according to reports.

DECEMBER 1998—IRAQI INTELLIGENCE PLOTS TO BOMB RADIO FREE EUROPE IN PRAGUE, CZECH REPUBLIC: Jabir Salim, the Iraqi Consul in the Czech Republic and the head of its intelligence operations, oversees a plot to bomb Radio Free Europe. The bombers plan to use a truck bomb loaded with explosives to collapse the headquarters. Salim has received $150,000 in two payments from Saddam's government to purchase untraceable explosives and recruit terrorists. Later that month, however, Salim defects and furnishes details of the plot to Western intelligence services.

DECEMBER 28, 1998—YEMENI TERRORISTS KIDNAP AND MURDER WESTERN TOURISTS: Sixteen Western tourists—12 Britons, 2 U.S. citizens, and 2 Australians—are kidnapped outside of Aden, Yemen, by the radical jihadist Aden Abyan Islamic Army. Four of the hostages are killed the next day during a raid by Yemeni security forces.

NOVEMBER 12, 1999—ROCKET ATTACKS TARGET U.S. INSTALLATIONS IN IS-LAMABAD, PAKISTAN: Six rockets are fired from improvised launchers in three vehicles at American and United Nations offices in Islamabad. The rockets are all fired within minutes of one another. The attacks are aimed at the U.S. Embassy in the Diplomatic Enclave, the UN headquarters inside the Saudi Pak Tower, and the American Center. Rockets also land on a parked vehicle outside of the UN World Food Program.

AUGUST 12, 2000—ISLAMISTS KIDNAP AMERICANS IN UZBEKISTAN: Four American mountain climbers are kidnapped by members of the Islamic Movement of Uzbekistan. They are able to escape six days later.

OCTOBER 12, 2000—TERRORISTS BOMB THE USS *COLE* IN THE PORT OF ADEN, YEMEN: Two men guide a tender boat alongside the USS *Cole,* a U.S. Navy Aegis destroyer docked in the port of Aden, and detonate explosives, blowing a hole 20 feet high and 40 feet wide in the hull of the ship. Seventeen sailors aboard the *Cole* are killed and 39 are injured.

DECEMBER 30, 2000—THE U.S. EMBASSY IN MANILA SURVIVES MULTIPLE BOMBINGS: Members of Jemaah Islamiyah, the South Asian terrorist operation for al Qaeda, explode five bombs in Manila, killing 22 people. One of the bombs detonates across the street from the U.S. Embassy.

SEPTEMBER 11, 2001

ACKNOWLEDGMENTS

This book has been a work of passion since the day I started it two years ago. As with most love affairs, there have been ups and downs. I am forever thankful for those who provided the ups when I was down.

First and foremost, I want to thank my wife, Nichole, who stands beside me in everything I do. While she wasn't crazy about the idea of me traveling to Iraq, she supported it and endured my need to get involved in yet one more military campaign. She thought she'd seen the last of those where I'm concerned. More importantly, she has brought into our world and raised three of the coolest people I've ever met: my daughter, Kylie, and our sons, Tanner and Chase. Their laughter and approaches to life inspire me, intrigue me, and keep me going.

Thanks also to Crown Forum and my editor, Jed Donahue. Jed also believed in me when things were difficult and I'm forever indebted to him for his patience and professional insight. I can honestly say that without his involvement and encouragement, this project would not have happened. Thanks to you, Jed, and the amazing group of associates you have at Crown. Thank you for your patience and perseverance.

I'm deeply indebted to my parents, Bob and Sandy Patterson, for their love and support throughout the years. I'm also thankful for the love and support of my wife's parents, Phil and Chris La-Grow, who have been my biggest cheerleaders. It might have been that tour of Air Force One that pushed them over the edge.

Finally, and most importantly, I want to acknowledge and thank the real heroes of this book: our men and women in uniform. Their devotion to service and professionalism in the face of constant and sometimes ugly naysaying motivated me to tell their story, the ground truth, with as much conviction and passion as I am able to muster. They are misunderstood, underappreciated, and vilified. They deserve so much more. Hopefully, this book is a step in that direction. There are the inspirational military bloggers Blackfive, Greyhawk at Mudville Gazette, Cassandra at Villainous Company, LT Smash, and Dadmanly, whose writing and reporting of the war convinced me early on that our nation was completely missing the point on Iraq and the greater war against Islamofascists. Along the way, I developed personal friendships with Major Eric Egland, First Sergeant Jeff Nuding, and Sergeant (soon to be Lieutenant) Joe Skelly. I'd go to combat with any of these proud American warriors on my wing any day. Thanks, guys, for your service, your time, and your support.

And thank you, Lord, for your continued blessings and involvement in my life. I can do all things through Christ who strengthens me.

NOTES

CHAPTER 1: THE UNHOLY ALLIANCE

1. Major Eric Egland, interview with author on September 16, 2005.
2. Professor Joseph Morrison Skelly, interview with author on October 19, 2005.
3. "Dean: US Won't Win in Iraq," woai.com, December 6, 2005, http://www.woai .com/news/local/story.aspx?content_id=C36A87B9-63A0-4CDE-AA91-B41571AF D3AF.
4. *CBS Evening News,* "Rockefeller: Bush Duped Public On Iraq," September 9, 2006.
5. Senator John Kerry, *Face the Nation,* CBS, December 4, 2005.
6. Edward L. Daley, "The Party of Treason," *Daley Times-Post,* December 7, 2005.
7. Jim Miklaszewski and and Mike Viqueira, "Lawmaker: Marines killed Iraqis 'in cold blood,' " MSNBC, May 17, 2006.
8. "Bill Clinton Calls Iraq 'Big Mistake,' " *USA Today,* November 16, 2005.
9. Markos Moulitsas Zúniga, dailykos.com, April 1, 2004, http://www.dailykos.com/ comments/2004/4/1/144156/3224#16.
10. Edward Epstein, "Deaths of GIs Stir Senate to Condemn Iraq Amnesty Plan," *San Francisco Chronicle,* June 21, 2006.
11. "The Rush to Hang Saddam Hussein," *New York Times,* December 29, 2006.
12. David Horowitz, *Unholy Alliance: Radical Islam and the American Left* (Washington, DC: Regnery, 2004).
13. "How North Vietnam Won the War," *Wall Street Journal,* August 3, 1995.
14. "Washington Retreat: Congress Sends the Wrong Signals to the Iraqis," *Wall Street Journal,* November 18, 2005.
15. Letter from al-Zawahiri to al-Zarqawi, Office of the Director of National Intelligence, http://www.dni.gov/release_letter_101105.html, October 11, 2005.
16. Michael Moore, "Heads Up . . . from Michael Moore," April 14, 2004, michaelmoore .com, http://www.michaelmoore.com/words/message/index.php?messageDate=2004-04-14.
17. "Full Transcript of bin Ladin's Speech," November 1, 2004, aljazeera.net.

18. Letter of May 8, 2006, from Mahmoud Ahmadinejad to George Bush, http://hosted.ap.org/specials/interactives/_documents/ahmadinejad0509.pdf.

19. Aaron Klein, "Terrorists Endorse Pelosi's 'Good Policy of Dialogue,'" WorldNet Daily, April 4, 2007.

20. Margaret Hunt Gram, "Professors Condemn War in Iraq at Teach-in," *Columbia Spectator,* March 27, 2003, p. 1.

21. John Perazzo, "Who Is the Fifth Column?" frontpagemagazine.com, March 2005.

22. Claire Cozens, "US Military 'Still Failing to Protect Journalists in Iraq,'" *The Guardian,* November 19, 2004, http://www.guardian.co.uk/Iraq/Story/0,2763,1355027,00.html, and Roderick Boyd, "A CNN Executive Says G.I.s in Iraq Target Journalists," *New York Sun,* February 8, 2005.

23. Ed O'Keefe, "Murtha: Marine Murder in Iraq?," *ABC News,* May 28, 2006.

24. HR 4655, The Iraq Liberation Act, October 31, 1998.

25. Richard Johnson, Paula Froelich, and Chris Wilson, "Sheen: What 9/11 Hijackers?," *New York Post,* May 23, 2006.

26. James Hirsen, newsmax.com, June 2005, p. 14.

27. Profile of Cindy Sheehan, discoverthenetworks.org, http://www.discoverthenetworks.org/individualProfile.asp?indid=2031.

CHAPTER 2: THE WAR WITHIN

1. Mary Hynes, "Ace in the Hole: A Special Welcome for Pilot Ace Steve Ritchie," *Las Vegas Review Journal,* April 25, 1997.

2. Robert L. Jamieson Jr., "Veteran Gets Rude Welcome on Bainbridge," *Seattle Post-Intelligencer,* July 9, 2004.

3. Ibid.

4. Army Private First Class Joshua Sparling, a paratrooper with the Army's prestigious 82nd Airborne Division, opened such a card in December 2005, while recuperating at Walter Reed Army Medical Center. At the time Sparling was just hours removed from being wounded in Ramadi, Iraq, an explosion having launched him 30 feet off the ground. Michelle Malkin, "Thank You Joshua Sparling," December 5, 2005, http://michellemalkin.com/archives/004021.htm.

5. Stephen Goode, "David Horowitz's Right Turn," *Insight Magazine,* January 27, 2004.

6. Robin Toner, "Trust in the Military Heightens Among Baby Boomers' Children," *New York Times,* May 27, 2003.

7. Mackubin T. Owens, "The Military: What Is It Good For?," The Claremont Institute, December 9, 1999.

8. Geoffrey Blainey, "After Iraq: The Road from Baghdad," *Policy,* vol. 19, no. 3 (Spring 2003).

9. Peter D. Feaver and Richard H. Kohn, "Project on the Gap Between the Military and American Society," Triangle Institute of Security Studies (TISS), 1998–2001, Table 1.23, p. 73.

10. "Murtha Says He Wouldn't Join Military Now," Reuters, January 3, 2006.

11. John McCain, "John McCain: Serve, Yes, but Not for Life," *The Navy Times,* January 24, 2000.

12. Jack Kelly, "Parent-Trap Snares Recruiters," *Pittsburgh Post-Gazette,* August 11, 2005.

13. Frank Schaeffer, "Thanking Our Troops," *Washington Post,* November 29, 2002.

14. Kathy Roth-Douquet and Frank Schaeffer, *AWOL: The Unexcused Absence of America's Upper Classes from Military Service—and How It Hurts Our Country* (New York: HarperCollins, 2006), p. 29.

15. Regina Herlinger, "My Ivy League Soldier," *Wall Street Journal,* April 2, 2003, editorial page.

16. Active-duty, Guard, and Reserve forces total approximately 2.3 million Americans. With a population of approximately 299 million, those serving in uniform represent .0077 percent of the total population. Sources: US Census Bureau and the Department of Defense.

17. House Committee on Veterans Affairs, "Veterans in 108th Congress," http://veterans.house.gov/vetlink/vetsincongress.html, and Roth-Douquet and Schaeffer, *AWOL,* pp. 6–7.

18. Anne Taubeneck, "All That He Can Be," *Northwestern Magazine,* Spring 2002.

19. Roth-Douquet and Schaeffer, *AWOL,* p. 10.

20. Testimony of John F. Kerry, Legislative Proposals Relating to the War in Southeast Asia, United States Senate, Committee on Foreign Relations, Washington, D.C., April 22, 1971.

21. Ibid.

22. Ibid.

23. Ibid.

24. See, for example, Michael Medved, *Right Turns: Unconventional Lessons from a Controversial Life* (New York: Crown Forum, 2004), p. 86. Medved, a former antiwar protest organizer and now a conservative talk radio host, writes, "For college students of the late 1960s, our strident opposition to the war didn't inspire our overriding determination to shun military service; rather, our overriding determination to shun military service inspired our strident opposition to the war."

25. Wallace Terry, *Bloods: An Oral History of the Vietnam War by Black Veterans* (New York: Random House, 1984).

26. *PBS News Hour,* "Vietnam's Legacy," April 5, 2000, http://www.pbs.org/newshour/bb/asia/jan-june00/vietnam_4-5.html.

27. Myra McPherson, *Long Time Passing: Vietnam and the Haunted Generation* (Garden City, NY: Doubleday, 1984), p. 132.

28. Tom Raum, "Bush, Kerry Duel over Draft," trentonian.com, October 16, 2004, available at http://www.zwire.com/site/news.cfm?newsid=13154631&BRD=1697&PAG=461&dept_id=44551&rfi=6.

29. Charles Rangel, "War's Burden Must Be Shared," January 7, 2003, http://www.house.gov/apps/list/hearing/ny15_rangel/shared sacrifice010703.html.

30. Charles Babington and Don Oldenburg, "House GOP Brings Up Draft in Order to Knock It Down," *Washington Post,* October 6, 2004, p. A01.

31. Michael Franc, "Kerry Echoes Liberals' Disdain for Military," The Heritage Foundation, November 4, 2006, http://www.heritage.org/Press/Commentary/ed11046a.cfm.

32. Ibid.

33. Cap Weinberger and Wynton Hall, "Have the Mainstream Media Ignored Our Heroes?," realclearpolitics.com, June 19, 2006.

34. Andy Rooney, "Heroes Don't Come Wholesale," *Montana Standard* (Tribune Media Services), April 8, 2004.

35. Bob Herbert, "Truth in Recruiting," *New York Times,* August 22, 2005.

36. Cynthia Tucker, "Working Class Fight War While Well-Off Defend It," *Atlanta Journal-Constitution,* March 26, 2006.

37. Jessica Werner, "Tim Robbins Pours His Anger into an Anti-War Play," *San Francisco Chronicle,* December 6, 2003.

38. Michael Moore, *Fahrenheit 9/11.*

39. "A Mind Is a Terrible Thing to Waste: A Guide to the Demilitarization of America's Youth & Students," published by Nuclear Age Peace Foundation, 2005, http://www.wagingpeace.org.

40. B. G. Burkett and Glenna Whitley, *Stolen Valor: How the Vietnam Generation Was Robbed of Its Heroes and Its History* (Dallas: Verity Press, 1998), p. 52.

41. Ibid.

42. Ibid., p. 48.

43. Arnold Barnett, Timothy Stanley, and Michael Shore, "America's Vietnam Casualties: Victims of a Class War?," *Operations Research,* vol. 40, no. 5 (September–October 1992).

44. Cynthia Gimbel and Alan Booth, "Who Fought in Vietnam?," *Social Forces,* vol. 74, no. 4 (June 1996).

45. Burkett and Whitley, *Stolen Valor,* p. 454.

46. John Perazzo, "Black Patriotism vs. Liberal Lies," frontpagemagazine.com, March 20, 2002.

47. Burkett and Whitley, *Stolen Valor,* p. 454.

48. "Vietnam Vets Battle Media Bias," newsmax.com, May 2, 2005.

49. Laura Ingraham, *Shut Up and Sing* (Washington, DC: Regnery, 2003), pp. 140–41.

50. Cortney Fielding, "Dem Stars Rally on Campus," *Pasadena Star News,* October 30, 2006. Audio of Kerry's speech available at http://www.kfi640.com/pages/JohnZiegler.html?feed=127993&article=457655.

51. Karl Zinsmeister, "Giving Thanks for America's Warrior Class," *American Enterprise Online,* http://www.taemag.com/issues/articleid.17810/article_detail.asp.

52. Jack Kelly, "Military Mockery," townhall.com, December 4, 2006, http://politicallyexposed.townhall.com/Default.aspx?mode=post&g=f9f852fc-a3d8-4c63-a7bd-605e9b8ce97c.

53. Gary Younge, "What About Private Lori?," *The Guardian,* April 10, 2003, http://www.guardian.co.uk/Iraq/Story/0,,933586,00.html.

54. "Who Is Volunteering for Today's Military?," http://www.defenselink.mil/news/Dec2005/d20051213mythfact.pdf.

55. Tim Kane, "Who Bears the Burden?: Demographic Characteristics of U.S. Military Recruits Before and After 9/11," The Heritage Foundation, Report #05-08, November 7, 2005.

56. Tim Kane, "Stupid Soldiers: Central to the Left's Worldview," The Heritage Foundation, November 3, 2006.

57. Kane, "Who Bears the Burden?"

58. "Who Is Volunteering for Today's Military?"

59. "Population Representation in the Military Services," U.S. Department of Defense FY2004, http://www.dod.mil/prhome/porep2004.

60. "Military Personnel: Reporting Additional Servicemember Demographics Could Enhance Congressional Oversight," U.S. Government Accountability Office, September 2005, GAO-05-952, p. 22, http://www.gao.gov/new.items/d05952.pdf.

61. DOD Report, "Population Representation in the Military Services, May 2006, http://www.dod.mil/prhome/poprep2004.

62. Franc, "Kerry Echoes Liberals' Disdain for Military."

63. Kane, "Who Bears the Burden?," and Tim Kane, "Who Are the Recruits?: The Demographic Characteristics of U.S. Military Enlistment, 2003–2005," The Heritage Foundation, October 26, 2006.

64. Department of Defense, Operation Iraqi Freedom—Military Deaths, March 19, 2003, through March 24, 2007, and Department of Defense, Operation Enduring Freedom—Military Deaths, October 7, 2001, through March 24, 2007, http://siadapp.dior.whs.mil/personnel/CASUALTY/oif-deaths-total.pdf and http://siadapp.dior.whs.mil/personnel/CASUALTY/OEFDEATHS.pdf.

65. Ibid.

66. Wesley Pruden, "But This Time, Boss, We've Got It Right," *Jewish World Review,* October 14, 2002.

67. Harris Poll, *Harris Confidence Index,* January 22, 2003.

68. Institute of Politics, Harvard University, "A National Survey of College Undergraduates" (Cambridge, MA: Harvard University, 2002), p. 2.

69. National Annenberg Election Survey, October 16, 2004.

70. Author interview with Sergeant Joseph Morrison Skelly, June 14, 2005.

71. Author interview with Corporal Matt Sanchez, February 3, 2007.

72. Author interview with Specialist Christopher R. Arnold, June 15, 2005.

73. Matt Pottinger, "Mightier Than the Pen," *Wall Street Journal,* December 15, 2005.

74. Gordon Trowbridge, "2003 Military Times Poll—We Asked. You Answered," armytimes.com, December 29, 2003.

75. Jeff Nuding, *It Is Well with My Soul,* dadmanly.com, June 14, 2005.

76. Author interviews conducted at Camp Victory, Baghdad, Iraq, July 11–14, 2005.

77. Daniel Ford, "God-Fearing Spartans," *Wall Street Journal,* September 22, 2005.

78. Karl Zinsmeister, "Facts v. Fiction: A Report from the Front," *American Enterprise,* January 2006.

79. Leonard Wong, Thomas A. Kolditz, Raymond A. Millen, Terrence M. Potter, "Why They Fight: Combat Motivation in the Iraq War," Strategic Studies Institute, U.S. Army War College, July 2003, p. 9–10.

80. Ibid., p. 18.

81. Ibid., p. 18.

82. Ibid., p. 19.

83. 1st Lt. Brian Donlon USMC, http://www.military.com/NewContent/0,13190, Defensewatch_032805_Marine,00.html.

84. Gerald Atkinson, "The Military/Civilian Culture Gap," July 4, 2002, http://www .newtotalitarians.com/MilitaryCivilianCultureGap.html.

CHAPTER 3: THE LEFT'S MADRASSAS

1. Rick Rodgers, "Navy Honors Four Marines' Valor in Combat," *San Diego Union-Tribune,* May 4, 2004; Wynton C. Hall and Peter Schweizer, "Campus Rads vs. Our Vets: The Antiwar Unwelcome on Campus," *National Review Online,* August 29, 2005.

2. Hall and Schweizer, "Campus Rads vs. Our Vets."

3. Ibid.

4. "The Odd Renaissance of Karl Marx," *Time,* May 14, 1973.

5. Todd Gitlin, "Varieties of Patriotic Experience," in George Packer, ed., *The Fight Is for Democracy: Winning the War of Ideas in America and the World* (New York: Perennial Books, 2003).

6. Robert Brustein, "What Price Correctness?," *Chicago Tribune Magazine,* January 16, 1994.

7. Stanley Rothman, S. Robert Lichter, Neil Nevitte, "Politics and Professional Advancement Among College Faculty," *The Forum,* vol. 3, issue 1 (2005), Article 2. http://www.cmpa.com/documents/05.03.29.Forum.Survey.pdf.

8. Howard Kurtz, "College Faculties a Most Liberal Lot, Study Finds," *Washington Post,* March 29, 2005, p. C01. Study was conducted by professors Stanley Rothman of Smith College, S. Robert Lichter of George Mason University, and Neil Nevitte of the University of Toronto.

9. Daniel B. Klein and Charlotta Stern, "Narrow-Tent Democrat and Fringe Others: The Policy Views of Social Science Professors," Swedish Institute for Social Research, Stockholm University, October 21, 2005.

10. David Horowitz and Eli Lehrer, "Political Bias in the Administrations and Faculties of 32 Elite Colleges and Universities," frontpagemagazine.com, August 28, 2003, http://www.frontpagemag.com/Content/read.asp.

11. "Political Bias in America's Universities," pamphlet produced by the Center for the Study of Popular Culture, p. 14–15.

12. Dr. William R. Forstchen, "Academia Goes to War?" *Asheville Tribune,* November 7, 2001.

13. Author interview with Matt Sanchez, February 3, 2007.

14. Suzanne Fields, "Honor Thy Soldiers," *Washington Times,* May 30, 2005, p. A23.

15. Kareem Fahim, "Columbia U. Senate Votes Against Return of ROTC," *New York Times,* May 7, 2005.

16. "Anti-Military Ruckus on Campus," *Macon Telegraph,* April 8, 2005.

17. Ibid.

18. Nick Rosenthal, "ROTC, You Are (Still) Not Welcome Here," *Columbia Spectator,* May 20, 2006.

19. James Thayer, "Shooting Down the Ace," *The Weekly Standard,* February 28, 2006.

20. Jake Ellison, "Anti-war Group Targets On-Campus Military Recruiters," *Seattle Post-Intelligencer,* February 4, 2005.

21. Lachlan Maclean and William Roller, "Students Protest Military Recruitment," *Xpress* (San Francisco State University), March 9, 2005.

22. Jamie Weinstein, "The Campus Left's War on ROTC," frontpagemagazine.com, April 5, 2005.

23. Cinnamon Stillwell, "OPINION: Supporting the Troops? Not on Campus," sfgate .com, May 4, 2005.

24. Jondi Gumz, "Students Protesting Military Recruiters Disrupt UCSC Job Fair," *Santa Cruz Sentinel,* April 6, 2005.

25. Anthony Paletta, "The Wisdom of Solomon?: The Right to Bear Armies," *National Review Online,* July 22, 2005, http://www.nationalreview.com/comment/paletta200507220822.asp.

26. Jane Roh, "Supreme Court Rules Against Schools in Military Recruiting Case," foxnews.com, March 6, 2006, http://www.foxnews.com/story/0,2933,186936,00 .html.

27. David Horowitz, "The Sick Mind of Noam Chomsky," frontpagemagazine.com, September 26, 2001.

28. Mark Steyn, "Devil Wears Striped Pants," *New York Sun,* September 25, 2006.

29. *New York Times* and *Guardian* quotes cited in Keith Windschuttle, "The Hypocrisy of Noam Chomsky," *The New Criterion,* vol. 21, no. 9 (May 2003).

30. Larissa Mac Farquhar, "The Devil's Accountant," *The New Yorker,* March 31, 2003.

31. Horowitz, "The Sick Mind of Noam Chomsky."

32. Norman Solomon, "Noam Chomsky—Saying What Media Don't Want Us to Hear," *Media Beat,* December 6, 2001, http://www.fair.org/media-beat/011206 .html.

33. Richard Todd, "The 'Ins' and 'Outs' at MIT," *New York Times,* May 18, 1969; Anders G. Lewis, "Noam Chomsky: Unrepentant Stalinist," frontpagemagazine.com, April 12, 2004.

34. Noam Chomsky, *At War with Asia* (New York: Vintage Books, 1970), pp. 259–87.

35. Windschuttle, "The Hypocrisy of Noam Chomsky."

36. Keith Windschuttle, "A Disgraceful Career," *The New Criterion,* vol. 23, no. 1, September 2004; Horowitz, "The Sick Mind of Noam Chomsky."

37. John Perazzo, "Who Is the Fifth Column?," discoverthenetworks.org, March 2005.

38. Noam Chomsky, "Hezbollah's Insistence on Keeping Its Arms Is Justified," *Al-Manar,* May 13, 2006, http://www.camera.org/index.asp?x_.

39. Malcolm Kline, "From Abject to Zinn," *Campus Report Online,* September 24, 2004.

40. Dan Flynn, "Master of Deceit," frontpagemagazine.com, June 3, 2003. Review of Howard Zinn's book *A People's History.*

41. Amir Butler, "Interview with Howard Zinn," *A True Word,* http://www.atrueword .com/index.php, August 28, 2002.

42. Howard Zinn, *Terrorism and War* (New York: Seven Stories Press, 2002), pp. 50–56.

43. Howard Zinn, "It Is Not Only Iraq That Is Occupied. America Is Too," *The Guardian,* August 12, 2005.

44. Ward Churchill, "'Some People Push Back': On the Justice of Roosting Chickens," Pockets of Resistance #11, September 2001, http://www.kersplebedeb.com/mystuff/s11/churchill.htm.

45. "Dismantling the Politics of Comfort: The *Satya* Interview with Ward Churchill," *Satya*, April 4, 2004, http://www.satyamag.com/apr04/churchill.html.

46. Churchill, "'Some People Push Back.'"

47. Jim Kirksey and Amy Herdy, "CU Prof Defends Military Remarks," *Denver Post*, June 30, 2005.

48. David Horowitz, *The Professors: The 101 Most Dangerous Academics in America* (Washington, DC: Regnery, 2006), p. xxi.

49. Jacob Laksin, "The Record of a Radical," frontpagemagazine.com, February 10, 2005.

50. Ibid.

51. Mark Burch, e-mail of October 12, 2005, to the Center for the Study of Popular Culture, "Subject: Re: New Study Reveals Significant Bias in Law and Journalism Schools."

52. Margaret Hunt Gram, "Professors Condemn War in Iraq at Teach-In," *Columbia Spectator*, March 27, 2003.

53. "Farrakhan for Columbia," *New York Sun*, January 10, 2005

54. David Horowitz, *Unholy Alliance: Radical Islam and the American Left* (Washington, DC: Regnery, 2004), p. 89.

55. Noemie Emery, "Look Who's Waving the Flag Now," *The Weekly Standard*, October 15, 2001.

56. Robert Jensen, "A Defeat for an Empire," *Fort Worth Star-Telegram*, December 9, 2004.

57. Jonathan Calt Harris, "A Berkeley Prof's 'Intifada' Against America," frontpagemagazine.com, April 15, 2004.

58. HNN Staff, "The Historian Who Denounced the Military for 'Baby-Killing Tactics,'" History News Network, April 10, 2005.

59. Ibid.

60. Peter Kirstein, "How I Define Patriotism," George Mason University's History News Network, October 13, 2003, http://hun.us/articles/1745.html.

61. Mike Rosen, "Another Nutty Professor," November 25, 2005, realclearpolitics.com, http://www.realclearpolitics.com/Commentary/com-11_25_05_MR.html.

62. Thomas Ryan, "RNC Forecast: Severe 'Weather' Watch," frontpagemagazine.com, August 30, 2004.

63. Thomas Ryan, "Hamilton College's Other Leftist Problem," frontpagemagazine.com, February 3, 2005.

64. Ronald Radosh, "Don't Need a Weatherman," *The Weekly Standard*, October 8, 2001, vol. 007, issue 04.

65. Dinitia Smith, "No Regrets for a Love of Explosives: In a Memoir of Sorts, a War Protester Talks of Life with the Weathermen," *New York Times*, September 11, 2001.

66. Hope Reeves, "The Way We Live Now: 9-16-01: Questions for Bill Ayers; Forever Rad," *New York Times Magazine*, September 16, 2001.

67. Duncan Campbell, "Most Wanted," *The Guardian*, October 18, 2001.

68. David Horowitz, "Allies in War," frontpagemagazine.com, September 17, 2001.

69. "Vet Strikes Back," soundpolitics.com, March 21, 2005, www.soundpolitics.com/archives/004019.html.

70. Susan Paynter, "School's Stage Was Set for a Stark Lesson," *Seattle Post-Intelligencer,* March 16, 2005.

71. "Vet Strikes Back."

72. Jeff Jacoby, "Antimilitary Bigotry," *Boston Globe,* November 19, 2006.

73. Joel Andreas, *Addicted to War* (Oakland, CA: AK Press, 2004), pp. 16, 21, and 54.

74. Ibid., back jacket.

75. *Rethinking Mathematics: Teaching Social Justice by the Numbers,* edited by Eric Gutstein and Bob Peterson (Milwaukee: Rethinking Schools, Ltd, 2006).

76. Michelle Malkin, "Brainwashing Preschool Peaceniks," townhall.com, April 16, 2003.

77. Marc Fencil, Letter to the Editor, *The Post* (Ohio University), April 8, 2005, http://thepost.baker.ohiou.edu/articles/2005/04/08/opinion/4561.html.

CHAPTER 4: STEALING THEIR HONOR

1. "Report from Vietnam," Walter Cronkite, *CBS Evening News* broadcast, February 27, 1968, http://www.alvernia.edu/cgi-bin/mt/text/archives/000194.html.

2. Deborah Potter, "Anchors Overboard?," *American Journalism Review,* June–July 2005.

3. Jack Kelly, "Iraq, Vietnam, the MSM & Dan Rather," realclearpolitics.com, June 23, 2006.

4. Ibid.

5. Steven Hayward, "The Tet Offensive," *Dialogues,* April 2004, http://www.ashbrook.org/publicat/dialogue/hayward-tet.html.

6. Peter Braestrup, *Big Story: How the American Press and Television Reported and Interpreted the Crisis of Tet 1968 in Vietnam and Washington* (Boulder, CO: Westview Press, 1977), p. 493.

7. Ibid., p. 508.

8. Stephen Young, interview with Colonel Bui Tin, *Wall Street Journal,* August 3, 1995.

9. Mackubin Thomas Owens, "Defeated by Defeatism," *National Review Online,* November 21, 2005.

10. John Keegan, "Bush Is Wrong: Iraq Is Not Vietnam," *Telegraph,* October 20, 2006.

11. Letter from al-Zawahiri to al-Zarqawi dated July 9, 2005, Office of the Director of National Intelligence, October 11, 2005, http://www.dni.gov/release_letter_101105.html.

12. "Hizbullah Secretary-General Hassan Nasrallah: When We Were Young, I Cannot Forget the Sight of American Forces Leaving Vietnam, and the Americans Abandoning Their Vietnamese Allies, I Anticipate the Same for Our Region," Al Jazeera, October 31, 2006, http://www.memritv.org/Transcript.asp?P1=1309.

13. Letter from al-Zawahiri to al-Zarqawi.

14. Author interview with Major Eric Egland via phone from Iraq on September 16, 2005.

15. "Global Islamic Media Front Discusses, Plan for Penetrating US Media," World News, http://www.xignite.com/xWorldNews.aspx?articleid=GMP20060824342002.

16. Daniel Pipes, "They're Terrorists, Not 'Activists,' " September 7, 2004.

17. J. Michael Waller, "War and the Role of the Mass Media," *Insight Magazine*, November 26, 2001, and James S. Robbins, "Press vs. Military," *National Review Online*, October 29, 2001.

18. Claire Cozens, "US Military Still 'Failing to Protect Journalists in Iraq,' " *The Guardian*, November 19, 2004.

19. Roderick Boyd, "A CNN Executive Says G.I.s in Iraq Target Journalists," *New York Sun*, February 8, 2005.

20. Joe Strupp, "New Survey Finds Huge Gap Between Press and Public on Many Issues," *Editor & Publisher*, May 15, 2005.

21. William Arkin, "The Troops Also Need to Support the American People," WashingtonPost.com, January 30, 2007, http://blog.washingtonpost.com/earlywarning/2007/01/the_troops_also_need_to_suppor.html.

22. Martin Lukacs, "There has never been an American army as violent and murderous as the one in Iraq: Pulitzer-winning investigative journalist Seymour Hersh slams Bush at McGill address," *The McGill Daily*, vol. 96, no. 15, October 30, 2006.

23. Paul Whitefield, "Apocalypse Again—Call Up the Vietnam Vets: Where Else Can Bush Get 21,500 Trained Soldiers for His 'Surge'?," *LATimes.com*, January 21, 2007.

24. Sherrie Gossett, "Boston Globe Publishes Bogus GI Rape Pictures," worldnetdaily.com, May 12, 2004.

25. Sharon L. Bond, "The Few, the Proud—but Surely Not AWOL," *St. Petersburg Times*, March 26, 2005.

26. Robert Scheer, "History? What History?," *The Nation*, April 16, 2003.

27. Quoted in Chris Weinkopf, "Looting and Loathing," June 11, 2003.

28. Rich Noyes, "The Media vs. The War on Terror: How ABC, CBS and NBC Attack America's Terror-Fighting Tactics as Dangerous, Abusive and Illegal," Media Research Center, September 11, 2006, http://www.mediaresearch.org/SpecialReports/2006/sum/sum090806.asp.

29. Rich Noyes, "TV's Bad News Brigade: ABC, CBS and NBC's Defeatist Coverage of the War in Iraq," Media Research Center, October 13, 2005.

30. James Q. Wilson, "The Press at War: The Patriot Reporter Is Passé," *City Journal*, Autumn 2006.

31. Norman Podhoretz, "The War Against World War IV," *Commentary*, February 2005.

32. Arthur Chrenkoff, "Bad News from Iraq," January 21, 2005, http://chrenkoff.blogspot.com/2005_01_16_chrenkoff_archive.html.

33. Karl Zinsmeister, "Facts v. Fiction: A Report from the Front," *American Enterprise*, January 2006.

34. Noel Sheppard, "Media's Conveniently Changing View of Zarqawi," *American Thinker*, June 12, 2006, http://www.americanthinker.com/2006/06/medias_conveniently_changing_v.html.

35. NBC's *Today* show, August 17, 2005.

36. "Press Freedom in the U.S.: A National Survey of Journalists and the American Public," University of Connecticut Department of Public Policy, cited in Mark Jurkowitz, "Survey: Press, Public Not on Same Page," *Boston Globe*, May 16, 2005.

37. "Can You Trust the National Media?: Part Two," *Investor's Business Daily,* October 17, 2006.
38. "Media Bias Is Real, Finds UCLA Political Scientist," *UCLA News,* December 14, 2005, available at http://www.newsroom.ucla.edu/page.asp?RelNum=6664.
39. Peter Jennings appearing on *Larry King Live,* CNN, April 10, 2002.
40. Evan Thomas, *Inside Washington,* PBS, May 12, 1996, profile detailed at discover thenetworks.org, http://www.discoverthe networks.org/individualProfile.asp?indid=1873.
41. Howard Fineman, "The 'Media Party' Is Over: CBS' Downfall Is Just the Tip of the Iceberg," msnbc.com, January 11, 2005, http://www.msnbc.msn.com/id/6813945/.
42. Michael Isikoff appearing on MSNBC's *Hardball,* December 2, 2005.
43. Rory B. Quinn, "A Generation Transformed," *International Herald Tribune,* August 5, 2005.
44. Fred Barnes, "A War Without Heroes?" *The Weekly Standard,* December 26, 2005.
45. Ibid.
46. Karl Zinsmeister and Joseph Light, "Media Priorities," *American Enterprise,* September 2005, p. 13.
47. Rich Noyes, "Touting Military Misdeeds, Hiding Heroes," Media Research Center, June 12, 2006.
48. Andy Rooney, "Heroes Don't Come Wholesale," *The Montana Standard,* April 8, 2004.
49. Joel Stein, "Warriors and Wusses," *Los Angeles Times,* January 24, 2006.
50. Author interview with Command Sergeant Major Jeff Nuding, U.S. Army, September 5, 2005.
51. Author interview with Major Eric Egland via phone from Iraq on September 16, 2005.
52. Sergeant Eddie Jeffers, "Hope Rides Alone," February 1, 2007, http://www.newmedia journal.us/guest/e_jeffers/02012007.htm.
53. Ma Deuce Gunner, *"Newsweek's* Exemplary 'Faux Pas,' " May 17, 2005.
54. "Letter From Iraq—Airman Angry at the Media," blackfive.com, May 25, 2004, http://www.blackfive.net/main/2004/05/letter_from_ira.html.
55. Captain Steve Alvarez, "Commentary: Support for the Troops Never Stronger," American Forces Information Network, June 24, 2005, http://www.defenselink.mil/Utility/PrintItem.aspx?print=http://www.defenselink.mil/news/Jun2005/20050624_1845.html.
56. Major General William McCoy, Commanding General, Gulf Region Division/Director, Project and Contracting Office, Multi-National Force-Iraq, in letter to the editor, *Washington Post,* August 6, 2006.
57. "CCN Despicable—Marines Say," blackfive.com, January 5, 2006, http://www.blackfive.net/main/2006/01/cnn_despicable_.html.
58. "A Soldier's Take on *Newsweek's* Unsourced Mayhem," theanchoress.com, May 16, 2005, http://theanchoressonline.com/2005/05/16/a-soldiers-take-on-newsweeks-unsourced-mayhem/.

59. John Leo, "The Media in Trouble," *U.S. News & World Report,* May 30, 2005.
60. Janet Reitman, "The Baghdad Follies: Hunkered Down with the Press Corps in Iraq," *Rolling Stone,* June 16, 2004, http://www.rollingstone.com/news/story/_/id/6186837?rnd=1098283669179&hasplayer=true&version=6.0.12.1040.
61. MSNBC, *Connected Coast to Coast,* July 13, 2005.
62. "NBC Airs New Quran Desecration Rumors," newsmax.com, May 18, 2005.
63. Toby Harndon, "Hoping for the Worst," *The Spectator,* May 15, 2004.
64. Lieutenant Colonel Tim Ryan, "Aiding and Abetting the Enemy: The Media in Iraq," blackfive.com, January 2005, http://www.blackfive.net/main/2005/01/aiding_and_abbe.html.
65. Joe Garofoli, "Conservative Talkers Taking Radio Shows on Road to Iraq," *San Francisco Chronicle,* July 7, 2005.
66. Paul Rieckhoff, "Radio 'Truth Tour' Ignores the Hard Facts," huffingtonpost.com, July 22, 2005, http://www.huffingtonpost.com/theblog/archive/paul-rieckhoff/radio-truth-tour-ignore_4513.html.
67. Kelly Beaucar Vlahos, "Critics Call Radio Hosts' Trip Propaganda Mission," foxnews.com, July 6, 2005.
68. Author interview with First Sergeant Jeffrey Nuding.

CHAPTER 5: STAR WARS

1. Rich Lowry, "Sgt. Rafael Peralta, American Hero," *National Review Online,* January 11, 2005.
2. President George W. Bush, Speech to National Hispanic Prayer Breakfast, Washington, DC, June 16, 2005.
3. Oliver Stone profile, discoverthenetworks.org, http://www.discoverthenetworks.org/individualprofile.asp?indid=628.
4. Michael Medved, "War Films, Hollywood and Popular Culture," michaelmedved.com, May 19, 2005, http://www.michaelmedved.com/site/product?pid=20016.
5. Diana West, "With Eyes Wide Shut to Terror," *Washington Times,* April 29, 2005.
6. Ibid.
7. Ibid.
8. Gary Gentile, "Hollywood Executives Asked to Help with War on Terrorism," Associated Press, November 11, 2001.
9. "Disney/Miramax Set to Release Film Depicting America Military as Drug Dealers, Criminals; Timing Seen Fueling Iraq War Controversy," drudgereport.com, July 13, 2003, http://www.drudgereport.com/bufsol.htm.
10. Benjamin Harvey, "Turkish War Film Set in Iraq Demonises US Troops," *The Scotsman,* February 3, 2006.
11. Dennis Lim, "Dante's Inferno: A Horror Movie Brings Out the Zombie Vote to Protest Bush's War," *The Village Voice,* November 29, 2005.
12. For an excellent factual point-by-point refutation of *Fahrenheit 9/11,* see Dave Koppel, "Fifty-nine Deceits in Fahrenheit 9/11," http://www.davekopel.com/Terror/Fiftysix-Deceits-in-Fahrenheit-911.htm.
13. Charlotte Higgins, "Fahrenheit 9/11 Could Light Fire Under Bush," *The Guardian,* May 17, 2004.

14. Specialist Joe Roche, Amy Ridenhour, National Center for Public Policy Research, July 26, 2004, http://www.nationalcenter.org/2004/07/fahrenheit-911-and-its-impact-on.html.

15. John McCaslin, "Inside the Beltway," *Washington Times,* July 12, 2004.

16. Richard Sisk, "G.I. Pans '9/11' role," *New York Daily News,* August 15, 2004.

17. Ibid.

18. Koppel, "Fifty-nine Deceits."

19. Alister Bull, "Iraqi Group Uses Michael Moore Film to Mock Bush," Reuters, August 18, 2006.

20. Michael Moore, "Head's Up from Michael Moore," April 14, 2004, http://www.michaelmoore.com/words/message/index.php?messageDate=2004-04-14.

21. Brian Reade, "The Awkward Conscience of a Nation," *Daily Mirror,* November 3, 2003.

22. David Brooks, "All Hail Moore," *New York Times,* June 26, 2004.

23. newsmax.com, June 6, 2004.

24. Victor S. Navasky, *Naming Names* (New York: Penguin Books, 1991), p. 202.

25. Kenneth Lloyd Billingsley, "Hollywood's Missing Movies: Why American Films Have Ignored Life Under Communism," reasonline, June 2000, http://www.reason.com/news/show/27732.html.

26. Sean Smith and David Ansen, "Oscar Roundtable: Prize Fighters," *Newsweek,* February 6, 2006.

27. Patrick Goldstein, "25 Years After Vietnam: A Seismic Cultural Shift," *Los Angeles Times,* April 16, 2000.

28. Ibid.

29. Ibid.

30. Dr. Lawrence H. Suid, "Hollywood and Vietnam," *Air University Review,* January–February 1983.

31. Peter S. Scholtes, "Shoot 'Em All!," *City Pages,* August 22, 2001, http://citypages.com/databank/22/1081/article9770.asp.

32. Jo Piazza and Chris Rovzar, "With War Still On, Hollywood Looks to Start Shooting," *New York Daily News,* May 15, 2006, http://www.nydailynews.com/news/gossip/story/417861p-352969c.html.

33. "50 Cent Gets Real with Iraq War Film," MSNBC, May 24, 2006, http://www.msnbc.msn.com/id/12958293/.

34. See http://www.libertyfilmfestival.com/libertas/.

35. James Hirsen, *Tales from the Left Coast* (New York: Crown Forum, 2003), pp. 83–84.

36. Media Research Center, Cyber Alert, October 3, 2002, vol. 7, no. 153, http://www.mediaresearch.org/cyberalerts/2002/cyb20021003.asp#5.

37. Adam Sweeting, "How the Chicks Survived Their Scrap with Bush," *The Telegraph,* June 15, 2006, http://www.telegraph.co.uk/arts/main.jhtml?xml=/arts/2006/06/15/bmdixie15.xml.

38. Don Feder, "Maggie Gyllenhaal's 'Courage' to Hate America," frontpagemagazine.com, April 29, 2005.

39. Megan Basham, "Oscar-Winning Monster Mouths Off," townhall.com, February 8, 2007.

40. Woody Harrelson, "I'm an American Tired of American Lies," *The Guardian*, October 17, 2002.

41. "Woody's on Side: US Actor Defends George Michael's Anti-Bush Single," *Mirror* online edition, August 9, 2002. http://www.mirror.co.uk/news/allnews/page.cfm ?objectid=12103357&method=full&siteid=50143.

42. Sean Penn, CNN's *Larry King Live*, January 11, 2003, http://transcripts.cnn.com/ TRANSCRIPTS/0301/11/lklw.00.html.

43. Humberto Fontova, *Fidel: Hollywood's Favorite Tyrant* (Washington, DC: Regnery, 2005), p. 11.

44. Andrew Stuttaford, "Pretty Useless: Julia Roberts, Our Favorite Ingénue," *National Review Online*, March 24–25, 2001.

45. "Jane Fonda Fears 'Entire World' Will Unite Against U.S. After Iraq War," Associated Press, April 9, 2003.

46. David Schmader, "Last Days: The Week in Review," *The Stranger*, November 19–25, 2000, http://www.thestranger.com/seattle/Content?oid=5493.

47. Mark Binelli, "Hollywood's Hottest Chick," *Rolling Stone*, September 4, 2001.

48. Alan Johnson, "Hollywood Should Clean Up Its Act, Says Actor Sheen: 'West Wing' Star Rallies Democrats on Dayton Visit," *Columbus Dispatch*, September 24, 2000.

49. Larry Elder, "Hollywood 'Experts' Speak Out," *Jewish World Review*, February 27, 2003.

50. Robert Avrech, "Help! I'm a Hollywood Republican," frontpagemagazine.com, August 22, 2005.

51. Michael Medved, "War Films, Hollywood and Popular Culture," michaelmedved .com, May 19, 2005, http://www.michaelmedved.com/site/product?pid=20016.

52. Plato, *The Republic*, XXXII—Socrates—Glaucon.

CHAPTER 6: THE DHIMMICRATS

1. Steven F. Hayward, *The Real Jimmy Carter: How Our Worst Ex-President Undermines American Foreign Policy, Coddles Dictators, and Created the Party of Clinton and Kerry* (Washington, DC: Regnery, 2004), p. 157.

2. Quoted in Byron York, "Clinton Has No Clothes: What 9/11 Revealed About the Ex-President," *National Review*, December 17, 2001.

3. "Dean: America Can't Win in Iraq," worldnetdaily.com, December 5, 2005.

4. Larry Elder, "Kosovo: Clinton 'Lied,' People Died?," *Jewish World Review*, December 1, 2005.

5. David Gelernter, "The Danger of the Kennedy Quagmire," *Los Angeles Times*, July 1, 2005.

6. Brad Wright and Jennifer Yuille, "Kennedy: 'Iraq Is George Bush's Vietnam,'" cnn.com, April 6, 2004, http://www.cnn.com/2004/ALLPOLITICS/04/05/kennedy .speech/.

7. Margaret Talev, "Senate Democrats promise 'relentless' flood of anti-war legislation," *Kansas City Star*, February 17, 2007, http://www.kansascity.com/mld/kansas city/news/politics/16723415.htm.

8. Art Moore, "Democratic Senator Praises Bin Laden," worldnetdaily.com, December 20, 2002.

9. "Gore Assails Bush's Iraq Policy," *Washington Post,* September 23, 2002.

10. Stephen F. Hayes, "The Baghdad Democrats," *The Weekly Standard,* vol. 8, issue 5 (October 14, 2002).

11. Chris Suellentrop, "The Anti-War Democrats," slate.com, October 2, 2002, http://www.slate.com/id/2071879/.

12. Floor speech of Senator Hillary Rodham Clinton on S.J. Res. 45, A Resolution to Authorize the Use of United States Armed Forces Against Iraq, October 10, 2002, http://clinton.senate.gov/speeches/iraq_101002.html.

13. Norman Podhoretz, "Who is Lying About Iraq? A campaign of distortion aims to discredit the liberation," *National Review Online,* November 14, 2005.

14. Ibid.

15. Mark M. Alexander, "Call them what they are—TRAITORS," townhall.com, November 19, 2005, http://www.townhall.com/columnists/column.aspx?UrlTitle= call_them_what_they_are_—_traitors&ns=MarkMAlexander&dt=11/19/2005& page=full&comments=true.

16. Dick Morris, "Hillary's Badwill Tour," *New York Post,* December 2, 2003.

17. Rick Klein, "Kerry's Skills on Display in Mideast Trip," *Boston Globe,* January 4, 2005.

18. Borzou Daragahi, "Kerry Cheered in Baghdad, Decries Bush Blunders," *San Francisco Chronicle,* January 6, 2005.

19. Jim Krane, "Gore Laments U.S. 'Abuses' Against Arabs," Associated Press, February 12, 2006.

20. Ted Barrett, " 'Unwinnable' Comment Draws GOP Fire," CNN.com, May 10, 2004.

21. Edward Epstein, "Murtha Calls for Immediate Withdrawal of U.S. Troops from Iraq," *San Francisco Chronicle,* November 17, 2005.

22. Charles Babington, "House Rejects Iraq Pullout After GOP Forces a Vote," *Washington Post,* November 19, 2005.

23. Barrett, " 'Unwinnable' Comment Draws GOP Fire."

24. "Rep. John Murtha Urged Somalia Pullout in '93," newsmax.com, November 21, 2005.

25. Congressman John Murtha, *Meet the Press,* NBC, June 11, 2006.

26. Congressman John Murtha official website, Murtha press conference transcript on Iraq, May 18, 2006, http://www.house.gov/list/press/pa12_murtha/PRiraqtrascript .html

27. Ed O'Keefe, "Murtha: Marine Murder in Iraq?," *This Week,* May 28, 2006, http:// abcnews.go.com/ThisWeek/story?id=2013939&page=1.

28. Letter from Lieutenant Colonel Christopher J. Stark to Congressman John Murtha, Pennsylvania, November 21, 2005, http://uncooperativeblogger.com/2005/12/16/ letter-to-john-murtha/.

29. "Biden Urges New Course in Iraq," cnn.com, June 21, 2005, http://www.cnn.com/ 2005/POLITICS/06/21/biden.iraq/index.html.

30. Colonel Jim Vosler, Director, Strategic Communications, US Central Command, "Indicators of Progress: As of June 28, 2005."

31. "Gen. Barry McCaffrey: Biden's Iraq Troop Numbers Bogus," newsmax.com, August 28, 2005.

32. Author interview with General Abdul Qadr Jassim, Iraq Army, Baghdad, Iraq, July 13, 2005.

33. Mark Steyn, "The Civil War that Wasn't," *The Australian,* February 1, 2005.

34. Amy Fagan, "Democrats Call Zarqawi Killing a Stunt," *Washington Times,* June 8, 2006.

35. Michael Barone, "Democrats are Winning . . . Except at the Polls," realclear politics.com, June 12, 2006, http://www.realclearpolitics.com/articles/2006/06/democrats_are_winning_except_a.html.

36. Nathan Burchfiel, "Zarqawi Killing Great, but Pull Troops, Say Kerry, Murtha," cnsnews.com, June 8, 2006.

37. Ben Johnson, "The Left and the Death of Zarqawi," frontpagemagazine.com, June 9, 2006.

38. Testimony of John F. Kerry, Legislative Proposals Relating to the War in Southeast Asia, United States Senate, Committee on Foreign Relations, Washington, DC, April 22, 1971.

39. John Kerry, *Face the Nation,* CBS, December 4, 2005.

40. Barbara Starr, "Details of Army's Abuse Investigation Surface," cnn.com, January 21, 2004, http://www.cnn.com/2004/US/01/20/sprj.nirq.abuse/.

41. Adam L. Penenberg, "Searching for the *New York Times,*" Wired News, July 14, 2004, http://www.wired.com/news/culture/0,1284,64110,00.html.

42. Byron York, "Republicans Love It When Gore Gets Mad," *National Review Online,* May 27, 2004.

43. Catherine Donaldson-Evans and Major Garrett, "Senate Condemns Iraqi Prisoner Abuse," foxnews.com, May 11, 2004.

44. Shailagh Murray, "Durbin Apologizes for Remarks on Abuse," *Washington Post,* June 22, 2005.

45. Michael Crawford, "MILNET Opinion," July 2005, www.milnet.com/opinion/Hollywood-Fiction-Attach.html.

46. Author interview with Major Eric Egland, September 16, 2005.

47. Author interview with U.S. Army specialist, Camp Victory, Baghdad, Iraq, July 14, 2005.

48. Gordon Cucullu, "Gitmo Jive," *American Enterprise,* September 2005.

49. Gordon Cucullu, "Mothering Terrorists at Gitmo," Democracy Project, June 28, 2005, available at http://www.democracy-project.com/archives/001673.html.

50. Hugh Hewitt, "The Durbin Effect," *The Weekly Standard,* June 23, 2005.

51. Cassandra Vinograd, "Carter: Guantanamo Detentions Disgraceful," Associated Press, July 30, 2005.

52. Lionel Barber and Paul Taylor, "Clinton Adds Voice to Criticism of Guantánamo," *Financial Times* (London), June 19, 2005.

53. "Hillary Clinton Attacks Cheney on 'Torture,' " newsmax.com, November 16, 2005.

54. Jimmy Carter, *Our Endangered Values: America's Moral Crisis* (New York: Simon & Schuster, 2005), pp. 126, 129.

55. Ben Johnson, "No Torture Occurred," frontpagemagazine.com, July 18, 2005.

56. Brandon Bosworth, "Sidelights," *American Enterprise,* October–December 2005.

57. Heather Mac Donald, "How to Interrogate Terrorists," *City Journal,* Winter 2005.

58. Ibid. See also Secretary of Defense Donald Rumsfeld, Memorandum for the Com-

mander, US Southern Command, April 16, 2003, available at http://www.gwu.edu/~nsarchiv/NSAEBB/NSAEBB127/03.04.16.pdf.

59. Mac Donald, "How to Interrogate Terrorists."

60. "Hillary Clinton Launches Charm Offensive," newsmax.com, February 7, 2006.

61. Victor Davis Hanson, "Hitler, Hitler Everywhere," *Jewish World Review,* June 28, 2005.

62. "Kerry Blasts Foreign Policy, Says U.S. Has Become 'International Pariah,'" fox news.com, January 28, 2007, http://www.foxnews.com/story/0,2933,247484,00.html.

63. John Seward, "Fifth Column General: Tom Hayden's Plan to Defeat America in Iraq," frontpagemagazine.com, December 6, 2004.

64. Frank J. Williams, "Abraham Lincoln and Civil Liberties: Then & Now—The Southern Rebellion and September 11," *New York University Annual Survey of American Law,* vol. 60 (January 14, 2005), p. 481.

CHAPTER 7: THE WAHHABI LOBBY

1. John J. Tierney, "The Politics of Peace: What's Behind the Anti-War Movement?," Washington, D.C., Capital Research Center, March 2005.

2. Stéphane Courtois, Nicolas Werth, Jean-Louis Panné, Andrzej Paczkowski, Karel Bartosek, Jean-Louis Margolin, and Mark Kramer, *The Black Book of Communism* (Cambridge, MA: Harvard University Press, 1999).

3. David Horowitz, "The Peace Movement Isn't About Peace," frontpagemagazine.com, April 7, 2003.

4. Tierney, "The Politics of Peace."

5. Christopher Hitchens, "Ramsey Clark in Baghdad," frontpagemagazine.com, December 5, 2005.

6. John Perazzo, "The Many Faces of Socialist 'Peace' Activists: The International Action Center," discoverthenetworks.org, March 17, 2006, http://www.discoverthenetworks.org/Articles/themany.html.

7. Ibid.

8. Ibid.

9. Ibid.

10. Profile of Brian Becker, discoverthenetworks.org, http://www.discoverthenetworks.org/individualProfile.asp?indid=1104.

11. Profile of the Revolutionary Communist Party (RCP), discoverthenetworks.org, http://www.discoverthenetworks.org/groupProfile.asp?grpid=6197.

12. John Perazzo, "Maoists for 'Peace,'" frontpagemagazine.com, February 28, 2003.

13. Http://www.notinourname.net/statement_conscience.html.

14. Ibid.

15. Profile of World Can't Wait, discoverthenetworks.org, http://www.discoverthenetworks.org/groupProfile.asp?grpid=7213.

16. "World Can't Wait: Agendas, Activities, and Affiliates," discoverthenetworks.org, December 2005, http://www.discoverthenetworks.org/Articles/wcw.html.

17. The World Can't Wait official website, worldcantwait.net.

18. United for Peace and Justice official website, http://www.unitedforpeace.org/article.php?list=type&type=16.

19. United for Peace and Justice official website, http://www.unitedforpeace.org/article.php?id=1737.

20. Official website of Global Exchange, http://www.globalexchange.org/about/.

21. Profile of Medea Benjamin, discoverthenetworks.org, http://www.discoverthenetworks.org/individualProfile.asp?indid=626.

22. Medea Benjamin, "Response 3: Toward a Global Movement," *The Nation,* April 3, 2003.

23. "Relatives of US Servicemen Killed in Iraq to Hold Vigil on Jordan Border," Agence France-Presse, December 31, 2004.

24. Profile of Code Pink, discoverthenetworks.org, http://www.discoverthenetworks.org/groupProfile.asp?grpid=6149.

25. Profile of Iraq Occupation Watch, discoverthenetworks.org, http://www.discoverthenetworks.org/groupProfile.asp?grpid=6785.

26. Robert D. Novak, "Cindy Sheehan's Allies," townhall.com, August 20, 2005.

27. Marc Morano, "Anti-War Protests Target Wounded at Army Hospital," cnsnews.com, August 25, 2005.

28. Ibid.

29. Sergeant Mark Leach, U.S. Army, Afghanistan, http://andisworld.typepad.com/welcome_to_andis_world/2005/10/a_reservist_pus.html.

30. Froggy Ruminations, "Hating Our Troops American Style," August 25, 2005, http://froggyruminations.blogspot.com/2005/08/hating-our-troops-american-style.html.

31. David Henson, "Bush, Sheehan Share Moments," *The Vacaville Reporter,* June 24, 2004.

32. American Gold Star Mothers official website, http://www.goldstarmoms.com/agsm/WhoWeAre/History/History.htm.

33. Dave Kopel, "Sheehan's Radical Views Little Noted," *Rocky Mountain News,* August 27, 2005.

34. Maureen Dowd, "Why No Tea and Sympathy?," *New York Times,* August 10, 2005.

35. Joe Kovacs, "Sheehan: Other Moms of Slain 'Brainwashed,' " worldnetdaily.com, August 29, 2005.

36. Ben Johnson, "Hillary Agrees to Meet Cindy Sheehan," frontpagemagazine.com, September 22, 2005

37. Kopel, "Sheehan's Radical Views Little Noted."

38. James Taranto, "The Sad Story of Cindy Sheehan," opinionjournal.com, August 12, 2005.

39. Ben Johnson, "Exploiting the Dead," frontpagemagazine.com, August 12, 2005.

40. Kopel, "Sheehan's Radical Views Little Noted"; Johnson, "Hillary Agrees to Meet Cindy Sheehan."

41. Sergeant Walter J. Rausch and 1st Platoon, 101st Airborne Division (Air Assault), Sergeant Hook, Taste of Freedom, November 17, 2005, http://sgthook.com/2005/11/17/taste-of-freedom/.

42. C. J. Grisham, "Open Letter to Cindy Sheehan," asoldier'sperspective.us, http://www.soldiersperspective.us/?p=519.

43. Code Pink for Peace official website, http://www.codepink4peace.org/article.php?list=type&type=48.

44. Rocco DiPippo, "The Left's War Against the Military at Home," frontpagemagazine.com, July 11, 2005.

45. Brooke Shelby Biggs, "Hellraiser: John Sellers," *Mother Jones*, September–October 2000.

46. The Ruckus Society official website, http://www.ruckus.org/article.php?list=type&type=43.

47. Ben Johnson, "57 Varieties of Radical Causes: Teresa Heinz Kerry's Tax-Exempt Donations," http://www.discoverthenetwork.org/articles/TeresaHeinzKerry%5B1%5D.htm.

48. Central Committee for Conscientious Objectors official website, http://www.objector.org/ccco/people.html.

49. Central Committee for Conscientious Objectors official website, http://www.objector.org/moos/moos_poster.html.

50. Central Committee for Conscientious Objectors official website, http://www.objector.org/before-you-enlist/hazardous.html.

51. "A.W.O.L.: Youth for Peace and Revolution, Military Out of Our Schools Now!" http://www.objector.org/Resources/AWOL3.pdf.

52. Profile of Veterans for Peace, discoverthenetworks.org, http://discoverthenetworks.org/groupProfile.asp?grpid=6244.

53. See http://www.warresisters.org/Roots/newsite12.html.

54. Campus Anti-War Network official website, http://www.campusantiwar.net/.

55. Charles Sykes and K. L. Billingsley, "How the Ford Foundation Created Multiculturalism," frontpagemagazine.com, January 9, 2004.

56. The Ford Foundation Annual Report 2005, http://www.fordfound.org/about/financial6.cfm.

57. Profile of the Ford Foundation, discoverthenetworks.org, http://www.discoverthenetworks.org/funderprofile.asp?fndid=5176&category=79.

58. Remarks by Susan V. Berresford at the Federation for Community Planning's Human Services Institute. Cleveland, Ohio, April 5, 2002, official website of the Ford Foundation, http://www.fordfound.org/news/view_speeches_detail.cfm?news_index=117.

59. Profile of the Tides Foundation and Tides Center, discoverthenetworks.org, http://www.discoverthenetworks.org/funderProfile.asp?fndid=5184.

60. Profile of the Ford Foundation, discoverthenetworks.org, http://www.discoverthenetworks.org/funderprofile.asp?fndid=5176&category=79.

61. Profile of the Center for Constitutional Rights, discoverthenetworks.org, http://discoverthenetworks.org/groupProfile.asp?grpid=6148.

62. Profile of Lynne Stewart, discoverthenetworks.org, http://www.discoverthenetworks.org/individualProfile.asp?indid=861.

63. Official website of the National Lawyers Guild, http://www.nlg.org/about/aboutus.htm.

64. William Hawkins, "The Biggest Funder of the Left," frontpagemagazine.com, July 23, 2003.

65. Chip Berlet, "Abstaining from Bad Sects: Understanding Sects, Cadres, and Mass Movement Organizations," http://www.resistinc.org/newsletter/issues/1999/12/berlet.html.

66. "National Lawyers Guild," discoverthenetworks.org, http://www.discoverthenetworks.org/groupProfile.asp?grpid=6162.

67. Ibid.

68. Profile of the Ford Foundation, discoverthenetworks.org, http://www.discoverthenetworks.org/funderprofile.asp?fndid=5176&category=79.

69. Jamie Glazov, "The ACLU vs. America," frontpagemagazine.com, September 26, 2005.

70. James Taranto, "The Sad Story of Cindy Sheehan," *Opinion Journal*, August 12, 2005.

71. "Ohio Mourns More Marines Killed in Iraq," *USA Today*, August 13, 2005.

72. "Other Ways to Grieve," Chrenkoff, August 15, 2005, http://chrenkoff.blogspot.com/2005/08/other-ways-to-grieve.html.

CHAPTER 8: THE MEASURE OF A NATION

1. Public Broadcasting System (PBS), *Frontline*, "Interview with Osama bin Laden," http://www.pbs.org/wgbh/pages/frontline/shows/binladen/who/interview.html.

2. Author interview with Major Eric Egland, May 20, 2005.

3. Rory B. Quinn, "A Generation Transformed," *International Herald Tribune*, August 5, 2005.

4. Victor Davis Hanson, "The Surreal World of Iraq," *National Review Online*, June 27, 2003.

5. Bryan Appleyard, "Why Do They Hate America?," *Sunday Times* (London), September 23, 2001.

6. Brian Donlon, "A Marine's Farewell to Iraq," military.com, March 28, 2005, http://www.military.com/NewContent/0,13190,Defensewatch_032805_Marine,00.html.

7. "Letter from Fallujah," 2Slick's Forum, http://2slick.blogspot.com/2004/11/letter-from-fallujah.html.

8. "Saluting the 3rd ACR," *The Mudville Gazette*, February 16, 2006, http://www.mudvillegazette.com/archives/004167.html.

9. Kevin Ferris, "Veterans Day: Let's Give Thanks," philly.com, November 15, 2005.

10. Letter from Zawahiri to Zarqawi dated July 9, 2005, Office of the Director of National Intelligence, October 11, 2005, http://www.dni.gov/release_letter_101105.html.

11. Author interview with Sergeant Joe Skelly, July 25, 2005.

12. Sergeant Eddie Jeffers, February 1, 2007, "Hope Rides Alone," http://www.newmediajournal.us/guest/e_jeffers/02012007.htm.

13. President's Address to a Joint Session of Congress and the American People, United States Capitol. Washington, DC, September 20, 2001.

INDEX